HATING JAZZ

HATING JAZZ

A History of Its Disparagement, Mockery, and Other Forms of Abuse

Andrew S. Berish

The University of Chicago Press   Chicago and London

The University of Chicago Press, Chicago 60637
The University of Chicago Press, Ltd., London
© 2025 by The University of Chicago
All rights reserved. No part of this book may be used or reproduced in any manner whatsoever without written permission, except in the case of brief quotations in critical articles and reviews. For more information, contact the University of Chicago Press, 1427 E. 60th St., Chicago, IL 60637.
Published 2025

34 33 32 31 30 29 28 27 26 25   1 2 3 4 5

ISBN-13: 978-0-226-83833-5 (cloth)
ISBN-13: 978-0-226-83835-9 (paper)
ISBN-13: 978-0-226-83834-2 (e-book)
DOI: https://doi.org/10.7208/chicago/9780226838342.001.0001

Library of Congress Cataloging-in-Publication Data

Names: Berish, Andrew S., author.
Title: Hating jazz : a history of its disparagement, mockery, and other forms of abuse / Andrew S. Berish.
Description: Chicago : The University of Chicago Press, 2025. | Includes bibliographical references and index.
Identifiers: LCCN 2024039496 | ISBN 9780226838335 (cloth) | ISBN 9780226838359 (paperback) | ISBN 9780226838342 (ebook)
Subjects: LCSH: Jazz—Social aspects—United States. | Jazz—History and criticism. | Music and race—United States. | Jazz—Analysis, appreciation. | Jazz—Humor. | Hate.
Classification: LCC ML3918.J39 B47 2025 | DDC 306.4/84250973—dc23/eng/20240904
LC record available at https://lccn.loc.gov/2024039496

To Robert Walser

Contents

1 · Defining Jazz Hatred 1
2 · What Do You Mean You Hate Jazz? Taste, Race, and the Orchestration of Sensibilities 30
3 · Jazz Is Stupid: Hating Jazz through Satire and Ridicule 66
4 · The Musicians Suck: Contempt and Disgust in the Historical Reception of Jazz 99
5 · The Ethics of Hating Jazz 129

ACKNOWLEDGMENTS 153
NOTES 157
BIBLIOGRAPHY 189
INDEX 209

1
Defining Jazz Hatred

"Hatred of jazz," writes jazz critic Ben Ratliff, "whether sincere or fashionable or reflexive, as a kind of sorry-not-sorry joke—runs strangely deep in American culture."[1] Ratliff is responding to the treatment of jazz in director Damien Chazelle's 2016 film *La La Land*. The film's male lead, Seb (Ryan Gosling), is a pianist and passionate advocate for what he believes is authentic jazz. He holds his nose as he plays with Keith (John Legend), the leader of a popular R&B act. Ostensibly, the film is a defense of jazz, a celebration of its artistic integrity, but Seb's rigid devotion to a particular notion of jazz pushes him awfully close to parody: the male jazz snob oblivious of everything but his own taste. The film is sympathetic to Seb's point of view, suggesting that serious art is uncompromising in its mission, the uneducated mass audience be damned. The film's message about the authenticity and integrity of jazz provided the excuse for a larger debate about the music's precarious place in American culture, especially its role as a go-to cultural punching bag. "What's with This Uncool Surge in Jazz Bashing?" reads the headline of Ted Gioia's article in the *Daily Beast*.[2] The jazz historian cites several examples: a *Washington Post* article by Justin Wm. Moyer, "All That Jazz Isn't All That Great"; a *Deadspin* essay by Jason Gubbels, "Jazz Needs a Better Sense of Humor"; a *New Yorker* satirical piece involving Sonny Rollins; and the acidic Twitter feed @JazzIsTheWorst.[3]

But what does it mean to hate jazz? What is the object of hate? The genre? A specific manifestation of the genre? Is hating jazz merely a rhetorical gesture, a strong way of conveying dislike? Or is it something more substantial, an intense negative affective engagement with the music? Does the hatred come from outside the jazz community or from within it? And is hating jazz a response to a sonorous phenomenon or just a reflection of culturally predetermined inclinations? Taking jazz hate seriously provides a way to explore how jazz—really all music—gives shape and meaning to our lives. A great deal of scholarship and popular writing has focused on the rise and development of jazz into a respected art form.[4] But this is only half the picture. By focusing on the rejection of the music, we see more holistically its complicated place in American cultural life. In his essay on *La La Land*, Ratliff offers us a start: hating jazz is tied up in matters of race, gender, class, and generation, issues that interact with a sensual engagement with the sounds of the music.[5] This makes hating jazz exceedingly complicated. Just as loving jazz takes many forms, so does hating it. Jazz hate runs from mild dislike and annoyance to angry denunciation and fiery contempt. Although it has its own logic, jazz hating is frequently entangled in other kinds of hate, specifically racism and misogyny. Jazz hatred, I will argue, is not an idiosyncratic product of an individual encounter between listener and music, but a meeting of cultural, political, and historical forces. Although usually expressed in the language of the personal, jazz hatred is always a social phenomenon.

The semantic indeterminacy of jazz has been central to its reception. To tell the story of jazz hating is to also tell a parallel story about the changing definitions of the music. As Guthrie Ramsey notes, jazz has been "singular" in its "social mobility—its ability to move among 'folk,' mass culture and 'high' art discourses."[6] Is it America's classical music or is it a modernized example of folk music?[7] Is it the symbol of a multicultural United States, the paradigmatic example of a "mulatto" American culture?[8] Or is it Black American Music, the product of Afro-diasporic creativity and adaptability, rooted in a unique African-derived aesthetic?[9] Drummer Max Roach famously critiqued the word *jazz* for ways it has absorbed the worst of America's racial history. For Roach, *jazz* was synonymous with cultural prejudice and condescension. To explain this history, the drummer planned to write a book titled *I Hate Jazz*.[10] The nature and intensity of one's feelings toward the music depend not only on one's definition but also on what kind of musical practices are being discussed: small group or large, improvisation or notated composition, nightclub or concert hall music, swing feel or rock. A generic label such as jazz is not an empirically verifiable thing but a messy social process. Ramsey writes that genres "establish a framework for the communication of meaning, provide a context for interpretation, and serve as a starting point from which to discern changes or innovations." Designating a genre, he concludes, "speaks to both purely musical issues and to larger social orders."[11]

While working on this book, I've had many conversations with people who say they hate jazz. They are often candid about their experiences, describing a music they find perplexing or unpleasant. Many people have told me they just don't understand what they are hearing or feel unsure about how to react to what is happening in the music. They want to know if I can tell them anything about why they hate the music. I tell them that I can't do that. But what I can do is talk about the history of jazz hating—the written and spoken historical record that chronicles other people's hate for the music. Jazz hating has historically taken certain forms for certain historical reasons. For example, feeling put off by the music because of its reputation as difficult and requiring specialized training is rooted in a tradition of writers and musicians who cultivated exactly this attitude.

Our musical dislikes feel intensely personal, but they are not. We are social creatures, and so is our experience and judgment of music. There are important shared cultural patterns underlying each of our individual reactions. These patterns, though varying through time and place, share a preoccupation with the nature of affect, how the music makes one feel, and the music's relationship to race, particularly whiteness and Blackness.[12] In this way, jazz hate has important similarities with the hate expressed toward other twentieth-century popular musics rooted in Black musical practices, genres such as rock 'n' roll, R&B, disco, and rap and hip-hop. But jazz hate also overlaps in interesting ways with criticism leveled at musics not always associated with Black culture, such as heavy metal and country music. Throughout my survey, I will point to these other reception histories to highlight the similarities but also draw out some important differences. As is probably clear by now, my study is focused on jazz in the US with some attention to the broader English-speaking world (Canada, Australia, and the UK). And while I touch on jazz hate in Europe in my discussions of Adorno, Nazi Germany, and the Soviet Union, I do not explore in depth the rich and complicated reception history of jazz across the continent.[13] I also do not consider jazz hating in Africa or Asia—areas particularly understudied in Anglo-American scholarship.[14] Thankfully, there is more and more research, in many different languages, on jazz across the globe. With this context in mind, my book may seem overly narrow, but I hope the general framework I provide will inspire and guide further research.

My overarching argument in the book has three components: (1) jazz hate is variable but always social and is never just about an individual judgment of certain sounds; (2) jazz hate is an *affective practice*, an ongoing, dynamic engagement with the music that combines feeling and knowledge; (3) jazz hate is about race, most often Blackness and whiteness. To some readers, this may all sound obvious: people don't like jazz because they don't like how it makes them feel. But the way we write and talk about music often obscures this notion. When thinking about our experiences with music, we often adopt—even without always knowing it—an evaluative language rooted in a historical notion of the aesthetic. This post-eighteenth-century, post-Kantian idea holds that art is a special experience between artist and the individual. It is direct, unmediated, and, even if transcendent, always open to judgment. Art may touch on social life, but its evaluation is independent of this messiness. The music we listen to is good or bad. We may argue about these evaluations, but, at some point, there is no disputing that certain music is great and other music terrible. Aesthetic hierarchies can change—the Beatles and J. S. Bach are both great artists—but the basic discursive framework is still much the same. Yet, despite this hegemonic discourse, our discussions of music are shot through with alternative, even contradictory ways of thinking: art is subjective and there is no judging other people's taste. Or: this music speaks to my community or my national, racial, religious, or class identity. One goal of this book is to unpack the tensions in our conventional ways of talking about art and music. I am especially interested in taking apart a mode of engagement that emphasizes art as an individual experience, removed from day-to-day life, and open to objective evaluation. By flipping reception history on its head—studying how jazz has been hated rather than loved—we can see much more clearly how dominant ways of discussing jazz have obscured issues of sociality and feeling. Loving or hating jazz is always, inevitably entangled in the complexities and contradictions of our social lives.

JAZZ HATE IS SOCIAL

Hate is a complicated word. As both a thing (noun) and an action (verb) the word names a complicated mixture of cognitive and emotional characteristics such as intense dislike, loathing, and animosity. In psychology (and much of philosophy), emotions are most often described as "intentional states that conjoin bodily experience of intensified relevance with our descriptive and moral languages about the world."[15] This understanding combines several traditions of thought about emotions—the bodily sensation school most famously articulated by William James and Carl Lange; the brain-based or "limbic" theories of Walter Cannon, James Papez, Paul MacLean, and others; and the cognitive theories such as Magda Arnold's appraisal theory. In this body-brain-cognitive synthesis, *hate* is the name for a particular confluence of bodily arousal (such as heart pounding or sweating) with judgment toward something in the world (in the language of psychologists, an "intentional object").[16] As a bodily sensation, hate is an intensely "negative and difficult emotion" often characterized by "rage, resentment, or unconcern."[17] But, paradoxically, hate can also result from love, where the desire to protect or defend the beloved can turn into hate for any actual or perceived threat.

In our day-to-day understanding of emotions, we often conceptualize our thoughts and feelings as bounded, as being specific to ourselves. Hatred, in this view, is something generated from within and directed outward toward something or someone in the world. But, as many scholars have argued, hate is fundamentally social. Neither "pre-social nor naturally given," emotions are "closely intertwined with social norms and shared meanings," as Birgitte Johansen notes; they are, in other words, "culturally-embedded and socially-patterned." Hating is learned and shared. It may feel private, especially when it is not communicated, but the nature of that experience—the feelings, attitudes, and behaviors that make up the "emotion"—is always, at root, communal. This characteristic of hatred, and emotion generally, has other implications. Most importantly, for my purposes, it starts to undo the distinction between *what* is hated, person or thing. Affect theory, in particular, offers a more radical understanding of feeling as "something that reaches across bodies, objects, and space." This idea moves emotion from "psyche to situation."[18] Hating a thing, such as jazz, is never just about sounds; it is always about people in their time and place.

Hatred has some additional characteristics that will be important to my survey. As Aristotle famously argued, the object of hatred is often extended to a class or group of objects that have similar characteristics.[19] This extension of hate also tends to narrow judgment to one or more "intolerable traits," a development that almost inevitably objectifies the hated.[20] In this way, hate *hypostatizes* and *reifies*, turning judgments of characteristics or behaviors into fixed and defining attributes that generalize to a whole category of things or people. For some thinkers, this characteristic of hatred sets it apart from anger, resentment, and indignation—emotions focused on actions that offer the possibility of remediation. Hate "tends to have the entire being of someone [or something] as its object." There is no action that can repair the hated; "change or redemption [appear] impossible." And unlike most emotions that are episodic, the hypostatizing and reifying nature of hate often makes it "deep-seated and enduring."[21] The only way to deal with the hated persons or objects is to remove, expel, or annihilate them. Hatred, in other words, requires an adversary. "The discourse of hatred," Niza Yanay writes, "always constitutes an enemy; there is no hatred without an enemy."[22]

The intensity of hatred can sometimes turn even against the loved. Freud, for example, saw love as fundamentally "ambivalent," accompanied by impulses of hate toward the loved object.[23] In his 1915 essay "Instincts and Their Vicissitudes," Freud situates hate as part of the ego's development as it moves from a primary narcissism outward to the objects of the world. "If the object is a source of unpleasurable feelings, there is an urge which endeavors to increase the distance between the object and the ego.... We feel the 'repulsion' of the object and hate it; this hate can afterwards be intensified to the point of an aggressive inclination against the object—an intention to destroy it." Love, on the other hand, is the "pleasure-relation of the ego to its sexual object." Despite being part of the polarity "love-hate," Freud argues that hate has "no such intimate connection with sexual pleasure and the sexual function." For Freud, "the true prototypes of the relation of hate are derived . . . from the ego's struggle to preserve and maintain itself." He goes further, asserting that hate "as a relation to objects" is older than love, "deriving from the narcissistic ego's primordial repudiation of the external world with its outpouring of stimuli."[24] In this analysis, hate—whatever its form or target—is rooted in a need to protect the self. Freud's ideas about the mobility and ambiguousness of hate will be very helpful later, when I discuss the contempt often expressed within the jazz world, especially when haters feel a threat, conscious or unconscious, to their values or sense of self. Musical boundaries become entangled with the boundaries of subjectivity—the threat to one is a threat to the other.

So where does this leave us when talking about hating music? Hate and hating have "bad standing in most modern, liberal contexts as something to be either fought or overcome."[25] Hatred is misogyny. It is racism. It can lead to real-world violence. Yet we use the word all the time in day-to-day life to talk about virtually anything and everything—sweaters, mothers-in-law, films, and music. Nearly every example I use in this study uses the word "hate," and I chose these specific examples for that reason. Throwing the word around initiates a complex and sometimes contradictory set of meanings and associations. Literary historian Daniel Karlin helpfully divides this complex usage into two categories: a strong one and a weak one. In its strong version, hate indexes, in Samuel Johnson's words, a "violent commotion of the mind," an intensity of feeling that disorders perception. This is hate as generalizing, hypostatizing, and reifying. But in its weaker version, hate is "merely an intensified or rhetorically heightened way of expressing a taste or preference."[26] In *La La Land*, when Mia tells Seb she hates jazz, she is really just expressing a dislike for jazz. Today this kind of hate often takes the form of *hating on*, defined by Lara Langer Cohen and Brian Connolly as the "joyous ethics of solidarity that come from hating."[27] The recent development of "anti-fandom" studies offers a relatively new scholarly structure to studying the ways hate, in all its variability, is deployed in modern mass culture.[28] As I will discuss later in terms of satirical attacks on jazz, hating on very quickly slides into something more venomous, a hate that dehumanizes and demonizes.

The dislike of jazz is not one thing but many, and it is tied to historical contexts. For example, the contempt of many early commentators in the late 1910s and the harsh critiques of swing by writers in the mid- and late 1930s, despite having some surface similarities (an obsessive focus on repetitive riffs and rhythms), represent very different historical moments shaped by very different notions of race and music. Between 1917, the year of the Original Dixieland Jazz Band's "Livery Stable Blues," the recording that established the commercial popularity of jazz, and 1935, the year that Benny Goodman was coronated the "King of Swing," a series of events reshaped not just American life but basic notions of national identity. The mobilization for World War I, the demographic upheavals of the Great Migration, the economic boom followed by a devasting collapse—these developments initiated a profound rethinking of American identity by writers, intellectuals, and politicians. The notion of a white protestant America was gradually being replaced by a pluralistic understanding that embraced European immigrants.[29] Being American was now less about family lineage and more about adhering to a certain set of abstract values such as freedom of thought, representative democracy, and free market capitalism (the last contested by a revitalized Left during the Great Depression).[30] These ideas were given additional support by revolutions in sociology and anthropology that fundamentally redefined notions of race and culture.[31] The critical dismissal of jazz musicians at these different moments was thus motivated by very different understandings of American identity and culture. For some early critics, jazz was the unwelcome triumph of racial Others—Blacks and immigrants.[32] But by the mid-1930s, attacks on jazz began from a very different place: What was the best music for a pluralistic society? Was swing an authentic voice of youth or a precursor to fascism? Race and racism did not disappear, but the terms of the debate—what could and should be said in mainstream American newspapers and magazines—had radically changed.

JAZZ HATE IS AFFECT

My second core argument is that, despite its historical variability, all the forms of jazz hatred I examine share a concern with socially mediated affect, the way jazz makes people in certain times and places *feel* something. This is a different, but related, project to the study of musical emotion, a subfield that focuses narrowly on musical analysis or more broadly on individual psychological responses.[33] To talk about the history of jazz hating we need a tool like affect, one that moves beyond these more narrow, individualistic accounts to embrace the ambiguity and sociality of feeling. The academic study of affect has some broad parameters: "the circulation of power through feeling and emotion."[34] Musicologist Anahid Kassabian describes one influential version of affect theory: "Affect is the circuit of bodily responses to stimuli that take place before conscious apprehension. Once apprehended, the responses pass into thoughts and feelings, though they always leave behind a residue."[35] Kassabian's definition, useful as a starting place, reflects a particular strain in the scholarship that argues for the "autonomy" of affect. In her critique of affect theory, Ruth Leys summarizes this doctrine: "affects must be viewed as independent of, and in an important sense prior to, 'ideology'—that is, prior to intentions, meanings, reasons, and beliefs." They are "non-signifying, autonomic processes that take place below the threshold of consciousness awareness and meaning."[36] This assumption, articulated most strongly by Brian Massumi (following Gilles Deleuze and Felix Guattari), argues that affects' autonomy challenges the linguistic and discursive focus of contemporary social theory.[37]

I don't believe affect theory is antihermeneutic, nor do I think that it would be very useful if it were. Affect theory is a large field with a range of positions. Massumi's notion of autonomy, the idea of a strict divide between feeling and cognition, is a popular view, but many works about affect do not endorse it. Scholars such as Ben Anderson, Ben Highmore, Lawrence Grossberg, and Margaret Wetherell offer more fluid models, ones that recognize a continuum between immediate, preconscious, autonomic bodily processes and mental interpretations of these experiences.[38] In these models, affect is a "trajectory toward emotion," where feeling (bodily arousal and sensations) and thought (cognition) intermingle, shaping and reshaping each other.[39] In Wetherell's formulation, affect is also practice, "a figuration where body possibilities and routines become recruited or entangled together with meaning-making and with other social and material figurations."[40] Wetherell's choice of "practice" defines affect as a fluid event, what she calls "pattern[s] of unfolding." These patterns "unfurl, become organized, and effloresce with particular rhythms" and interact with existing social and bodily patterns and templates—what Pierre Bourdieu labeled "habitus," a "universe of ready-made feelings and experiences."[41] These "ready-made" feelings often have gender, class, and racial attributes that can include or exclude those who don't adopt the required practices. Wetherell, though, argues that these feeling templates are multiple, allowing for the creation of new affective practices that don't fit comfortably into any one defined set.

Wetherell's approach is close to the dominant research paradigm in psychology and neuroscience where researchers are looking for emotion as the meeting of bodily response and cognition. By emphasizing the role of context, scholars like Wetherell are also able to accommodate the real social determinations of feeling. Now-classic works of anthropology by Lila Abu-Lughod and Michelle Zimbalist Rosaldo have "definitively undermine[d] any idea" that the same feelings are common to all people everywhere.[42] Place, time, and culture shape emotions and our understanding of them in complex ways. But by retaining elements of affect's immediacy, the way bodies react constantly to the world around them, these scholars of affect provide analytical tools that go beyond social constructionism to something deeper, an analysis that grapples explicitly with the interplay of sensation and thought. This is especially important when dealing with music, a phenomenon that appears to be both an unmediated and abstract "language of emotion" and a readable text overflowing with meaning.[43]

JAZZ HATE IS ABOUT RACE

The third component is something that has already been suggested: jazz hate has always been about race. Although jazz hating is intertwined with other social ideas—gender and class, for example—race occupies a special, foundational place. This is because jazz is first and foremost the product of Black creativity. The music's growth and expansion were structured by what Ronald Radano and Philip Bohlman call the "racial imagination," the "shifting matrix of ideological constructions of difference associated with body type and color that have emerged as part of the discourse network of modernity." Ideas of race and racial difference have been "crucial aspect[s] in the constitution of identities and groups." But that doesn't mean these ideas are fixed: "the racial imagination remains forever on the loose." "Race," Radano and Bohlman argue, "defines not fixity, but a signification saturated with profound cultural meaning and whose discursive instability heightens its affective power."[44]

The racial imagination contains many different formations, but I will focus mostly on the important binary of Black and white. The Black-white division is rooted deep in American social and political life, exemplified by the widely, long-held idea of the "one-drop rule" that determined who was Black by the presence of any African ancestry. When other nonwhite groups have sought recognition and justice, they often have had to frame their place in US society in reference to this color line. Historically, the cultures of jazz have echoed this. The Black pioneers of the style invented the music from a fusion of Anglo-European, African, Caribbean, and Latin American musical styles. The music's "Spanish tinge," to use pianist Jelly Roll Morton's famous phrase, testifies to the Spanish-speaking musicians from the Caribbean and Latin America who helped create and develop the music. That proximity was a source of complex musical and social interactions, as "brown" musicians negotiated the nation's unyielding Black-white binary. In the first half of the twentieth century, lighter-skinned musicians such as Puerto Rican valve trombonist Juan Tizol could pass for white, a situation that frequently caused confusion as he traveled and performed with Black orchestras such as Duke Ellington's.[45] Darker-skinned Afro-Caribbean musicians such as conga player Chano Pozo were treated unequivocally as Black.[46] Asian American musicians faced similar issues, locating their "yellow" identity in relation to the Black-white divide. As musicologist Loren Kajikawa writes, for Asian American musicians of the 1980s, "Black music [was] not simply a voice from the margins but rather a set of deeply embedded cultural forms that pervade a variety of racialized contexts." These musicians were acutely aware that they were "working a cultural field sown by African American artists," and consciously positioned their music as an extension of Black cultural practices.[47]

In his book *The Color of Jazz*, Jon Panish argues that *Black* and *white* are "hybrid and complex" signifiers. These words, although fluid and changeable over time, nonetheless mark out a definable discourse that has dominated American life since at least the eighteenth century. Blackness is not a transcendental or essential fact, but "a combination of cultural inheritances and diasporic experiences."[48] Whiteness, on the other hand is different, distinct from Blackness but developed in tandem with it. Lacking fixed content, whiteness becomes an amorphous category, an unacknowledged norm against which racial difference is measured. It is a racialized identity "unlike any other because it is the dominant, normalized location."⁴⁹ But, as George Lipsitz reminds us, whiteness is more than an identity: "It is a structured advantage that is impersonal, institutional, collective, and cumulative." These advantages create a self-perpetuating system, what Lipsitz calls a "possessive investment in whiteness." Whiteness, Lipsitz argues, "exaggerates small differences in appearance to create large differences in condition. . . . It manifests itself through practices that create differential access to wealth, health, housing, education, jobs, and justice."⁵⁰ But these advantages, as well as the boundaries of whiteness, are historically specific and changeable even while remaining a persistent source of injustice and inequality. This changeability evidences the performative nature of whiteness, that it is "acted out" and made real through conscious and unconscious habits. As Kelsey Klotz, quoting Judith Butler, describes it, "a performance of race understands the racialized body as the site of a 'legacy of sedimented acts rather than a predetermined or foreclosed structure, essence or fact.'"⁵¹ From the hierarchical racial catalogs and rankings of the 1911 *Dictionary of Races or Peoples*, published by the US Immigration Commission, to the World War II–era idea of the white ethnic melting pot (the movie army platoon of Italians, Jews, and even Mexicans), the contours of whiteness have shifted, contracting and enlarging in response to historical change.⁵²

The jazz hate I write about works within the Anglo-American "racial imagination." And within this racial imagination, Blackness has remained an underlying framework for white engagement with the music. Not just musicians but musical sounds were understood against a "sonic color line," a real, if slippery, notion highly dependent on the interaction of social, visual, and sonic cues.⁵³ To understand this dynamic, I borrow Eric Lott's notion of the Black mirror. If Black Americans live with what W. E. B. Du Bois called "double consciousness," white Americans—those that self-identify or are socially or politically determined as white—see their world through the Black mirror: "Not unlike drag, black mirroring seeks less to reproduce blackness with any accuracy than to activate it for white purposes, in the first instance those of social dominance and self-regard." Lott argues that "classic American literature, Hollywood film, pop musical artistry, and concerned social commentary . . . summon blackness in order to redeem the Republic and instead reveal their supremacist redundancy."⁵⁴ Playing with Blackness, jazz musicians are also solidifying whiteness. This characteristic of the American racial imagination extends back to the nineteenth century and blackface minstrelsy. As Matthew D. Morrison writes, "the performance of blackness in blackface by ethnic whites not only determined how black people came to be seen and treated in the United States, but provided a proxy for whiteness to imagine itself as other than 'Other.'"[55]

An important context for the Black mirror is the asymmetry of American cultural borrowing and experimentation: culture may be flexible, allowing for hybridity, but as Panish (drawing on Raymond Williams) points out, it is only "relatively autonomous" from ideology and social structures.[56] Racism governs cultural interactions, creating an environment where whites can easily borrow and try on other identities, like Blackness, with little social, political, or economic risk. As Ingrid Monson notes, "white Americans since the 1960s seem to have been interested primarily in the fun parts of African American culture: music, dance, sports, fashion, and that elusive quality of hipness."[57] They have not, generally speaking, been willing to think hard about the discrimination and racism that also comes with Blackness in American society. African Americans, on the other hand, do not operate within the same parameters and cannot freely participate in cultural experiences without regard to race. The historical difficulty of Blacks and other nonwhites in performing European opera and concert music is only one of many examples that show this cultural asymmetry. Over and over again in American musical history, enthusiastic young white musicians have always been able to freely engage Black styles, from ragtime to jazz to rock 'n' roll to hip-hop. "In a racially stratified society," Monson writes, "structural differences remain though musical aesthetics have spread beyond their original borders." Jazz musicians, critics, and fans "mobilize the resources and discourses available to them in order to cope with the situation." These "resources and discourses" are an inextricable mixture of race and aesthetics shaped by historical context.[58]

Not only has jazz—the musicians, the writers, and the fans—been defined through notions of Blackness and whiteness, but the music itself becomes a "complex signifier" of race. "The imagination of race not only informs perceptions of musical practice," write Radano and Bohlman, "but is at once constituted within and projected into the social through sound." Jazz is a "soundtext" that carries and introduces racial meanings as it circulates. The musical sounds propagate notions of Blackness and whiteness.[59] Affective engagements with jazz, even when focused on the music itself, are still caught in the netting of the racial imagination. Although not always explicit, hating jazz has always been about the nature of Blackness in American life, and the implications of that for whiteness.

AFFECT, RACE, AND MUSIC

Many scholars of music have begun to explore affect theory. Two edited collections, *Sound, Music, Affect: Theorizing Sonic Experience* (edited by Marie Thompson and Ian Biddle) and *Sound and Affect: Voice, Music, World* (edited by Judith Lochhead, Eduardo Mendieta, and Stephen Decatur Smith), provide theoretical overviews of affect and its history in musical writing and scholarship.[60] Thompson and Biddle focus on explaining the various strands of affect theory and collecting together a variety of approaches, whereas Lochhead, Mendieta, and Smith concentrate more on connecting historical notions of musical affect with current theorizing. The most recent historical investigation of musical affect is Roger Mathew Grant's *Peculiar Attunements: How Affect Theory Turned Musical*. Grant explores the relationship between contemporary understandings of affect and those of eighteenth-century Europe, particularly through the idea known as *Affektenlehre*, or the "doctrine of affects."[61] All this recent work demonstrates what Lochhead, Mendieta, and Smith describe as the "conceptual openness" of affect as an analytical and theoretical category, the ways affective orientations open up new views of old subject matter at the same time that they break down disciplinary perspectives.[62]

Musical sound is crucial to making sense of the affective engagement with jazz. As Kassabian reminds us, music can move us, figuratively and literally, like few other experiences: "Sound and music have the capacity to modulate our bodily states with a mere fraction of a second's intervention and without our conscious consent."[63] The history of Western music is dominated by writers reaffirming and analyzing music's tremendous power to shape our individual and collective feelings, moods, and emotions. Beginning with Plato's admonishments against certain musical scales, music has been consistently portrayed as a powerful, often uncontrollable force on our affective lives. Sociological and psychological studies confirm that most people listen to music for the ways it allows them to evoke and manage emotions. Although other art forms work in similar ways, music's intimacy—how it surrounds us and penetrates us—makes it bodily in ways other arts are not. The explosion of recorded media has made this intimate experience ubiquitous, bathing our daily lives in all kinds of musical sounds, many we choose and just as many we do not.[64] In his book *Music and Embodied Cognition*, Arnie Cox provides a comprehensive typology of the ways musical sound shapes our individual affective responses. His "eight avenues of Musical Affect"—mimetic participation, anticipation, expression, acoustic impact, analysis, associations, taboos, and ephemerality—show the complex ways bodily experience, cognition, and culture work together to generate affective responses to music.[65] Together this body of writing demonstrates that the sonic component of musical experience is inextricably linked to feeling. The need to judge and evaluate music—a critical part of popular music culture—is related to its insistent affective demands on us.

The affective engagement with jazz has focused on a variety of musical characteristics. Form and melody have often been the focus of debates between jazz lovers and haters. Despite being organized tightly around song structures for much of its history, the music has a reputation for formlessness, or, as critic Mike Hobart describes it, "noodling around . . . a sound and fury signifying nothing."[66] The accusation of noodling is repeated in newspapers, magazines, blogs, and reddit boards. The idea of noodling—aimless improvisation—is also part of jazz musician lingo (it should be avoided!). The sense of formlessness is closely related to the perceived absence of melody. Of course, there is lots of melody, but what dismays many listeners is the absence of anything clear and transparent, a melody that can be easily followed. This is a critique that seems to emerge with each new African American musical practice—just as critics of ragtime in the late nineteenth century lamented its "primeval conception of music" focused just on rhythm, later critics in the 1980s lamented rap as nothing more than "rhythmic chant."[67] Jazz writers have recognized this common complaint and tried repeatedly to defend the music. Martin Williams titled his 1961 introduction to jazz appreciation *Where's the Melody?* Thirty-six years later, writer and pianist Jonny King titles the first chapter of his jazz appreciation book the same way.[68]

But more than form or melody, the focal point of jazz reception and evaluation has returned, over and over again, to rhythm, paradoxically to both its repetitiveness ("groove" and "swing") and its unpredictability (syncopations and polyrhythms). When the music first grabbed the national consciousness, critics fixated on its rhythms. As Radano argues, the white fascination with Black rhythm predates jazz, extending back to the first white encounters with music by enslaved people in the New World and extending up through ragtime, the immediate commercial predecessor of jazz. The grooves and syncopations of Afrodiasporic musics were heard as primal and precivilized, described as "hot," infectious, and sometimes dangerous. Radano writes that "the modern figure of hotness, which by the 1920s had become the informing epithet for the more rhythmically dynamic versions of jazz, seemed to conflate all the qualities of excess, from drunkenness to fever, from violence to sexual promiscuity."[69] But the obsession with rhythm as the defining feature of the music continued across the twentieth century and into the present. Loving and hating jazz depended a great deal on how one felt and interpreted jazz rhythms. There are few more concise signifiers of "jazz" than the swing pulse of a ride cymbal. The interpolation of that gesture into a performance immediately unfolds a complex set of jazz associations.

But focusing just on the sounds is insufficient. Affect is overdetermined, the product of an array of forces—aesthetic, political, and historical. For those who hate (and love) it, jazz is far more than sound; it is a cultural "site" saturated with affect.[70] Not a single object, jazz circulates in several mediated forms—as "abstract" musical sounds, recordings, televised performances, soundtracks to films, and discourse. And although feeling appears to reside in jazz, this is an illusion caused by "the erasure" of the "production and circulation" processes that create the objects we care so much about.[71] Understanding jazz as a circulating array of mediations helps break one of the most distorted understandings of music and affect: that it is the music itself that is the sole carrier of meaning and feeling. I will discuss the sounds of the music, but these are not enough to understand the historical affective engagements with jazz.

Many discussions of jazz hating, at least in music history circles, begin with the German philosopher Theodor Adorno. A leading thinker of the Frankfurt school, Adorno wrote extensively about music and its role in modern life. A trained musician and composer, Adorno was partial to the avant-garde practices of early twentieth-century classical music, specifically the atonal and twelve-tone works of Arnold Schoenberg, Alban Berg, and Anton Webern (Adorno befriended and studied with Berg). Although Adorno wrote on a diverse range of topics, music became an important vehicle for his deeper philosophical concerns, particularly the psychological and sociological damage wrought by the modernity of industrial capitalism. For Adorno, popular culture, including music such as jazz, was actually, despite its promises of pleasure and escape, a tool of subjection. Its pleasures were deceptive—rather than liberating people from the drudgery of their impoverished lives, popular cultural forms such as jazz reinforced the imprisoning ideologies of modern life: instrumental reason and free market capitalism.

Over his career, spanning the early 1930s through the late 1960s, Adorno returned several times to jazz, a music that he believed encapsulated all his concerns about the delusions of what he, along with Max Horkheimer, would term the "culture industry." Adorno's preoccupation with jazz has, in turn, become a preoccupation for the music's defenders. The list of authors who have directly engaged with Adorno's jazz writings is large and growing.[72] His essays on the genre span twenty years, with the first, "Farewell to Jazz," published in 1933 and the last, "Perennial Fashion—Jazz," appearing in 1953, although he returns to the subject in lectures from the early 1960s (collected and published in 1962 as *Introduction to the Sociology of Music*). In this late volume, jazz is subsumed under a broader analysis of popular music.[73] Despite the upheaval of Adorno's life during this period—exile to England then the US, and a return to postwar West Germany—Adorno's writings on jazz are consistent in their basic approach and conclusions. His critique of jazz is an integral part of his larger analysis of modern music generally, one that embraces Western art music as well as jazz and other popular forms.

Once you place Adorno's jazz writings in that larger philosophical context, the question becomes more general: not why he hated jazz but what is it about popular music more generally that so worried him. Seeing Adorno as a jazz hater is primarily the result of a narrow understanding of his critical project and, perhaps more, about reading off negative affects from his often hyperbolic prose. It is true, as Fumi Okiji notes, that Adorno never fully took into account race, especially the way jazz enacts its own self-critique of Western modernity.[74] Adorno's rhetoric is indeed harsh, often contemptuous, but there are some complications with a one-to-one matching of Adorno's feeling toward jazz and his analytical critique. First, Adorno's rhetoric is hard to disentangle from his analysis. He adopted exaggeration and hyperbole as a strategy to force confrontation with a very strong and adaptable foe, Western bourgeois ideology.[75] Second, his attacks on jazz, although unforgiving, are matched in intensity with his attacks on other musics and musicians such as Stravinsky.[76] The question for scholars is not what Adorno feels about jazz, but what he thinks is the role of affect in the musical experience of popular culture.

Recent work on Adorno has turned to the place of affect in his writing.[77] In her book *Adorno and Democracy: The American Years*, political scientist Shannon L. Mariotti argues that affect was essential to Adorno's thinking. For Adorno, "thinking and feeling are not distinct; they rely on each other." A critical consciousness, a recognition of the alienation of modernity, is fueled by "our feelings, from pain and suffering, both bodily and mental. . . . The sense of suffering tells us that something is wrong with the world around us."[78] In *Negative Dialectics*, Adorno writes, "The physical moment tells our knowledge that suffering ought not to be, that things should be different. 'Woe speaks: "Go." ' "[79] To live authentically is to feel shock and disruption at the broken world around you. Adorno was concerned deeply with art's affective power, especially its ability to overwhelm critical thought. The "jazz monopoly," he writes, "rests on the exclusiveness of the supply and the economic power behind it. But it would have been broken long ago if the ubiquitous specialty did not contain something universal to which people respond. Jazz must possess a 'mass basis,' the technique must link up with a moment in the subjects—one which, of course, in turn points back to the social structure and to typical conflicts between the ego and society."[80] The affects produced by mass culture dull our responses to the material and psychic violence of our present social system. We are unable to pause, to really examine the world. If we could, we would be startled—"shocked," in Adorno's language—by the ways our ideas do not, and cannot, cover objective reality. This realization of the "non-identical" is the first step toward repairing our damaged lives.[81]

In "On Popular Music," Adorno devotes the end of the essay to the affect of the jitterbug. His analysis begins where many contemporaneous accounts also begin, with the apparent fanaticism and mass hysteria of youth enthralled by swing. But Adorno's analysis then moves in a very different direction, folding back in on itself in typically dialectical fashion. For Adorno, the jitterbug's intense emotional engagement is "fictitious": although there are genuine responses to rhythmic stimuli, "mass hysteria, fanaticism, and fascination themselves are partly advertising slogans after which the victims pattern their behavior." The jitterbug can "switch off his enthusiasm as easily and suddenly as he turns it on."[82] At the root of this performance is an ambivalence that turns into "spitefulness," a resentment the jitterbug feels at accepting the will of an external force, in this case a culture industry that forces a person to accept its products or be marked as antisocial.[83] Adorno is not entirely clear about what psychological level this spitefulness occurs at, suggesting only that it is not fully unconscious (in the Freudian sense) but also not fully obvious to the person feeling it. The ambivalence seems to exist in some middle state, not unlike affect itself: a feeling that is strong and real but whose cause is only dimly perceivable. The ambivalent acceptance of the culture industry, the loss of control to "domineering standardization," mutates into an intense *positive* affect toward the cultural commodity provided and an intense *negative* affect—spite and even fury—toward criticism of that commodity.[84] These hostile feelings emerge, for example, when the jitterbug is confronted with "corny," outdated sounds: "Any rhythmical formula which is outdated, no matter how 'hot' it is in itself, is regarded as ridiculous and therefore either flatly rejected or enjoyed with the smug feeling that the fashions now familiar to the listener are superior," Adorno writes. "Likes that have been enforced upon the listeners provoke revenge the moment the pressure is relaxed."[85] These antipathies, although misguided, are evidence for Adorno of a struggle, of a sense of subjectivity fighting back, even if futilely, against social forces too strong for it.

Given his complex aesthetics, Adorno spurned nearly all the music around him (and from before his time too!). His rhetoric does appear contemptuous (jitterbugs as grotesque and abject insects), but reading the jazz essays next to his other musical writings shows a consistent rhetorical strategy—to shock and jolt the reader from a too-ready acceptance of easy answers to very difficult questions. Affect suffuses Adorno's writings—anxiety, fear, despair. These affects were grounded in his personal history: the latent fascism and authoritarian tendencies that underpinned putatively democratic systems. The falseness of jazz, its demand for conformity, signaled a deeper societal falseness and conformity.

Jazz scholars have only recently taken up the role of affect in the creation and reception of jazz. In his article "'My Foolish Heart': Bill Evans and the Public Life of Feelings," Paul Allen Anderson uses the reception of pianist Bill Evans to consider the larger discourse on emotional expression in jazz. Although Evans played hard-swinging blues and up-tempo numbers, music critics focused largely on his lush, romantic ballad playing. Anderson's ingenious essay explores the "public life" of "private" emotion through a distinction he makes between "introverted anthems" and "extroverted anthems." Evans's ballad playing was an example of the former: "musical gestures of masculine sentimentality found a home in poignant introverted anthems."[86]

In contrast to Evans's cultivation of "poignancy" and "finer feelings," other jazz performers of the era, especially the avant-garde purveyors of "the new thing," sought out different modes of musical-emotional communication. John Coltrane's quartet recordings of the early 1960s featured "unprecedented and hypnotic waves of energy." The saxophonist's searching, obsessive exploration of motives, rhythms, and timbres created a swirl of hard-to-pin-down feelings. These were neither introverted nor extroverted anthems: unlike Evans's balladry, they did not signify "poignancy," but they also did not signify the kind of public affirmation of feeling that the era's rock and soul music did. In Coltrane's wake came a new school of like-minded musicians such as Archie Shepp, Marion Brown, and Cecil Taylor. Critics frequently, and notoriously, read these musicians as sounding "angry." Coltrane was dismayed by this appellation: "I've been told my playing is 'angry,'" but musicians "have many moods, angry, happy, sad."[87]

The labeling of Black avant-garde players as angry echoes a broader discourse around Black male musicians. Nichole Rustin-Paschal explores the music and career of another "angry black musician," bassist Charles Mingus.[88] Taking up where Anderson's essay on Bill Evans leaves off, Rustin-Paschal explores the music's public emotions but now with an explicit focus on the intersections of race and gender. "The language of emotion," she writes, "is fundamentally about gender in jazz culture." To emphasize this, Rustin-Paschal speaks not of jazz musicians but of "jazzmen" and "jazzmasculinity." Like Anderson, Rustin-Paschal also focuses on the social life of emotion rather than its individual psychology: "The shorthand of 'emotion' circulates in and through jazz culture primarily as a term inclusive of subjectivity and experience, rather than physiological expression of feeling." The discourse of emotion is "an ever-evolving political language, capable of wrestling with the meaning of the contemporary moment."[89]

Hatred, as literary historian Daniel Karlin writes, "covers a multitude of sins": "The house of hatred has many mansions, but it remains one house in part because of the sign over the door."[90] As Anderson and Rustin-Paschal demonstrate, two of those "mansions" in hate's large house are racism and misogyny. Anti-Blackness, as a specific form of hate, plays an undeniable part in many examples of jazz hatred. As a mode of expression rooted in the Black American experience, evaluations of jazz inevitably become entangled with a history of racial thinking. For example, expressions of love for jazz, or Black music more generally, have played an important role in white affirmation of the Black experience of racism and injustice. A love of jazz has often become a symbol of understanding, both for Black and non-Black writers. As we will see with Black writer Stanley Crouch, an appreciation for jazz provided him a pathway to what he believed was a clearer understanding of the fundamental nature of the African American experience.

Similarly, misogyny has played an outsized role in many forms of jazz hatred. Early critics of the music emphasized its power to weaken self-control, unleashing all kinds of licentious behavior. Before listeners realized what was happening, they were engaging in all kinds of socially destructive, animalistic behaviors such as "sexual permissiveness, interracial mixing, [and] lewd and lascivious behavior."[91] This attack on self-control made the music implicitly feminized: women, whether through biology or social conditioning, were seen as constitutionally unable to restrain their emotions the way men could. But as jazz gained in popularity and the culture developed in the mid- to late 1920s—a world of nightclubs, recordings, and competitive jam sessions—jazz became heavily masculinized. Misogyny was now often directed at women trying to break into the music or at musicians who challenged the homosocial world that had developed. Racism and misogyny are key players in my story, but in the cases I consider, the hater typically foregrounds the music and its maker(s) as the object of hate, justifying that hate through a jazz-specific aesthetic language. That rejection, however, nearly always partakes of other kinds of hate such as racism and misogyny.

Although jazz is the center of my study, I see this book as part of a larger investigation into the history of emotions and affect, what Raymond Williams famously called "structures of feeling," a way to capture "practical consciousness" in its time and place. As Williams explains it, structures of feeling involve affect but are not limited to it (he also proposes "structures of experience" as a way to capture the concept's wider embrace). For Williams, the goal is to describe the "present-ness" of experience, the ways it develops and changes, and by this to avoid the reductionist errors of earlier Marxist analyses of culture. The history of jazz hating represents different structures of feeling, with their own "characteristic elements of impulse, restraint, and tone" and their own "affective elements of consciousness and relationships."[92] Although these structures of feeling have a kind of independent coherence, they are closely connected to other social structures, such as class, gender, and race. Hating jazz in the 1910s and '20s was definably different, if still connected, to the way jazz was hated in the '30s and '40s. Mocking jazz today echoes the satirical attacks of the 1960s, but they also embrace some very different attitudes and values connected to very different social experiences.

JAZZ RECEPTION, PAST AND PRESENT

Hating jazz is about a lot of things, but first it is about evaluation and judgment. I listen, contemplate, and then decide if it is good or bad, art or trash. Either I keep that to myself, or I speak or write about that judgment. As Simon Frith has pointed out in regard to rock and pop, evaluation and judgment represent fundamental ways we engage with popular music. It connects us to communities of listeners who share our evaluations. It can also mark out difference, separating lovers and haters. Labeling some music as bad, Frith writes, is "a way we establish our place in various music worlds." "Not to like a record," he continues, "is not just a matter of taste; it is also a matter of argument, an argument that matters."[93] The focus of my study is the public expression of that negative evaluation of jazz: Why and when do people communicate their dislike? What is at stake? What historical conditions trigger and frame such public expressions of hate?

I should be clear at the beginning that I love jazz. I've played and studied it for many years, as a drummer and more recently as a guitarist. Jazz, in its many varieties, continues to be an integral part of my life as a scholar and a fan. Although my instrumental study and listening preferences reside in the "mainstream" of the music—the mostly acoustic, small-group, postbop improvisational style—I listen widely and, I hope, with an open mind to all kinds of jazz, including Latin jazz, European-based free jazz, and smooth jazz. Even as I have tried to cultivate broad listening habits, I often fall back on evaluative language when describing my listening to other people: this music is good (innovative, creative, or new); that music is bad (boring, uninteresting, or clichéd). I am also implicated in the same racial dynamics that have defined jazz since its emergence. As a white musician and a scholar, I came at the music through the Black mirror. Jazz musical culture, in its virtuosities and grooves, offered something powerful to me, an affective experience that was compelling and not otherwise available. It also opened a door into a larger, deeper Black aesthetic. The historical account of jazz hating that follows is inevitably shaped by my own experiences and, like all histories, is partial and incomplete. But reflecting on my own tendencies has helped me understand the ways race, affect, and evaluative language intertwine in jazz discourse, both academic and journalistic.

In scholarship, issues of evaluation and judgment have most often been examined in "reception" studies such as Kathy Ogren's work on early jazz, David Stowe's and Lewis Erenberg's writings on swing, Paul Lopes's writing on the rise of jazz as an art music; Scott Saul's and Eric Porter's work on jazz musicians as thinkers and activists; John Gennari's writing on jazz critics; and Tony Whyton's research on the canonization of jazz musicians.[94] But issues surrounding the evaluation of music—aesthetic, social, and political—are engaged by many jazz scholars, if only in passing. Landmark works by Paul Berliner, Scott

DeVeaux, Ingrid Monson, and David Ake, for example, in carefully describing the social and musical processes of jazz musicians, inevitably touch on taste, feeling, and evaluation.[95] Unlike the narrower historical scope of these books, mine takes a more wide-ranging one. Organized thematically around issues of taste, humor, and genre, my study spans the history of the music, taking up some familiar topics such as the attacks on swing and bebop in the 1930s and '40s and the hand-wringing about Kenny G and the popularity of smooth jazz in the '90s. But I also investigate some lesser explored corners of jazz history: the '60s satire of jazz insiders like George Crater, and the early twenty-first-century work of innovative musicians like pianist Robert Glasper. And although I do talk about the specifics of musical performances, my book focuses more on the ways listeners, fans, and musicians have talked and written about what they think of the music. I concentrate on what is generally thought of as the more intangible aspect of reception—how people have *felt* about the music. Since there are already many accounts of why people love jazz, it seemed more interesting and useful to consider the opposite: Why do people hate jazz? Where do negative affects come from and what do they mean? Why and when do people voice their dislike, disapproval, or displeasure with jazz?

The historical record is not short on haters. In my years reading, researching, and writing about jazz, I have been fascinated by these critical voices. Many of these voices, as I will show, have been racist, classist, and ignorant, but many more have been progressive, intelligent, and intellectually adventurous. The hatred of jazz has come from all kinds of people. All of it deserves closer scrutiny. Perhaps most significant has been the realization that the strongest rhetoric has consistently come from *within* the jazz community. It was remarkable to see so many jazz lovers—critics, musicians, and fans—express so much anger, aggression, and contempt toward others in the jazz world, be they musicians, producers, record executives, or other fans. Talking about hating music focuses our attention on our affective engagement with the music from the "other side," and forces us to see music in its full relation to our lives. Looking toward hate we also see how all sorts of unpleasant moods are basic to musical enjoyment.

Although my study is focused on jazz, broadly understood, the themes I raise are applicable to other genres of popular music. Hate and hating are part of the discourse of the whole field of popular music. There are already several excellent books and articles that cover some of this territory. Simon Frith's *Performing Rites: On the Value of Popular Music* is a broad survey of the ways listeners value popular music. The role of judging music, Frith argues, is essential to popular music culture. Although jazz makes an appearance, the essays in Christopher Washburne and Maiken Derno's *Bad Music: The Music We Love to Hate* cover a lot of musical territory, including discussions of country, pop, world music, folk, film music, punk, rock, and electronic music. In *Good Music*, John J. Sheinbaum offers a nuanced and historical discussion of changing value systems across musical genres. Carl Wilson's now classic, *Let's Talk about Love: A Journey to the End of Taste*, weaves together the story of Celine Dion's musical career with a concise survey of academic discussions of taste. Wilson offers a reassessment of a much-derided pop star, demanding that we think through the consequences of our dislike: What or whom are we hating when we hate Celine Dion? An honest answer leads to an uncomfortable recognition of damaging class and ethnic prejudices. Finally, in *Hearing Luxe Pop: Glorification, Glamour, and the Middlebrow in American Popular Music*, John Howland offers an innovative cross-genre study of "luxe pop," the product of a "longstanding tradition of merging popular music idioms with lush string orchestrations." Howland traces this phenomenon through multiple musical genres and styles from the 1920s through the present, in the process demonstrating the ways that the fusion of strings with commercial popular music signified "glamour, sophistication, prosperity, and social mobility." Although not explicitly a history of taste, the history of luxe pop is closely tied to variations in American understandings of middle-class and middlebrow culture.[96]

As these books show, the dislike of music is interlaced with enjoyment: loving something intensely often means aggressively protecting it from forces that appear to diminish or demean it. It is difficult to tell the history of any popular genre without addressing the criticism leveled at it. The development of rock 'n' roll, country, and rap, for example, were defined and shaped by the intense, often obsessive hatred of writers, politicians, and community leaders. The contempt directed at these forms was a tangled mess of musical and social judgments. Criticism of the music became inextricable from ideas about race, class, gender, and sexuality.[97] And although the height of these attacks occurred when these genres emerged on the national scene, the shape of that early criticism persisted, providing the template for later attacks. As Nadine Hubbs shows in her book *Rednecks, Queers, and Country Music*, for many white middle-class Americans, country music remains a potent signifier of "rusticity, southernness, stupidity, or lack of sophistication." Even as our tastes have changed over the decades, becoming more multicultural and omnivorous, many Americans still claim they like "anything but country."[98]

These associations can spur something much stronger than a statement of taste preference. They can spark intense antipathy. You don't just dislike it; you hate it. One of the most notorious examples of hating country music comes from jazz drummer Buddy Rich during an appearance on a 1971 episode of *The Mike Douglas Show*. Rich was notorious for his arrogance and strong opinions as well as a frightening temper, so his attack on country music was not out of character. During the interview, Rich lambastes the music for its simplicity and lack of intelligence. Country music is "so simple that anybody can sing it, anybody can do it, anybody can play it on a string." "I think," he continues, "it's about time that this country grew up in its musical tastes rather than making the giant step backwards that country music is doing."[99] Rich not only appears to dislike the music, but he believes it represents all that is stupid and ignorant in the country.

Rich's contempt demonstrates several important things. First, his remarks show the lasting power of certain ideas regarding musical styles, how musical stereotypes quickly shift into social insult (country musicians and fans are stupid). This process—the move from musical to social criticism—is often fueled by very strong affective engagements such as anger, disgust, and contempt. But the interview also shows the ways this kind of affective-evaluative rhetoric suffuses the popular music landscape. The evaluation game is played by all. Rich is also a jazz musician—one of the best known in its history—and his reactions, if not typical, show the ways affects are intertwined with modes of evaluation. Rich, for example, draws on familiar tropes of jazz appreciation: jazz is hard work, jazz is complex and sophisticated, jazz is an authentic artistic expression. Although I focus on jazz hating, I hope to demonstrate that my discussion applies to other genres and styles of twentieth- and twenty-first-century American popular music as well. I wish to open a space for more scholarship that looks at the ways affect shapes both the acceptance but also the dismissal of popular musical genres and styles.

PLAN OF THE BOOK

Chapter 2 considers jazz hate in terms of taste—the process of choosing cultural objects in a commercial marketplace. Much writing on taste is indebted to the landmark work of French sociologist Pierre Bourdieu. In *Distinction: A Social Critique of the Judgement of Taste*, Bourdieu argued that taste is not a separate faculty but a tool in a larger social struggle, the need to mark out class distinctions. But this analysis shortchanges our affective experiences. In his essay "Taste as Feeling," Ben Highmore tries to bring affect back into the study of taste, arguing that taste "orchestrates sensibilities" in the confines of a specific ideological and material reality. One of the defining characteristics of this reality in the US is race and racial thinking, especially the idea of Blackness. The chapter then considers two historical moments in jazz reception—one from the 1940s and another from the 1950s—to show how immediate taste judgments, especially negative ones, need to be understood in a larger social and historical context, particularly America's involvement in World War II and its aftermath and the ways that experience reinforced but also challenged racial thinking.

Chapter 3 looks at one of the most powerful ways Americans engage with jazz: humor. Making fun of jazz represents a different strand of affective engagement with the music, one that, although sometimes wrapped up in taste, is distinct from it. Although the meaning of jazz has shifted over its hundred-plus-year history, there are certain themes that have remained central. Jazz has been, from the start, associated with urban life and especially Black urban life. It has also developed a passionate fan base. And while it has appealed to women and men, the music has always been strongly linked with men and masculinity. All these associations have been surprisingly resilient over the years, even as context inflects them in new ways: jazz is a self-selecting activity of city elitists, and its performers and fans are self-obsessed, too serious to see the absurdity in a music that seems to have no melody and no structure.

Although many jazz musicians have been happy to laugh at themselves, this chapter focuses primarily on humor from outside the jazz community, on humor that is negative, what Freud called "tendentious." Mockery and ridicule are two kinds of humor animated by strong negative affects. The aggression that drives ridicule and mockery of jazz is, not surprisingly, tied very closely to race and the role of Blackness in American life. Nearly every example of derision I found was created by white writers, actors, and comedians. Mocking jazz is to always be looking in Lott's Black mirror. What the mocker sees is whiteness and its seeming emptiness next to the fullness of Blackness. The chapter surveys a continuum of jazz ridicule, from the benign to the acid.

But what happens when the humor is stripped away? What you are left with is only the tendentious: contempt, aggression, anger, and disgust. In chapter 4 I look at jazz hate from inside different jazz cultures, places where we find some of the most extreme rejections of the music.[100] These reactions have emerged most often at moments of crisis and change, both musical and historical. As with taste and ridicule, expressions of these strong negative affects are shaped by both gender and race. To hate some expression of jazz has frequently been a way to express contempt for women or some manifestation of Blackness. In the chapter, I focus on examples of vehement critical dismissal by critics and also musicians. These attacks have sometimes fused with misogyny and racism. The chapter ends with a discussion of two of the most famous recent examples of contempt from within the jazz world: Pat Metheny's tirade against Kenny G and Stanley Crouch's attack on late-career Miles Davis. Crouch's writing also provides a way back into the fundamental place of race in all forms of jazz hating. Hating jazz— expressing contempt, anger, or disgust—is ultimately a reflection on much more than the music: it is a recognition of the powerful and damaging ways race continues to structure American life.

In chapter 5 I turn more explicitly to the ethics of hating music. The most extreme example of jazz hatred is, of course, the Nazis, who attacked popular music to forward their racist and nationalist agenda. Their celebration of certain musics and condemnation of others— jazz being a notable target—was part of a larger ideological project, one that directly supported mass murder on a devastating scale. The Nazis' rhetorical assault on jazz is arguably the best example in the book of the strongest form of hating, where the rejection of a musical style was explicitly yoked to the need to purge undesirable people. But as Michael Kater shows, the rhetoric differed from the regime's far more pragmatic and calculated management of jazz.[101] Thus even in the Third Reich, affective responses to the music were ambiguous, caught between official prohibition and denunciation, and actual, and sometimes encouraged, practice.

But is all jazz hating a slide toward social hatred, even violence? Is hating jazz ever justified and socially beneficial? I end the book with a brief consideration of the ethics of jazz hating. Many scholars have argued that hate, if defined and carefully directed, can be a positive thing, leading to social unity and progressive political ends. I am far more cautious: contempt, anger, aggression, and disgust too often slip into reification, fusing undesirable sounds with undesirable peoples. It is very difficult to harness such strong feelings and rhetoric into balanced, self-aware political goals. Hating jazz leads too often to hating people, a dangerous proposition given the music's intimate connection to Black life. Although I would prefer a world without such antipathy, my primary goal here is to illuminate the ways hating jazz, just as much as loving it, is foundational to the music.

2

What Do You Mean You Hate Jazz?

TASTE, RACE, AND THE ORCHESTRATION OF SENSIBILITIES

>   SEB: *What do you mean you hate jazz?*
>   MIA: *[It] just means that when I listen to it, I don't like it.*

A key scene in the film *La La Land* happens early, at the beginning of the romance between Seb (Ryan Gosling) and Mia (Emma Stone). Walking on the backlot of a movie studio, Mia confesses something that may stand in the way of their developing relationship: "I should probably tell you something now, get it out of the way: I hate jazz." Seb stops: "What do you mean you hate jazz?" To defend herself, Mia says she just doesn't "like" it. Seb asks her what she is doing now, and Mia says "nothing." The scene cuts to the interior of a jazz club, and as the camera pulls back, we see the couple seated at a table with Black jazz musicians playing in the background. As the conversation continues, we learn that Mia has no problem with the people who make or listen to the music; she just doesn't care for it when she hears it. It turns out that Mia's notion of jazz is mostly based on music she heard on a local radio station, which played "smooth jazz" artists such as Kenny G. "Elevator music," she adds. "Jazz music that I know." A frustrated Seb attempts to talk Mia through the formal properties of the performance they are listening to while telling her about the music's exciting, sometimes dangerous, history, about what is "at stake" in the music. Mia's "hate" is, by her own admission, based on little experience. Seb believes exposure can lead to appreciation, and he passionately tries to convince Mia of the music's nobility and dynamism. She is clearly entranced by Seb's passion, although we don't have any indication she has changed her opinion of the music.

Mia's hate is not characterized by what the eighteenth-century writer Samuel Johnson called a "violent commotion of the mind."[1] Her "hate" is really a mild dislike, "an intensified or rhetorically heightened way of expressing a taste or preference."[2] In this chapter, I will explore the kinds of jazz hating that happen in the domain of taste discrimination: the evaluation of music as good or bad. Once we understand judgments of taste as the intersection of affect, race, and gender, we can better understand why certain music impinges on us and other music simply passes us by. One species of jazz hatred manifests in a passionate dismissal of the music on the grounds that it is ugly and reflects a deficient or missing sense of taste. But affective engagement does not emerge from an isolated, individual judgment; it is always social, happening in particular times and places.

After introducing the concepts of taste and the aesthetic, I turn to the role of affect, the way feelings interact with social determinants to guide our evaluations of music. The issue of race—Blackness and whiteness—although not always explicit, is foundational, and in the following section, I explore the ways that taste judgments are rooted in racialized affect. The evaluation of jazz is implicated in a "racial imagination," one concerned with defining and controlling Blackness. With all this in mind, I look at the specifics of jazz, exploring the common reasons for disliking it. I then consider two connected moments of jazz reception—swing in the 1930s and '40s and bebop and cool jazz in the mid-'50s—to illustrate the ways racialized affect and taste interact with concerns about identity and the role of public emotion in American life.

TASTE AS FEELING

Taste is a concept that fuses sensory experience with evaluation and judgment. As Raymond Williams writes, *taste* has been used in the English language since at least the thirteenth century to describe not just the experience of eating and drinking but also touch and feel. By the following century, references to the term show an expansion of meaning through metaphor. Key to that expansion was the idea of discrimination. Taste described not only a sensory property or an act of consumption but the related ability to determine good from bad.³ By 1778, the term had taken its modern form. In his *Encyclopédie* article, Voltaire writes that taste, "this sense, this gift for distinguishing our foods[,] has produced in all known languages the metaphor that uses the word . . . to express sensitivity to the beauty and defects of all arts."⁴ The eighteenth century was consumed with this idea. Writers such as Lord Shaftesbury, Francis Hutcheson, and David Hume explored the nature and characteristics of taste. In their writings, the concept retains its noun-verb ambiguity; taste is both a property of the mind (noun) and the act of sensing and feeling the things of the world (verb). This concept soon fixes itself into an "abstraction of a human faculty" and then to a "generalized polite attribute"; with this reification, "good taste" becomes a thing that one can acquire.⁵ The concept evolved further as the industrial capitalism of the nineteenth century gave way to consumer capitalism in the twentieth: good taste became entangled with notions of individual consumer choice in a marketplace filled with goods and services. That connection has made taste an especially volatile notion that leads to a recognition that there is no "objective 'good' taste . . . only an evanescent, culturally and historically specific preference for certain things."⁶ The connection between taste and consumerism is so close that we nearly always assume "that the viewer, spectator, or reader is a *consumer*, exercising and subsequently showing his taste."⁷ For historian Luca Vercelloni, taste, although never completely losing its connection to active, sensual experience, has largely become inextricable from modern bourgeois life; taste is "a tool of mediated preference . . . of socially and commercially conditioned choice."⁸

The role of taste in capitalist societies has inspired potent Marxist critiques. Taste is ideology—a belief that we have choices when we really do not. As philosopher Theodor Adorno wrote, "In the field of entertainment the freedom of taste is hailed as supreme." To challenge this freedom amounts to the "suspicion that individuality may have disappeared altogether."⁹ A similar but separate strand of this mass culture critique emerged in the mid-twentieth century with scholars and critics such as Paul Lazarsfeld, Dwight Macdonald, and Clement Greenberg.¹⁰ Later writers, notably Herbert Gans and Lawrence Levine, offered strong rebuttals to these earlier, overwhelmingly negative analyses of popular culture.¹¹

The most influential study of taste, though, remains French sociologist Pierre Bourdieu's massive *Distinction: A Social Critique of the Judgement of Taste*. Bourdieu's writing echoes Gans but takes things a step further, focusing not just on who likes what but on how certain social groups deploy taste. Bourdieu is more interested in how taste is used than in what it consists of. In the West, he argues, "taste is a practical mastery of distributions which makes it possible to sense or intuit what is likely (or unlikely) to befall—and therefore to befit—an individual occupying a given position in social space."[12] In other words, taste is not simply preference in the marketplace of culture and commodities, it is about identity and social positioning. Taste is a means of social orientation that helps situate the individual in the "right" place. In France, this translated into social class: What are the right things to like as a factory worker or a junior executive? Bourdieu's work has been challenged for its ethnocentricity and its rigid mapping of class to cultural choices. Sociologist Richard A. Peterson has offered an influential critique focused on "cultural omnivores," tracing the way tastes cross social hierarchies. Against the social determinants of taste, Peterson's research shows that "people within higher occupational groups were no longer exclusive in their tastes," freely incorporating examples of popular or mass culture into their experiences.[13] In a different way, sociologist Antoine Hennion challenges Bourdieu by emphasizing taste's fluid, multidimensional determinations. Taste is a "reflexive activity," one that allows individuals and groups to "transform sensibilities and create new ones" and not just simply to "reproduce an existing order without knowing what they do."[14]

Despite its frequent abstraction into a thing, in common usage taste retains some of its active meaning: the act of choosing well in a crowded and confusing world of people and things. Taste is inherently fluid and changing, a characteristic that has often marked it as feminine or feminizing. It is no coincidence that fashion is the paradigmatic example of the concept: an industry built around a fundamental acknowledgment that tastes are ephemeral and contingent.[15] Debates on the nature of taste were greatly intensified in the twentieth century with the emergence of mass consumer culture. This new world—a world of passive consumption driven by the whims of taste—was often criticized as emasculating, representing the loss of a world of active producers.[16] But taste is also closely connected to the more elevated concept of the aesthetic—how to know and define what is beautiful. The mixing of taste and the aesthetic are part and parcel of modern capitalism, and it is not a coincidence that the two discourses developed in the industrializing and colonizing world of eighteenth-century Europe. For the rising bourgeoisie, questions of choice suddenly became urgent. Rationalizing the beautiful and our choices of beautiful things went hand in hand with a society driven by increasing industrialization and commodification.[17]

In the discussion and analysis of taste, both in popular and academic discourse, the role of feeling is often pushed to the side, as something either irrelevant (in the Kantian aesthetic tradition) or too personal and amorphous to describe. But affect always finds its way back into the discussion. In his essay "Taste as Feeling," Ben Highmore tackles the issue of taste and affect directly. For Highmore, Bourdieu's framework of taste as a proxy war over class positioning ignores the fluid ways in which we "attach ourselves to the sensorial worlds." It is not that taste doesn't have class dimensions, but that the Bourdieu model can't take hold of how "microsensitivities," such as why we like a particular pop record, connect to "macro-orchestrations," such as late capitalism's "ubiquitous taste for 'convenience.'" To capture this active, sensory dimension, we need to treat "taste as an agent that orchestrates sensibilities and that potentially alters our social environment (rather than simply reinforcing already established social relations), generating new liberating possibilities and new 'coercive freedoms.'"[18]

By focusing on taste as feeling, we not only return the concept to its etymological origins in the experience of food, but we make the term active again—as a verb, "to taste"—and not a thing. Highmore is especially concerned with the materiality of taste, "an energy that orients us toward things . . . [a] modality of our attunement toward sensorial culture." Taste is "the shape and color that our attachments take in the world."[19] Taste is not a discrete on-off relationship but a fluid register of engagement. In other words, taste is part of affect, what Melissa Gregg and Gregory J. Seigworth describe as "an impingement or extrusion of a momentary or sometimes more sustained state of relation as well as the passage (and the duration of passage) of forces or intensities."[20] Highmore's argument sits at the most general level of taste, one that embraces all the myriad choices we make in our daily lives, from where to eat, how to dress, and what to do after work. Art, and specifically music, are also described well by Highmore's ideas. Our taste for any particular music is a meeting of the sensible and the social. Likes and dislikes in music run on a continuum of intensities generated by the interaction between "micropractices"—individual encounters—in the context of "macropractices," the social world that enables and constrains us.

JAZZ, TASTE, AND RACIALIZED AFFECT

Reconceptualizing taste as the intersection of social positioning and affect is transformative, but when considering jazz, it falls short. Much of the attraction to jazz—and repulsion from it—has been tied to ideologies of race, particularly whiteness and Blackness.[21] In both the celebration and criticism of jazz—the loving and the hating of it—there has been a consistent undercurrent of racialized thinking. Although there are exceptions, most writers on jazz since the 1920s have recognized the music's origin in Black life. That association, however, often merges with essentialist notions of Blackness—that the music's unique characteristics are the result of some biological specificity of African Americans. Sometimes the racism is explicit, but just as often it is implicit. The slippage from association to essentialism happens most often when explaining the music's affect, the way it grabs listeners' minds and bodies. In his study of early New Orleans jazz, Charles Hersch writes, "Even the harsh criticism of the music can be seen as a kind of repressed wish for the forbidden: in a time of increasing routinization and restraint, whites condemned Blacks for emotionality and the pursuit of pleasure at the expense of work precisely because they (whites) were drawn to those qualities."[22]

From the moment of its birth in New Orleans, white leaders combined fears of the music's affect with concerns of race mixing. Like ragtime before it, jazz "recklessly unleashed the passions, especially sexual ones, threatening to make whites as uninhibited as Blacks were said to be." Critics equated jazz's impudent rejection of musical rules with a rejection of social norms and values. Hersch writes, "To its critics, music at 'ratty' [jazz] clubs mirrored and encouraged the unrestrained behavior of its listeners." New Orleans officials tried their best to contain the music, passing laws that restricted the hours of bars and clubs that featured this low-class, provocative music. They also sought to contain it spatially: "blacks, prostitution, and jazz all threatened contagion and needed to be quarantined" into segregated and geographically defined areas of the city.[23]

As jazz grew in popularity, these same critiques would be voiced again and again—a fear of affective contagion and racial mixing or contamination. In *The Appeal of Jazz*, one of the earliest sustained analyses of the music, British music critic and jazz enthusiast R. W. S. Mendl summarizes the common objections to the new sounds. Although describing the British reception of jazz, Mendl's list echoes similar writing happening in the United States at the time. Focusing on those who expressed "sweeping condemnations" rather than "mild dislike," Mendl finds critics who "can discover no value of any sort or kind on the object of his hatred." For these writers, jazz is objectional because of its "sensuality," "noisiness," "stupidity," and "cynical grotesqueness." Mendl takes each objection apart, showing how jazz compares favorably to the highbrow world of European classical music. But he finds it more difficult to tackle the final objection: "There are some people whose hostile reaction to syncopated dance music is attributed by them to their antipathy towards everything connected with the n[*****]."[24] Even here, however, the situation is not what it seems:

> It is all very well to say that the presence of a black man, though you feel goodwill towards him and would even try to help him and sympathise with him in trouble, gives you gooseflesh, and that this is the reason for your antagonism to a form of music which is undoubtedly connected both in its origins and in its present manifestations with n[*****] traditions. But one of the principal negro elements in this music is that quality which it has inherited from the darky folk songs, and we usually find that the beauty of these songs is acknowledged even by those who are most averse from "the n[*****] business." The early jazz bands of the negroes were doubtless crude, if not vulgar. A certain amount of original coarseness has, possibly, survived even in the white man's recent elaborations which take the form of the syncopated dance orchestras of to-day. In so far as it does so, we are doubtless justified in accounting for our animosity towards modern jazz music partially by our aversion from its n[*****] source. But we should beware of laying

too much emphasis on this. For the colours of the modern jazz band, which we may pronounce to be ugly or too bizarre for our liking, are far removed from that primitive artless stock, and therefore we could not fairly expect to find the sole ground of our dislike of them in any preconceived antipathy towards the negro.[25]

In this passage Mendl solidifies a link between affect and race. Interestingly, he starts not with the feelings engendered by musical sounds but with more general feelings about Black people, who give the jazz hater "gooseflesh." Mendl goes on to argue that this "negro" hater is mistaken because the music has altered and developed in the hands of the "white man's elaborations" and is now far removed from the "primitive artless stock" of Black folk expression. Even though he attempts to distinguish the feelings aroused by the "n[*****]" and the feelings aroused by the "vulgar" early Black jazz bands, Mendl still ends up conflating social and musical affect, reinforcing the slippage between association and essentialism, between those who despise the music because of their "antipathy towards everything connected with the n[*****]" and those who despise jazz because it is "crude" and "primitive." Mendl's passage illustrates the total imbrication of race, affect, and musical sound.

The roots of this fusion of race and affect, though, goes much further back. Taste, as an intellectual project, has been wrapped up in ideologies of race since its emergence in the eighteenth century. As literary historian Simon Gikandi argues, enlightenment thinkers produced a discourse "predicated on the need or desire to quarantine one aspect of social life—the tasteful, the beautiful, and the civil—from a public domain saturated by diverse forms of commerce, including the sale of black bodies in the modern marketplace." The discourse of taste and aesthetics was a way of "managing the world engendered by commerce." That management meant excluding from taste any mention of slavery, one of the dominant engines of economic expansion in the eighteenth century: "the establishment of a realm of taste, or even the valorization of ideals of beauty, depended on systematic acts of excluding those considered to be outside the systems of explanation that were being established as norms." Gikandi concludes that the figure of the enslaved person was "the informing yet interdicted symbolic in the representation of the culture of taste, outside or excessive of the epistemological framework of modernity."²⁶ Taste, in other words, is built on notions of race and difference from the start.

Jazz is exemplary here because the issue of race has been so immediately present in the discourse around the music from the earliest writings in the late 1910s and early 1920s. Given the music's origin and central place in Black life, jazz reception has always interacted with notions of racial difference. The explicit racism of Mendl's discussion—the unselfconscious use of *n[*****]*, for example—becomes rare after the 1920s, but critics—mostly white ones—who loved the music also gave evaluative assessments suffused with racial ideas and thinking. Even though an improvement over the naked racism of earlier writers, these critics' conflations of taste, aesthetics, and race were just as often rooted in myth and stereotypes.

Many Black musicians and writers have responded forcefully to this fusion of musical taste and racial thinking. As John Gennari notes, these writers "have tended to emphasize the social messages embodied in the music." Jazz is not just a collection of sounds but "a way of living in the world."²⁷ One of the most famous statements of this perspective is Amiri Baraka's landmark essay, "Jazz and the White Critic," first published in *DownBeat* magazine in 1963 and then republished as part of Baraka's monograph, *Black Music*. For Baraka, most white critics of jazz, though enthusiastic and well-meaning, have been unwilling or unable to write about its true social, historical, and political context, "its social and cultural intent." They treat the music as a kind of spontaneous expression and not the product of an "intelligent body of socio-cultural philosophy." "The notes *mean something*," Baraka writes, "and the something is, regardless of its stylistic considerations, part of the black psyche as it dictates the various forms of Negro culture." But the white critics are not Baraka's only target: he also calls out the taste arbiters of the Black middle class, such as the Howard University professor who complained to Baraka how much "bad taste the blues contain[s]." If the white critic is often ignorant, Baraka's Black middle-class critic is self-hating, embracing a white middle-class standard of sterile American culture.²⁸

Although aimed at jazz criticism, his argument is also implicitly about taste as an inherently racialized category. Taste—in the essay synonymous with aesthetic evaluation—is socially and culturally specific. Earnest and sincere white critics cannot simply judge the music "good" or "bad" based on what they hear. Appreciation must give way to understanding. The music was produced from a unique historical and cultural experience, "a constantly evolving social philosophy directly attributable to the way the Negro responds to the psychological landscape that is his Western environment."[29] More than simply criticizing white critics for writing poorly and ignorantly about jazz, Baraka is implicitly making an argument about taste as white bourgeois ideology. Taste is not only a marker of class distinction, it is part of an extensive white supremacist project. Here he prefigures Gikandi's arguments about the twin birth of modern racism and the discourse of taste and the aesthetic. Jazz can and should be evaluated, but within a framework developed from the specificities of Black American culture. What John Gennari calls the "critics pose," the formalized and aestheticized critical position historically practiced by many white jazz critics, not only separates the critics from the masses but also from the material realities of Black life.[30]

In a self-published statement from 1973, trumpeter Wadada Leo Smith, writing as a member of the Association for the Advancement of Creative Musicians, takes this criticism a step further, arguing that Black "creative music" cannot be criticized at all:

> can creative music (an improvisational music) be criticized, as was [Euro-American] musical composition? as in all cases of something that comes into existence with absolutely no mate to it anywhere in the world, it naturally brings its own rules of understanding, of interpretation, and technique of expression. so it was with the coming of the twentieth century when we entered a new dimension of art, a dimension of art-music that never before existed: creative music, the improvisors. and so, the answer is no, creative music cannot be criticized.[31]

His point is general, but elsewhere in the statement Smith makes it clear that Black creative music must be independent of the control and judgment of the white culture industry, the "powerMAN," that has consistently deprived Black artists of their aesthetic and financial independence. That industry includes not just the discriminatory practices of its white leaders, but also white supremacist structures such as copyright laws, "barbaric type laws" that, by focusing on a leader, deprive contributors to creative music their fair share of royalties.

Smith's critique echoes the Black nationalist ideas of the mid- to late 1960s' Black Arts Movement (of which Baraka was an important member).[32] In its strongest form, such as in the writings of Ron (Maulana) Karenga, art was to be a force for Black revolution, and should be judged on "social criteria" alone.[33] More recently, bell hooks argues that, while the Black Arts critique of taste and Western aesthetics was correct, the conclusions that Baraka and others drew—"that everything black was good and everything white bad"—was ultimately corrosive to Black arts production. Hooks, and scholars like George Lewis, argue for an "aesthetic mobility," one that recognizes the distortions of a racialized European aesthetic tradition but without closing down avenues for creative engagement, borrowing, and reworking: "Working from a base where difference and otherness are acknowledged as forces that intervene in western theorizing about aesthetics to reformulate and transform the discussion, African-Americans are empowered to break with old ways of seeing reality that suggest there is only one audience for our work and only one aesthetic measure of its value."[34]

Baraka, Smith, and hooks all disclose the underlying racism in taste evaluations: that taste in its Western formation is never "disinterested" in the Kantian sense; they all share, at least implicitly, Gikandi's assessment that the idea of taste is strongly connected to Western notions of white supremacy. Each writer suggests that taste evaluations by white critics and the white public are often missing something fundamental. There is an epistemological aporia at the heart of white evaluations of Black music. Some of what is missing can be attributed to an ignorance of Black history and Black struggle. But as Highmore argues, taste cannot be extricated from feeling. As scholar Katherine McKittrick writes, Black creative practices have historically not only critiqued "colonialism, racism, structural inequalities, and other forms of violence" but offered "neurological, affective, physiological pleasure, sadness, and reparative possibilities."[35] Black musics, such as jazz, need to be grasped not just in their historical and social context but in their affective dimensions as well.

Understanding taste as inextricable from both race and feeling has important implications for how jazz has been evaluated both positively and negatively. Being moved by Black expressive culture or being left cold by it does not indicate any understanding of the feeling—the affective texture—of Black life. Many important white jazz writers tell a story of falling in love with jazz, an encounter with the music that was so emotionally gripping that it changed their life.³⁶ In her study of white jazz autobiographies, Reva Marin documents the many variations on this basic story. But the adoption of Black cultural practices is deeply fraught, haunted by a social reality of inequality. Many white musicians struggled to reconcile their adoption of Black musical practices with a need to create an authentic identity, one complicated by a shifting discourse around who counts as white (as with immigrant or second-generation Jewish musicians in the early twentieth century such as Art Hodes, Benny Goodman, and Max Kaminsky).³⁷

Conversely, many white jazz critics have criticized Black musicians who did not seem to embody Black vernacular musical practices. Composer and pianist John Lewis, leader of the Modern Jazz Quartet, was criticized in the late 1950s and '60s for not sounding "funky enough," in other words, not "Black" enough.³⁸ At times, these critiques could take on an uncomfortably essentialist cast. Writing in 1971, journalist and scholar Albert Goldman lamented the "bleaching out" of jazz, the "loss of the black essence" that weakened the music's "emotive force." "Jazz," he writes, "is an art of taste. Everything the musician hears must be tested against a mental touchstone, a black Kaaba that dictates this *is* or this *is not* jazz." Goldman smuggles in an essentialism that, although not explicitly biological, echoes that discourse. For Goldman, when Black musicians bleached out jazz, they were betraying some foundational truth about themselves.³⁹

EVALUATING JAZZ

When asked why they don't like jazz, most listeners start with the sounds. A Reddit thread from 2008, "To all the Jazz-Haters on Reddit, what is it that you dislike about Jazz?," lists the most common complaints:

> To me it sounds like several very talented musicians playing different tunes at the same time.

> It's intrusive enough to distract me, yet not melodic enough or lyrical enough to hold my attention.

> I like jazz and have played saxophone since I was 14. I'm 42. But, there is one thing about jazz that drives me nuts. The improvised solos. Seriously. A solo should be a set number of measures. Not 5 minutes per instrument. Enough already.
>
> I would characterize the melodies and rhythm as too "chaotic" for my taste. Most Western music follows a somewhat familiar pattern, introduce a phrase, deviate from it for a time and return back to the original phrase, producing a sense of resolution or returning home. Jazz just wanders around aimlessly at times, like a drunk hobo.
>
> I can do some types of jazz but usually it is too "unstructured" for me and I feel anxious listening to it.
>
> Don't even get me started on solos. Some of them just boil down to a narrative that goes as this: "Oh yeah, listen to me play whatever I want without regard to the rest of the group. You hear that part? Yeah, I think that sounded nice. Let me do the same thing with very little variation for about . . . 30 more times. Yeah. I'm forcing everyone else to be bored so I can force you to listen to this."
>
> It's boring. You can't dance to it. It's not fun and upbeat. It reminds me of being in a dentist's chair.[40]

These reactions—and you can find many, many similar exchanges elsewhere—often don't specify artists or offer any definition of the music they are talking about. People complain about specific elements of music they don't like—no melody, no form—and associate that with some music they believe is jazz. If jazz lovers tend to be very detailed about what they love, jazz detractors tend to be much more general. Further complicating matters is the historical fluidity of the genre: what has been defined as jazz has changed dramatically over time, shaped by writers as well as musicians and jazz fans. For example, the complaints about endless, meandering improvisation refer to the musical changes introduced by bebop musicians in the mid-1940s—swing-era musicians in jazz orchestras had tightly limited space for improvisation.

A common response to this vagueness has been to claim that the jazz hater just doesn't know the real thing (Seb's approach in *La La Land*). This is a consistent rhetorical move you can find in writings stretching back to at least the 1920s. Some scholars have asserted that German philosopher Theodor Adorno, arguably one of the most famous jazz haters, just didn't hear the real thing, that he had not heard or listened carefully to, for example, Louis Armstrong or Sidney Bechet.[41] But semantic indeterminacy seems characteristic of jazz hating. In my discussion, I will not be correcting for this fuzziness, and I won't offer any normative definition (as if that were possible). The mobility of the genre's meaning is essential to understanding the fluid and dynamic nature of jazz hating.

The dislike of jazz is better understood in a much broader framework, one that recognizes the fundamentally social nature of musical taste. "Value judgements underpinning negative criticism of music," Tony Whyton writes, "predominantly lie outside the world of 'pure' musical creativity, and in many respects, can be considered arbitrary," contingent on time and place.[42] Thus there is no bad jazz. It only becomes "bad" in a particular evaluative context, as part of an argument over musical value.[43] These contexts, however, are often obscured by the very language of evaluation. For example, the celebration of the jazz or pop standard has historically been expressed in the language of musical quality, skill, and sophistication—the works of the Great American Songbook transcending the ephemeral pop song. But the elevation of the standard in the 1950s reflected not transcendent artistry but the social position of its defenders, the "taste[s] of a culturally and economically dominant formation," represented by the pre–rock 'n' roll generation.[44]

Criticism of jazz most often falls into three categories: arguments about production, effects, and musical craft.[45] This typology is a starting point, and many examples I will talk about mix these types in various proportions. Production arguments, as Simon Frith terms them, criticize music as a thoughtless or meretricious product of mass culture. Bad music is bad because of the system that made it.[46] This has been an argument leveled at every form of commercial popular music since the late nineteenth century. "Taste panics" have defined the reception of nearly every new commercial musical form: Tin Pan Alley popular song, ragtime, jazz, all the way through attacks on 1990s boy bands such as *NSYNC or 2000s female pop stars such as Katy Perry. During the 1930s, the fierce partisans of 1920s small-group hot jazz, dubbed the "moldy figs" by swing proponents, railed against swing as a soulless product of the music industry. Rudi Blesh, one of the most strident moldy figs, believed that swing was the result of the "dilution and deformation of jazz" caused by "commercialism" and the adoption of the music by white bandleaders.[47]

A related production argument is what Frith calls "imitative" critiques, in which a song or musical performance is rated poorly because it is uncreatively derivative of an original record or performance. In a 1939 article for *Esquire* explaining swing, B. S. Rogers writes that "jazz and swing are synonymous. All swing is jazz, all jazz that is not swing is bad jazz or no jazz at all." "Commercial dance music," Rogers continues, "for example, the work of such men as Vincent Lopez, Guy Lombardo, and Eddy Duchin—is based on jazz devices and uses jazz techniques, but it isn't jazz in the pure and original sense of the word." People who say they can't understand swing just haven't heard the real thing, "a hot outfit playing hot music."[48] Although not the central point of his article, he makes it clear through his examples that true jazz is a form of African American music. Real jazz is the product of Black music making. And while many white bands have learned to play it well—Benny Goodman, for example—it is still imitative. Rogers's ideas were commonplace in much of the 1930s and '40s critique of "commercial" and "sweet" jazz. In his 1942 book, *The Real Jazz*, the influential French jazz critic Hugues Panassié frames a history of the music as one of bad white imitations of Black New Orleans musicians: "Unfortunately the majority of the white musicians paid little attention to the style of the Negro orchestras; they took over the Negro repertoire but played it in their own style, and as we have seen, the repertoire mattered little in jazz music. . . . The white musicians then, in adopting the repertoire and the instrumentation of the Negro orchestras while neglecting the interpretative style, adopted many accidental elements of jazz and missed the essential one. Such music can in all justice be called false jazz music."[49] Panassié's arguments echo loudly through the twentieth century, heard again and again by critics lamenting white "imitators" of Black styles such as R&B, soul, and hip-hop.

"Effects" argument, on the other hand, focus on an alleged causal relationship: bad music makes people do bad things, such as when Anne Shaw Faulkner wrote in 1921 that jazz put the "sin in syncopation."[50] In the 1920s, a New York City doctor warned that jazz was dangerous because it caused "drunkenness . . . [by sending] a continuous whirl of impressionable stimulations to the brain, producing thoughts and imaginations which overpower the will."[51] In the mid-1930s, at the height of the swing craze, the archbishop of Dubuque denounced the "cannibalistic rhythmic orgies" that were "wooing our youth along the primrose path to hell."[52] Other critics at the time feared that the mass popularity of the music was brainwashing young people, destroying their sense of independence and priming them to adopt fascism. These bad effects can be remedied when the music is eliminated and replaced by something morally sound.

This critique has been revived again and again in the twentieth century, perhaps most notoriously in the 1980s and early 1990s with the Parent Music Resource Center (PMRC). In her 1985 testimony in front of the US Senate Commerce, Science, and Transportation Committee on the need for the labeling of commercial music, Tipper Gore, founding member of the PMRC and wife of then senator Al Gore, asserted that "the element of violent, brutal erotica has exploded in rock music in an unprecedented way. Many albums today include songs that encourage suicide, violent revenge, sexual violence, and violence just for violence's sake." These messages, though, are not just threatening; they have contributed directly to the rising numbers of teen pregnancies, suicide, and other acts of violence. Gore goes on to directly attribute the suicides of several teens to the influence of songs by AC/DC, Metallica, and Ozzy Osborne.[53] With the rise of gangster rap in the late 1980s and early '90s the same arguments were trotted out again: lyrical or visual representations of violence were leading to real gang violence.[54] As with ragtime, jazz, and heavy metal, rap was an agent of social and psychological damage. Bad music caused people to do bad things.

Arguments about musical craft focus not on social or psychological effects but on something more technical: a set of normative practices that define good music making. They also suggest a communication failure. "Bad music," Frith writes, "is music that doesn't communicate—between musician and audience, between musician and musicians, between performers and composer."[55] Bad music impudently ignores the standards of musical excellence. To many early listeners, writes historian Neil Leonard, jazz was "full of wild excesses and formlessness, totally lacking in restraint and discipline."[56] This kind of criticism was especially common in the first few decades of jazz writing. In "The Age of Jazz," a 1929 essay published in the *Journal of Education*, author J. W. Studebaker laments the "atrocious execution of this music, augmented . . . by the unspeakably inane words accompanying the performance." But this same music, Studebaker continues, "played by a first-class orchestra takes on a definitely different aspect," one that gives it an appropriate place in the "scheme of modern music."[57] In a 1938 interview with the *New York Times*, bandleader Paul Whiteman's father, Wilberforce James Whiteman, says: "I hate jazz and swing music, and I despise crooning—there is no art in any of them." (Yet, he continues, "I think my son, Paul, is a humdinger.")[58] These kinds of criticism reappear throughout jazz history, for example in the attacks on Ornette Coleman and other avant-garde "free jazz" artists of the late 1950s and '60s, fusion artists of the '70s, and experimenters with jazz and hip-hop in the '80s and '90s.

These categories—production, effects, and craft—are helpful in understanding the ideologies that shape critical assessments of the music. But attached to these judgments are negative affects such as anger, envy, malice, and spite. Philosopher Max Scheler grouped these feelings under the phenomenon of *ressentiment*, a term he borrowed and reworked from Nietzsche. "*Ressentiment*," writes Scheler, is "a self-poisoning of the mind . . . a lasting mental attitude, caused by the systematic repression of certain emotions and affects, which, as such, are normal components of human nature." This repression "leads to the constant tendency to indulge in certain kinds of value delusions and corresponding value judgments."[59]

For Scheler, many aspects of daily life are suffused with *ressentiment*, a condition that develops when a person or group of people feels oppressed, unequal, or unable to access the social position or material goods of others. The intense, negative feelings this condition engenders are repressed and abstracted into an alternate value system. Scheler calls this rival system "delusionary," and its main function is to denigrate its opponent. "The formal structure of *ressentiment* expression is always the same: A is affirmed, valued, and praised not for its own intrinsic quality, but with the unverbalized intention of denying, devaluating, and denigrating B. A is 'played off' against B."[60]

Not all critiques of jazz are structured by *ressentiment*, but many of the most vituperative are. For example, as historian Neil Leonard argues in *Jazz and the White Americans*, the traditionalist attacks on jazz made in its early years construed it as not just a musical practice but an opposing value system. Although differing in emphasis, the two primary groups of critics—religious leaders and professional musicians and educators—attacked jazz for the ways it lacked everything they valued in musical art: jazz had no sense of proportion or propriety, and it could not transcend the basest aspects of human nature. Although focused on the characteristics of the music, these attacks were really part of a broader anxiety over post–World War I social changes. Urbanization, immigration, and commercialization were overturning the white Protestant dominance of American life. Feeling besieged and unable to turn the clock back, these critics played their value system against its opponent, metonymically represented by jazz. These new sounds, they argued, lacked any musical quality or spiritual substance. To them, the exuberance, joy, and vitality of jazz was a source of angst. In Scheler's words, they were justifying their "inner pattern of value experience" against a corrupt, alternate value system represented by jazz.[61]

Criticisms of jazz today are not all so easily explained by Scheler's *ressentiment*, but the idea is still useful. In his *Washington Post* article "All That Jazz Isn't All That Great," Justin Wm. Moyer declares, "Jazz is boring. Jazz is overrated. Jazz is washed up."[62] Moyer is a former musician (a reed player) who studied jazz at Wesleyan University before abandoning it because he "just didn't get" the music's aesthetics. "I found jazz generically pleasing," Moyer writes, "but insubstantial and hard to grasp." He offers five reasons for his judgment: jazz ruins great songs by removing lyrics; jazz improvisation is neither unique nor special; jazz is not evolving; jazz is unable to define itself; and jazz has been "co-opted" by capitalism. Moyer's rant is a hodgepodge of classic laments. There is the mass culture critique (jazz is an ill-defined commercial sellout), the modernist critique (jazz has not evolved), and the elitist critique (jazz ruins great popular songs; jazz improvisation is nothing special). Granted, a short newspaper think piece is not the venue for a sustained analysis, but Moyer's explanations and examples are both odd and highly selective. In the section on improvisation he offers passing insults to Phish and the Grateful Dead—both groups improvise a lot, and, he implies, are terrible. He then describes jazz guitarist Wes Montgomery's playing as serviceable background music for Barnes and Noble bookstores. When discussing the genre's lack of a clear identity, that it is "defined by little more than improvisation, sunglasses, and berets," he doesn't point out how amorphous other categories of music are, such as rock and hip-hop. He only offers substyles—rockabilly and twelve-tone serialism—musical types far more specific than the larger genre they are generally thought to fit under.

Scheler's *ressentiment* helps to explain what is otherwise a curious, spontaneous rant (Moyer appears to be triggered by the uproar over Django Gold's Sonny Rollins parody, discussed in chapter 3). The writing seethes with frustration. How does a music so underserving retain so much respect? How does jazz continue to be honored even though it long since did anything worthy of the accolades: "Jazz has run out of ideas, and yet it's still getting applause." Moyer's frustration points to a sense of powerlessness in the face of the music's cultural influence—everyone, Moyer suggests, is being duped. Musicians, writers, industry people—all seem convinced of the inherent worth of jazz (Ken Burns's documentary series on jazz, he notes, was twice as long as his Civil War documentary). From this position of impotence, Moyer can only shake his fist and claim that jazz is a false god. Moyer's *ressentiment* implies a dominant cultural system of artistic values that he finds pervasive and corrupt. Jazz does, indeed, have a relatively high cultural status today, but it only achieved that with great struggle and, arguably, at great cost. *Ressentiment*, though, is only one form of jazz hating—it is not always presented as a battle of competing, mutually exclusive value systems. In the next section, I will step back in time, to 1930s and '40s swing and '50s bebop and cool jazz—to show how Moyer's attacks are rooted in long-standing jazz-hating tropes. I will focus particularly on the way earlier writers fused criticism of musical details with broader attacks on the music's affective power.

HATING (AND LOVING) SWING

Critical evaluations of swing jazz of the '30s and '40s showed a deep concern for the ways music moved people. The love and hate of swing was driven not just by technical complaints (loud, repetitive), moral qualms (encouraging immoral behavior), or ideology (democracy vs. fascism), but by a deeper concern with the way jazz moved bodies and minds to act and be acted upon, almost in an involuntary manner.

In a 1936 piece in *Metronome*, Joseph V. Rubba defines swing as the "rhythmical expression of a melodic strain, set to the ideal tempo for the pattern employed, which will arouse in the dancer, the listener, and the performer, the desire to move in time with the rhythm beat." Everyone is susceptible to this affective power: "Watch the dignified dowager when Ozzie begins to swing his band. If she is not being too 'proper' you will see her tap her foot in time with the rhythm beat. Watch the staid old banker, the businessman, the politician. Their feet move, their heads or bodies sway, ever so slightly, in response to the swing urge. Then watch the younger set, the collegiates, the five-and-dime girls, the stenogs. They will go into the dance creation of the day only when the music has the swing appeal. Any other music leaves them cold, emotionless."[63] For Rubba, swing rhythm was a force that could make everyone move—men and women, adults and youth, the rich, the middle class, and the poor.

The frenzy of the jitterbug dancer was an object of special fascination and fear for the ways it threatened social cohesion, and later, wartime unity.[64] Swing seemed to have energized youth and brought them together, a counterforce to the anomie of Machine Age life; but this unity could override individuality and lead to fascism or communism. A youth revolution was also a potential threat to the social order, especially to traditional notions of gender roles and racial boundaries. Swing culture—as paradigmatic of mass culture—was often depicted as emasculating, a feminizing influence.[65] In contrast to early jazz—"the lusty music of negro men"—jazz critic Rudi Blesh saw swing as sentimental and trite, the antithesis of authentic jazz.[66] The presence of women jazz musicians—in all-female groups or as individual soloists in mostly male bands—intensified concerns about swing and gender norms.[67] Here I will mostly focus on the intersection of affect and race, but I will return to issues of gender, sexuality, and race in chapter 4 with a deeper look at the sexism and misogyny that has permeated the cultures of jazz for much of its existence.

The explosion of swing as a commercial phenomenon—the music had been played by Black bands well before 1935—triggered a flood of hand-wringing articles about the music and its effect on American society. As scholars such as David Bindas, Joel Dinerstein, David Stowe, Lewis Erenberg, and I have argued, these reactions to swing represented the meeting of a vibrant new musical style with many fundamental social changes: the rise of newly consolidated mass media (radio, recording, and film), the trauma of the Great Depression, the growth of Leftist politics, changing gender roles, a developing awareness of the African American civil rights struggle, and large-scale demographic shifts.[68] Although some critics at the time focused on the music's hedonistic immorality (a criticism that echoed earlier attacks on jazz), most critics had global developments on their mind, especially the rise of fascism in Europe. For these writers, swing represented fascist politics in cultural form. Watching masses of jitterbugging teenagers swarming ballrooms and concert halls, many writers worried that something was broken in American life and that young people, beaten down by the Depression, were revolting. In 1938, a Chicago journalist, reporting on the Swing Jamboree, an enormous free concert held at Soldier Field, described it as "jitterbug ecstasy," the "most hysterical orgy of joyous emotions by multitudes ever witnessed on the American continent."[69]

In his study of the 1940s, historian William Graebner frames this as a concern on the part of many intellectuals, politicians, and business leaders that the US did not have the right balance between part and whole. As the US grew closer to involvement in the global conflict, these leaders believed in the "necessity of sublimating the self to the larger whole, of melding the individual into the life of the group."[70] Yet these same leaders were also deeply suspicious of mass politics, not just of the fascist kind but communist too. America's great strength, they argued, was its celebration of individual liberty, something tied inextricably to the free market economy. In an influential February 1941 editorial in *Time* magazine, publisher Henry Luce offered a positive synthesis of these tensions, part of his plea for American involvement in the European conflict: "We have some things in this country which are infinitely precious and especially American—a love of freedom, a feeling for the equality of opportunity, a tradition of self-reliance and independence and also of co-operation." America, Luce argued, must engage the ongoing war, not just to save Europe but to save America itself, to preserve and expand its role as the purveyor of the "great principles of Western civilization—above all Justice, the love of Truth, and the ideal of Charity."[71] We must, Luce insisted, form a unity of individuals to protect Western, and specifically, American, values.

Swing music embodied these tensions in popular form. Bands, collections of individual musicians and the main vehicle for this music, were most often known by and celebrated for their leaders. Similarly, swing was a highly structured form with each section of the orchestra playing designated roles (horns, reeds, and rhythm section), but the heroes of the era were soloists who, briefly, claimed the spotlight, highlighting their individuality with hot solos. For some writers, particularly those on the Left, swing represented a quintessential American synthesis of individual and group, a thoroughly democratic music of the people. But for others, swing was a sign of decline, the drowning of the individual in grinding rhythms and blaring horn riffs, a form of "musical Hitlerism."[72]

Swing, however, made explicit an important element that was often glossed over: the role of race. What did American wartime unity mean when a significant minority of the population lived as a permanent underclass, discriminated against and unable to access the freedoms white Americans took for granted? Swing, as nearly every commentator recognized, was rooted in African American musical practices. Despite the segregation of the industry, divided into all-white and all-Black bands, the music was a constant, if sometimes very attenuated, reminder of Black humanity and creativity. Swing music, especially in its "hot" form—bluesy, riff-based, with a driving 4/4 rhythm—generated an affect with a racialized cast. White youth who embraced it were embracing Black ways of feeling and moving. Whatever political or sociological reading they preferred, critics were fascinated and often alarmed by the music's profound emotional appeal. The social concern with the exuberant youth culture that built itself around swing was thus part of a larger concern with managing emotions in a time of social crisis and war. Affect, if left unchecked, could easily collapse social life into chaos, undermining American values of freedom, individuality, and self-reliance. Swing threatened to unleash sexual energies that would upend family life and public morality (on this point, the war was disruptive enough). Racial progress may be necessary but not at the expense of national unity in the face of external threats. Even the "king of swing," Benny Goodman—a beneficiary of this adulation and a promoter of Black music and Black musicians—was disgusted by the emotional excesses he saw: "Their eyes popped, their heads pecked, their feet tapped out the time, arms jerked to the rhythm. They joined in background choruses, ran temperatures up and down in unison with the heat and coolness of the music."[73]

The fear of swing's affective power was part of a much broader anxiety about the consequences of unrestrained emotion in a time of economic crisis and war. The era saw a flood of books and articles from psychological and psychoanalytic professionals dealing with these concerns. These figures—nearly all white men—wrote books, gave interviews, and advised the US military. They promulgated "scientific" ideas about normal emotional psychology as well as the need for "mental hygiene." Throughout the war years, they wrote and talked about the need to regulate emotions and manage inherent psychic conflicts. In his best-selling book, *On Being a Real Person*, pastor Harry Emerson Fosdick distilled these psychological concerns into a publicly accessible form. He explained both the value of embracing emotional expression and the need for controlling it: "This fact of fear's necessity and usefulness, however, far from solving our problem, underlies its seriousness. . . . Like fire, it is a great and necessary servant but a ruinous master. When it becomes terror, hysteria, phobia, obsessive anxiety, it tears personality to pieces."[74] An American populace, anxious about war and experiencing large-scale demographic upheavals, was very receptive to these ideas.

The concerns with feeling and its impact on individuality and community are evident in jazz writing of the period. Musicians and critics struggled to reconcile notions of "good" music—what they liked and thought worthy of praise—with the emotional power of the era's jazz. In 1938, white bandleader Russ Morgan, a purveyor of "sweet" jazz, penned an article titled "Why I Hate Swing." In the essay, Morgan derides current popular jazz as full of false feeling. Swing, he writes, "doesn't mean playing loud, playing a hundred miles an hour like a racing car that's gotten out of control, it doesn't mean blasting the roof off with the brass section, and it certainly doesn't mean beating those drums until they're ready to bust." In contrast, "real" swing is "beautiful and full of feeling." Rather than engage in such fakery, Morgan chooses to perform his own style, "quiet, romantic, soft and velvety," because it is sincere, an honest kind of self-expression. A true swing band sounds unique:

> When a band expresses itself sincerely in swing it can't sound like any other band, just as no two people have the same fingerprints. In 1925, 1926 and 1927, there were two distinct groups of swingsters: the white and the colored musicians. It was natural enough that both should swing differently because a white man and a colored man have a

different soul. . . . Fletcher Henderson didn't sound like Duke Ellington, and Jean Goldkette didn't sound like Ben Pollack in 1926.[75]

It is significant that Morgan's reflections on the affect of swing eventually work their way to the question of race: despite both swinging sincerely, the best white and Black bands of the 1920s sounded different because a "white man and a colored man have a different soul." Even as Morgan separates out music of sincere emotion from fake, he also distinguishes musical affect by race. It is a passing reference—most of the article has Morgan reflecting on his time with Jean Goldkette's legendary band—but it is significant that not only does Morgan mark out true versus false feeling, he also racializes it.

Like Morgan, other critics struggled to parse out the music's affect from its quality as well as its racial associations. The November 1940 issue of *Music and Rhythm* vividly documents this debate. Alongside overheated articles praising and denouncing popular jazz musicians ("I Love Tommy Dorsey," "I Hate Tommy Dorsey," "Jazz Should Be Razzed," "Most Vocalists Are Terrible"), Paul Eduard Miller gives a sober analysis of current jazz. The experienced critic attempts to unemotionally evaluate swing. Toward that end, he advocates a step-by-step approach: "number one is the *listener* himself. Number two is the *music* itself. Number three is the *additional data* over and above that supplied by the actual sound of the music as it is performed." To hear things clearly, the objectivity of the "music itself" and the "additional data," the listener must contend with their "temperament": "It is scarcely necessary to point out the temperament of the listener has a great deal to do with the enjoyment or hatred of, or indifference to certain music." Listeners should suspend their urge to make snap judgments, the tendency to like what is familiar. They should restrain affective impulses and try to be impartial: "No one has ever passed a sound critical judgment on a piece of hot music if temperamentally he was predisposed to like or to hate the type to which he was listening."[76]

Miller largely avoided talking about race, but that was unusual. For most commentators, the connection between swing and emotion was inextricable from Blackness. The roots of the music's affective appeal rested in its connection to Black American culture, and even back to Africa itself. In a January 1938 article for the *New York Times Magazine*, Gama Gilbert traces the journey of jazz from the "hell-holes of New Orleans" to the "sanctum" of Carnegie Hall, where Benny Goodman was about to perform for the first time. The upcoming concert, Gilbert writes, was a landmark not only for Goodman but also for the music's popularity and critical respect. Gilbert's story has a clear narrative of rise, decline, and then rise again: jazz began as a Black, lower-class music; was taken up by white bands; and then spread around the world. Soon bandleaders such as Paul Whiteman arrived and transformed these rough sounds into a quasi-classical, respectable musical form. Small-group improvisation gave way to "symphonic jazz." This rise in respectability, however, created enervated, "sterile" music, divorced "from the urgency of human emotion." "Jazz," Gilbert writes, "had squandered its birth-right, betrayed its heritage. It has exchanged the blood of life which once beat in its veins for the wine of social acceptance. Its demise, due to pernicious anemia, was unlamented."[77]

But before it could die, the music was revived by "new sounds that bore a strangely familiar ring." This new jazz directly evoked the older style in its energy and wildness: "Old timers were minded [sic] of a rowdy, convulsive music that used to grate the Mississippi waters from the old excursion boats to the mainland." Here Gilbert makes clear that the music's dynamism and energy came from Black Americans: "It came from the hot lips and agitated fingers of a handful of darkies who had started life as stevedores, cotton pickers or river rats. One day they had put a horn to their lips, or grappled with an accordion, and music sounded. It came sweet and easy, and set them shivering with the glory of it." This origin story was a familiar one: jazz was a music created by unschooled Black men who played "instinctively," their sounds "indelibly colored with their own blood."[78]

When a young Benny Goodman heard these wild sounds in Chicago, it floored him. Unlike the "straight" commercial music of the sweet dance bands, Goodman found the music liberating. As Gilbert writes, everyone who cares about swing knows that "the soul of this music is its spontaneity, its elusiveness, its absolute freedom from technique or rules." Throughout his profile of Goodman, Gilbert focuses over and over on the music's affect: swing "sings with accustomed abandon," it is "mercurial and unpredictable," it is full of "a bubbling lilt and spirit that hardly seems able to repress itself." Swing "merits respect because it has deep, authentic feeling expressed in the fullest measure by its own terms and in a balanced design." It is, in other words, a music of authentic feeling: "It is hardly an exaggeration to say that swing is today the most widespread artistic medium of popular emotional expression."[79] Gilbert connects these emotional attributes directly to the "darkies" who invented it. Although he doesn't state it directly, Gilbert's point is clear: the emotional vitality of modern life is rooted in Black affect. When jazz loses this connection, it becomes lifeless, sterile in its modern respectability. But in the hands of musicians like Goodman, the music draws a connection to its racial source, creating a powerful new kind of jazz called swing.

Despite their different perspectives and agendas, each of these writers identifies affect as the core issue in the reception of swing. How the music moves listeners—emotionally and physically—is the foundation of its aesthetic character. For bandleaders like Morgan, swing is good music if it is emotionally honest, and too much of what is celebrated as swing is strained, full of false sentiment. But for jazz critics like Miller, identifying the best of the new style means putting feeling aside. Affect confuses things, misdirecting our attention to the music's real innovations. Swing was a stand-in for a pervasive worry about the role of affect in American life, a worry that became acute during the war, when scholars, policy makers, and government officials were obsessed with national unity and morale. The music not only centered affect but also tied it to race, a potent combination for these writers and politicians. Swing deserved scrutiny for the ways it offered paths toward unification but also divisions along age and racial lines. Evaluating the music, socially and aesthetically, meant, above all, characterizing its profound emotionally power.

HATING JAZZ IN THE 1950S

In 1954 RCA Victor released *Jazz for People Who Hate Jazz*, a follow-up to their 1953 *Classical Music for People Who Hate Classical Music*. The release features a mix of 1930s and '40s recordings from Fats Waller, Duke Ellington, Count Basie, Benny Goodman, and others. The album cover displays a squat, portly couple in evening clothes scrunching their eyes in discomfort as a small jazz band plays in the background. Above the couple, "jazz" is written in yellow capital letters. The marketing here is tongue-in-cheek. The record is clearly aimed at a broad middle-class audience, and the depiction of a well-dressed elderly couple completely incapable of appreciating jazz is poking fun at the curmudgeonly elite.

The marketing appeal is also ironic: you, the consumer, are presumably buying the record because you want to like jazz. If you really hated jazz, you probably wouldn't have bought it with the aim of becoming a fan. The record cover supports this: it doesn't depict you, the interested consumer. Instead, we see a snobby and ill-informed cartoon husband and wife, dressed for the concert hall or opera house. These people are ridiculous, and although we don't know exactly why this couple hates the music, their pained reaction suggest they believe it is horrible. The issue of race is muted and displaced: on the cover we see an alignment of whiteness with high social class (everyone in evening wear, including musicians), but we read the names of famous Black musicians such as Duke Ellington, Fats Waller, and Count Basie alongside equally famous white counterparts. The whiteness displayed on the cover is cartoonish and the record promises something else, something true and rewarding on the inside. Jazz, the record implies, is not lowly trash, it is something you will, if you listen thoughtfully, like or even come to love.

The cover encapsulates the mainstream presentation of jazz in the mid-1950s: a mildly resistant, racially pluralistic music that can be enjoyed by anyone. The affect of jazz, although it has a racial dimension (at least half of the music on the album is by Black artists), is safe and serious. Some of this feeling stems from the largely nostalgic selections on the record—a mix of early jazz and dance band music. Modernist jazz—bebop, cool "West Coast" jazz, hard bop—is absent, a music that had an association with social deviance and illegal drug use. But by the mid-1950s, even the edginess of bop and then hard bop, had been largely tamed, transformed into an acceptable and mainstream modernist aesthetic. The success of figures like pianist Dave Brubeck, especially with college students, "seemed to promise a jazz that would be more upscale, less interested in social protest, and whiter."[80] West Coast jazz, at least on the surface, exemplified these developments: most of the high-profile musicians—Gerry Mulligan, Chet Baker, Shorty Rogers, Jimmy Giuffre, and Shelly Manne—were white. The music favored "instrumental harmony, fluid execution, and polished teamwork . . . relying less on the blues and more on new melodies and old standards cloaked in pleasing harmony and counterpoint."[81] Visually, record covers and promotional materials reinforced this aesthetic, the musicians dressing casually, sometimes in short-sleeved shirts, and often wearing sunglasses. Other times, musicians were presented in dreamy, romantic poses. Chet Baker's movie-star looks made him a symbol of the style, conveying a mood of sensitivity and introspection. These sounds and images, along with a "colorblind" aesthetic rhetoric, helped reconfigure the music as a safe avenue for white self-expression.[82] Jazz, as Kelsey Klotz writes, "was newly acceptable" in white suburban homes.[83] By 1956, even the women's magazine *Good Housekeeping* would feature an article celebrating jazz as a boy who once had dirty hands, but "now, with clean hands," is to be found "in the concert halls, the music conservatories, and by way of respectable and carefully produced LP records, in the nicest living rooms."[84] It was the sonic template for an international midcentury modernist aesthetic.[85]

This transformation of a potentially threatening intersection of race and affect evokes the concept of containment. In work by cultural historians such as Lary May, Alan Nadel, and Robert Kolker, containment—a metaphoric extension of the Cold War policy of limiting communist expansion—explains attempts to manage the social tensions of the early Cold War era.[86] By the mid-1950s, the unruly racialized affect of jazz—so vividly evoked by Mendl in his early history of jazz—was "contained," remade into a safe variant of mainstream American modernism (of course, this imagery ignores the many West Coast Black musicians who played a variety of jazz styles). Jazz became a comfortable part of middlebrow consumer culture for the growing suburban white-collar class. It was a music that was educated but not overeducated. Neither highbrow like classical music nor avant-garde, jazz was also not lowbrow like R&B and rock 'n' roll.[87] It was a music of upward mobility, having the cachet of the nightclub and the concert hall.[88] Perhaps the most famous avatar of this social position is Stan Kenton and his "progressive" approach to jazz (significantly, Kenton's music makes a brief appearance in *Blackboard Jungle*, discussed below).[89]

These changes in the white mainstream attitudes toward jazz also reinforced gender norms. The celebration of jazz in the mid-1950s, as in the previous decades, was driven by male record collectors and aficionados. Jazz featured prominently in the pages of Hugh Hefner's fast-growing magazine *Playboy*, a publication that celebrated a new kind of postwar masculine ideal—the stylish, sexually liberated, upwardly mobile bachelor.[90] The Newport Jazz Festival, especially as captured by filmmaker and photographer Bert Sterns in *Jazz on a Summer's Day*, was a vivid and exuberant homage to jazz, juxtaposing the music with scenes of yacht races, hipster fans, and old Newport mansions. Not only was the musical jazz world overwhelmingly male—not a new development—but so were the writers who covered the music. Beat Generation writers such as Jack Kerouac and New Journalists such as Norman Mailer celebrated jazz and Black culture as a virile, invigorating force. In the tragic struggle of the Black man, they saw a model for revitalizing modern life. This racialized and masculinized version of jazz played an important part in the intellectual elevation of the music as a paradigmatic example of American modernist art. Not just West Coast jazz but the bluesier, gospel-influenced sounds of hard bop were also celebrated by artists and writers for their vigor and masculine energy.[91] The intersection of race, jazz, and masculinity would dominate understandings of the music within the genre and in the general culture.

The redirection of the music's racialized and masculinized affect into mainstream postwar American life also appears in a variety of other cultural texts. Kay Crisfield Grey's "The Lady Hated Jazz," published in the *Saturday Evening Post* in 1955, tells the story of Edward "Buster" Franklin, a onetime celebrated hot trumpeter in a jazz orchestra who becomes a suburban hardware store owner. Edward tries to court Liza, a local social studies teacher, but is rejected for no reason he can understand. Later, Edward finds out the truth: Liza's college roommate dated a musician who led a rumba band. When the roommate found out he was married with three kids, the young woman tried to kill herself. Liza got her to the hospital just in time to save her life. After that trauma, Liza "thinks all musicians are bums. Period." But after Edward serenades her with Gershwin's "Liza," the two reconcile, and Liza realizes that Edward, despite his musical past, is an upstanding, honest man.[92]

In the story, it is not jazz that is the problem but the music business. Music for the sake of music is fine. The story is significant not just for the ways it shows how the hatred of jazz was wrapped up with social anxieties, but also for the ways that attitudes toward the music were inextricably tied to a complex of intense feelings. For both Edward and

"The Lady Hated Jazz" text and illustration © SEPS licensed by Curtis Licensing Indianapolis, IN. All rights reserved.

Liza, there is no problem with the music itself—both believe it to be a conveyor of authentic and ennobling feeling. Even though there are no words spoken between them, we understand that Edward's private performance for Liza is a marriage proposal, a proposal that she finally accepts. The story endorses jazz as a positive aesthetic experience, so long as that experience is confined to a space outside the marketplace. Music is a powerful vehicle for private emotional connection: it is essential that Edward and Liza are alone for the culminating musical performance.

Liza's fear of jazz echoes two overlapping discourses: jazz as deviancy (nightclubs, drugs, prostitution) and jazz as juvenile delinquency (youth disrespecting adults and committing crimes).[93] But the story's focus on the genre is displaced: the urgent social concern at that moment was rock 'n' roll, the new musical style that signaled profound changes in the music industry. Jazz certainly had strong associations with depravity, but Liza's concern with the corruption of youth seems focused on the wrong thing. The year of Crisfield's story, Bill Haley's "Rock around the Clock" exploded in popularity. As with jazz, fears of rock 'n' roll were a panicked amalgam of race, gender, sexuality, and class concerns. Despite the commercial viability of jazz, its affective power in US culture waned dramatically in the face of the rock 'n' roll juggernaut.[94] As Keir Keightley argues, the rise of rock 'n' roll was part of a larger process of audience segmentation in mass culture: "Rock 'n' roll marks the point at which the discursively produced opposition between adult and teen audience segments is rendered most rigidly." This bifurcation meant that jazz—despite its long-racialized association with the seedy aspects of American life—became "adult" music. Next to rock 'n' roll's stripped-down aesthetic, jazz, with its reliance on popular song "standards," sophisticated harmonies, and instrumental virtuosity, represented "good music," if not highbrow, at least higher-brow, taste.[95]

The 1955 film *Blackboard Jungle* vividly shows jazz being overtaken by the new, bluesy, backbeat-driven style of rock 'n' roll. In the film, jazz has been fully digested into the decade's white middle-class world. The once-threatening racialized affect of early jazz and swing—those crazed Hitleresque jitterbugs—is now muted, transformed into the bookish hobby of a schoolteacher. As the youthful swing generation matured, they took their music with them.

In the film, Rick Dadier (Glenn Ford) is a new teacher at North Manual Trades High School, a tough place known for its difficult and often violent students. Struggling, Rick befriends fellow teacher and avid jazz fan Josh Edwards (Richard Kiley). Early in the friendship, Josh notes his "two first names, like Harry James," and asks Rick if he is a fan of swing. One day, Josh brings in his beloved collection of jazz 78s to share with one of his more advanced math classes ("Music," he says later, "is based on mathematics."). While Josh is listening alone in the classroom, Rick's tough students arrive. They immediately start hounding Josh to share his music. He reluctantly agrees, putting on Bix Beiderbecke's 1927 recording of "Jazz Me Blues." The students protest, "How 'bout some bop?" but Josh insists they give Beiderbecke a try. One student, Artie West (Vic Morrow), reaches into the stack of records and pulls out one to look at. "This is 'Cow-Cow Boogie,'" he says. Josh becomes alarmed, telling everyone to keep away from the records. Now provoked, Artie and the rest of the students begin throwing and smashing the records as a horrified Josh impotently looks on. A student removes the Beiderbecke record and puts on another one. This marks an audio transition from Josh's scratchy vintage Beiderbecke recording to the fuller, higher fidelity of film composer Charles Wolcott's own bop-inflected big-band tune (although the students continue dancing, drumming, and rioting to the music, blurring the distinction between diegetic and nondiegetic sound). After the students leave, Rick finds a despondent Josh alone, accompanied by the scratching of a needle at the end of the groove. "They broke my records. I don't understand, Rick. I just don't understand." In the next scene, Rick tries to get the students to take accountability by passing around a tin can and suggesting that, although the records were irreplaceable, they can put in money to help buy a new record player (an apparent inconsistency in the film, since the phonograph emerged from the chaos in working condition).

Even though the jazz records play a small part in the film—just another example of youth turned violent and disrespectful—they play a heavily symbolic role. *Blackboard Jungle* was not just another mid-1950s social problem film about juvenile delinquency (like *Rebel without a Cause*, also from 1955); it was also a warning about the exploding rock 'n' roll youth culture. The film opens with a scrolling prologue attesting to the film's social importance as a document of youth delinquency.

During the scroll, we hear a military-style snare drum solo that grows increasingly syncopated and swinging. Just after the scroll ends, the jazz-style drumming is cut short with the entrance of "Rock around the Clock" by Bill Haley and His Comets. That opening drum hit became a signal moment in the history of this new blues-oriented, backbeat-heavy music. The film turned the musical style and its cultural effects into an urgent public conversation. It also provided the contours for that debate: jazz, as Kevin Whitehead notes, was for old white men, rock 'n' roll was for multiracial youth.[96] Although this is the broad binary offered by the film, the position of jazz—as well as its Blackness vis-à-vis rock 'n' roll—is, nonetheless, ambiguous. The students in the film reject not jazz per se, but 1920s jazz and '30s and '40s swing (they smash not just the Beiderbecke record but also Charlie Barnet's "Cherokee" and Freddie Slack's "Cow-Cow Boogie"). The students specifically ask for bop, a style of jazz strongly marked as Black. Maybe they would have smashed Charlie Parker records too, but the film suggests that bop, unlike earlier jazz, was rebellious and in line with the students' cynical, cool, street-tough outlook on life. Also complicating things is Rick's discovery that the troubled student Greg Miller (Sidney Poitier) is a fine pianist who teaches spirituals to fellow Black students.

Popular music, the film shows, was registering a profound shift in attitudes and values, a shift that was felt across generational, race, and class lines. The youthful music that helped white veterans like Rick and Josh fight the Nazis was now dated, replaced by something newer and more raucous. In addition to Wolcott's jazz-oriented soundtrack (often blended with the diegetic jazz on radios, record players, and jukeboxes), the movie features two jazz recordings: Beiderbecke's "Jazz Me Blues" (1927), heard in the record-smashing scene, and Stan Kenton's "Invention for Guitar and Trumpet" (1953), selected by Josh on a bar jukebox where he is having a drink with Rick. As with his introduction to Rick, Josh never misses an opportunity to highlight his jazz fandom: "Stan the man. Terrific stuff." Jazz may still have had associations with sex, drugs, and crime—it was the default sound of film noir—but its musical language was also now fully integrated into the adult sound world.[97] It is rock 'n' roll that is more dangerous, the sound of a delinquent generation characterized by verbal, sexual, and physical violence.[98] By its end, however, the film offers hope: civic leaders, by espousing a 1950s racial liberalism, can manage the threat of rock 'n' roll and begin curbing the epidemic of youth delinquency. The filmmakers, in situating Greg Miller between these two worlds via his connection to Rick and his performance of spirituals, suggest that race is vital and that Black culture, if helped along, can mature.[99] With Rick and Greg committing themselves to staying the course, we hear the final strains of Bill Haley's "Rock around the Clock." Perhaps the racialized energy of rock 'n' roll, like jazz before it, can be usefully directed into supporting Cold War American values?

As Crisfield's story and *Blackboard Jungle* suggest, jazz, despite its associations with drug use and other social vices, was not a threat to the social order. The affective power of the music, if channeled appropriately—into heterosexual monogamy and aesthetic contemplation—was socially acceptable, even useful. The real threat was rock 'n' roll's unruly and distinctly Black masculine affect—its insistent beat, simpler structures, and suggestive lyrics. If the youth of *Blackboard Jungle* could be said to hate jazz, it is because it is anemic, a force for stasis and the status quo. Rock 'n' roll was energy and intensity; it spoke to the dynamism of the now.

During and after the war, American politicians and writers were concerned not with the existence of affects—the passions that captivate and motivate people—but with their management. If war planners sought to direct affect into wartime work, postwar leaders sought to redirect it into domestic life and the reestablishment of clear gender roles as a bulwark against communism. Loving or hating music, including certain popular, Black-originated styles, was deemed acceptable if controlled by family life and regular employment. The danger was with the "Blacker" sounds of rock 'n' roll, a music where affect and Blackness seemed dangerously intertwined and self-sustaining.

◉

One of the major tributaries of jazz hating is in the realm of taste—the separating out of good music from bad. A judgment of taste is not hate in its strongest form, for it does not usually argue for "annihilation"; good music can replace and correct for bad. But since taste discrimination is fundamentally social discrimination, it very easily slips into a rejection of people or communities. That kind of social generalization, combined with anger and aggression, can slide into an enduring, all-or-nothing kind of hate. Because jazz is rooted in Black American life, the stakes for this kind of social rejection are high. Attacking jazz, or some versions of jazz, as bad music, is inevitably implicated in an understanding of Blackness in American life. Still, the voices speaking today against jazz are small. The debates around *La La Land* happened mostly among a small group of jazz critics, musicians, and fans. For many Americans, jazz has little affective import; and when it does, it is because it is being laughed at. The most important affective responses to jazz today are in the realm of humor and satire.

• 3 •

Jazz Is Stupid

HATING JAZZ THROUGH SATIRE AND RIDICULE

Despite the perennial cries of its death or rebirth, jazz today is a marginal part of the American popular music landscape. Most engagement with the music comes not from live performance or even recordings, but from bits and pieces that show up in popular media. And when it does appear, it is most often treated humorously. Making fun of jazz is how many people today engage with the genre. For many listeners, jazz is mystifying, elitist, and cultish. If it moves them, it moves them to laughter. In a well-known sketch by the Canadian comedy troupe the Kids in the Hall, Bruce McCulloch, sitting on a stool with two white-haired musicians—a flutist and a bassist—playing behind him, tries to explain why he hates jazz:

> People say, "Bruce, what's this with you and jazz? What's the beef with you and jazz music?" I say, "Well, I really *hate* jazz." They say, "What do you hate about poor, old jazz?" I say, "The sound. The sound the jazz instruments make when they're being manipulated by jazz players for the delight of the jazz respondents. I think of it as musical barf." They say, "I don't think you've given jazz a chance." "Well," I maintain, "I haven't given suicide a chance, but... well, I did give suicide a chance. But that's only 'cause I was threatened with jazz. You know, jazz music."...
>
> You know what? I would like to declare this a jazz-free zone. About forty miles as far as the jazz-hatin' crow flies in any direction. Just paradise. Those guys [the musicians] would go to work, and it wouldn't be there.
>
> I'm gonna ask a question: What sort of music do you think there is in hell? You know, h–e–double hockey stick? Well, I think it's probably hateful, free-form jazz. And in heaven? Country and western music![1]

Cleverly staged as a stereotypical jazz poetry performance, it is a funny, over-the-top rant, very much in the absurdist style of the group. It is also ambiguous. Are we laughing with McCulloch? Is it funny because he is saying what we are all thinking, that jazz is stupid and someone just needs to say it out loud? Is he really celebrating country and western music over jazz? Or is he is mocking that too? Are we laughing *at* McCulloch, whose reaction is so over-the-top that it edges into silliness ("Jazz, schmazz. I'm sorry but I have to go that far: jazz, schmazz"), or with him? Who gets that riled up about any musical style?

◉

Jazz is easy to poke fun at because it has accumulated a lot of baggage over the years. Associations have changed, but at least since the 1930s the genre has been most closely associated with coolness and an outsider culture, one closely tied to Black life. The rise of bebop and the genre's commercial decline in the face of pop and rock only intensified these associations: jazz was an elitist urban genre adored by overly earnest aficionados. It was a masculine music that celebrated competitive individualism even as it pushed against mass culture and the marketplace. These tropes have been surprisingly consistent since the mid-twentieth century, and most of the humor directed at jazz has played off them. Humorous attacks on the music represent one of the core forms of jazz hating.

In this chapter I survey the sources of jazz ridicule. Why have so many critics, fans, and comedians made fun of jazz? I am especially interested in negative affects, the way even lighthearted attacks on jazz involve hurtful behaviors such as ridicule and mockery and negative feelings such as contempt and anger. A great deal of jazz humor is satirical: it laughs but it also judges, attacking the foibles and failures of people's behaviors and beliefs. When the moral position of the critic is unclear, the humor can become nihilistic, devolving into resentful bullying, what David Denby calls "snark."[2] To understand jazz in American culture, we need to understand what is being made fun of and why. Since humor represents one of the dominant ways people engage with the music—jokes about jazz get people's attention—we need to understand the specifics of this affective engagement. The satirical attacks, ridicule, and mockery of jazz, despite continuities, emerged from different historical contexts shaped by different arrangements of social forces. Given the space, I could cite many, many more examples from the US and around the English-speaking world.[3] With the music's global reach, I am certain that there are even more examples from across the globe, and in many other languages.

Making fun of jazz is often playful and silly. The long-running animated series *The Simpsons* has repeatedly featured the music: one of the primary characters, the precocious eight-year-old Lisa Simpson, is a jazz-playing baritone saxophonist who worships a fictional jazz and blues legend, Bleeding Gums Murphy. The show's treatment of the music and its culture has largely been admiring, gently poking fun at aspects of jazz (for example, Bleeding Gum's teacher, Blind Willie Witherspoon had unwittingly been playing an umbrella instead of saxophone for thirty years). Series creator Matt Groening is a jazz fan, and the show's references demonstrate a knowledge of the music and its history, deploying familiar jazz tropes.[4] In the 2006 episode "Jazzy and the Pussycats" (season eighteen, second episode), Bart learns to play the drums and joins a jazz band. The humor is knowing and mild: to learn the music, Lisa takes Bart to the Children's Bebop Brunch at Jazzy Goodtimes, where a waiter offers to scat the menu. Later in the episode, when the club hosts a benefit concert, the sign outside reads, 8-HOUR JAZZ BENEFIT. 2 SONGS WILL BE PLAYED. Throughout the episode, the show takes aim at other jazz clichés, such as its hipster lingo, penchant for nicknames, and commercial marginality. In the episode we hear respectable versions of Dave Brubeck's "Take Five" and Duke Ellington's "Caravan." The show also acknowledges the music's Black history: Bart's trio features two nonwhite musicians, Defonzo "Skinny" Turner and Marcus "Marbles" Le Marquez.

Although it didn't address jazz as often, the sitcom *Parks and Recreation* treated the music in a similarly lighthearted way. A 2013 episode (season five, episode eight) has Leslie Knope (Amy Poehler) on the local public radio station asking for public input on a new park. At the end of the interview, the radio host asks Knope to introduce the next segment: "Now it's time for jazz plus jazz equals jazz. Today we have a recording of Benny Goodman played over a separate recording of Miles Davis." We then hear exactly that, the cacophony of two jazz performances played simultaneously. Knope looks perplexed, but the host assures her that all is fine: "Research shows that our listeners love jazz." The joke is as much on the cluelessness of public radio stations as it is on the pretentiousness of jazz fans. It is a silly jab at snobbery—we all know that one recording of anything at a time is plenty! But, as with the many examples I will look at later, even this critique is tinged with something harsher: perhaps jazz fans are so out of touch that they really enjoy such ridiculous noise. As Michael Billig points out, humor today is often understood as a positive phenomenon.[5] To tell jokes and to laugh are understood to be productive ways to cope with an uncertain world. Humor helps balance the sorrow and hardship that is a part of our lives. But humor has a dark side; jokes are often made at the expense of people weaker than we are. Even when the butt of the joke or story is deserving, we are amused by the degradation of someone else. Ridicule and mockery are integral to humor.

There is a "coldness at the core" of humor, philosopher Simon Critchley observes, and, in the United States, that cold center is often occupied by fantasies of race.[6] Researching the history of jazz satire, I was struck over and over by how uniformly white it was. Whether the mockery came from inside the jazz community or outside, the instigators were nearly always white. Making fun of jazz is another example of what Eric Lott calls the "Black mirror": "the mechanics, dispositions, and effects of the dominant culture's looking at itself always through the fantasized black Other."[7] Mocking the insular and self-righteous world of jazz serves as an oblique attack on Blackness and related modes of being, such as "cool."[8] Early in jazz history, the ridicule was aimed explicitly at Black incursions into white culture. But by the 1930s and the rise of swing, the mockery of the Blackness of jazz became oblique, even unconscious, the jesters unaware of the underlying target. Jazz humor, especially in its aggressive forms such as ridicule and mockery, represent what Jon Panish would identify as a white discourse on Black culture.[9] As discussed later in this chapter, trumpeter Nicholas Payton derides a *New Yorker* satire of Sonny Rollins as "white people" humor. Echoing Lott's Black mirror, Payton argues that the failed satire represents all-too-familiar tropes of white engagement with Black life.[10]

THE PLEASURES AND PAINS OF HUMOR

The affect of humor is complex and multifaceted. Humor in its many forms is, at least on the surface, about pleasure. Commercial culture produces an enormous variety of mass media humor: sitcoms, improvisational shows, skit shows, stand-up performances, dramadies. Pleasure, though, is far too general to be of much use to us. All commercial popular culture is about pleasure. What is the specific pleasure of humor? The answer to that question involves a complicated mixture of thought and feeling. And while in practice these two are inseparable, it is helpful, analytically, to first consider feeling—the affective component—of humor's pleasure.

In his survey of humor research, Rod Martin writes that in the psychological literature, "scholars have not yet settled on an agreed-upon technical term" to describe the emotions related to humor. "The pleasant emotion associated with humor, which is familiar to all of us," Martin writes, "is a unique feeling of well-being that is described by such terms as *amusement, mirth, hilarity, cheerfulness,* and *merriment.* It is closely related to joy and contains an element of exultation and a feeling of invincibility, a sense of expansion of the self that the seventeenth-century English philosopher Thomas Hobbes referred to as 'sudden glory.'"[11] From these choices, Martin settles on *mirth* as the best word to encompass the set of emotional responses to humor, responses that can vary in intensity:

> Like other emotions (e.g., joy, love, sadness, fear), mirth can occur with varying degrees of intensity, ranging from mild feelings of amusement to very high levels of hilarity. Also like other emotions, mirth has physiological as well as experiential components. . . . The biological concomitants of the emotion of mirth form.[12]

Martin's view on emotion reflects a version of appraisal theory: the complex psychological and physiological responses we label as emotions begin with a "set of mental operations that serve to prepare the body for action."[13] As with many appraisal theories, Martin cannot account for feeling prior to appraisal. What about the many times we laugh at something without knowing exactly why? Affect theory is helpful here—it allows us to talk about the social and material factors conditioning that feeling without committing to an emotional concept such as mirth. The affect of humor is surprisingly complex. Mirth may indeed be a universal component, but it shares space with many incongruous feelings: anxiety, joy, sadness, pity, anger, contempt, and disgust. Affect in humor is always dependent on its context.

We find all kinds of things funny, even things that, from a different perspective, would be sad or cruel. In the early twentieth century, Freud and philosopher Henri Bergson both wrote perceptively on affect and humor.[14] Affect, for Freud, functions in contradictory ways. Intense affective engagement with a person or situation inhibits humor: "The comic is greatly interfered with if the situation from which it ought to develop gives rise at the same time to a release of strong affect." Watching your own grandmother trip on a toy is very different from watching someone else's grandmother or watching that enacted in a film. In the first situation, you have an intense affective engagement—a deep love that is fearful of a life-altering, or even life-ending, consequence of a fall. It seems unlikely that you would laugh. In the second and third situations, it might be wrong to laugh, but with less affective engagement, it is not uncommon for a fall to provoke laughter. We've all laughed at inappropriate times. "The generation of affect," Freud continues, "is the most intense of all the conditions that interfere with the comic.... For this reason it has been said that the comic feeling comes easiest in more or less indifferent cases where the feelings and interests are not strongly involved."[15]

Even as emotional investment can interfere with humor, jokes are, paradoxically, tied very closely to affect. Freud starts with the notion that humor involves a release of pleasure. But the nature of that pleasure is wide, involving a variety of positive and negative affects. "Humour," Freud argues, "is a means of obtaining pleasure in spite of the distressing affects that interfere with it; it acts as a substitute for the generation of these affects, it puts itself in their place." This substitution is part of an "economic" system of feeling: "the pleasure of humor... comes about... at the cost of a release of affect that does not occur: it arises from an economy in the expenditure of affect."[16] Humor is complicated, often involving displacements and substitutions: negative affects, such as contempt, are redirected into playfulness. Pleasure is always a component, but that pleasure can be connected directly or obliquely to a wide range of feelings. In the case of jokes, affects are experienced differently by who is telling the joke, who is listening, and who may be the object of the joke. In Freud's model, the pleasure of jokes, the comic, and the humorous (Freud's three categories of humor) are connected to basic psychosocial development, where childish or antisocial behaviors are suppressed or repressed. Safely evading these mechanisms is the primary generator of laughter.

Bergson takes a similar approach. Like Freud, he begins by setting aside affect—too much emotional engagement interferes with the distance needed to laugh at something. Key to Bergson's analysis is the axiom that all humor is social: "our laughter is always the laughter of a group." He analyzes humor as a kind of "automatism" that runs counter to the endless flow and diversity of life. People and animals become comic when they seem unable to adapt to changing demands and circumstances; they display a lack of the "tension and elasticity" that life's dynamism requires. Laughing at a man tripping as he walks down the street is funny because it shows "involuntary change," which is clumsiness. In a different register, a lawyer spouting legal reasoning in the face of a personal mishap—say a child misbehaving—also demonstrates inflexibility: the lawyer keeps "lawyer-ing" even though the situation demands a very different response. There is an automatism to one's identity, an inability to adapt to what life immediately demands.[17]

Bergson also notes that not only is laughter produced by automatism, it requires a certain psychological distance. Echoing Freud, Bergson argues that the person tripping must be treated in the abstract; care about the individual has to momentarily recede. This leads Bergson to make a larger claim about the role of affect in humor: "Here I would point out, as a symptom equally worthy of notice, the ABSENCE OF FEELING which usually accompanies laughter. . . . Indifference is its natural environment, for laughter has no greater foe than emotion."[18] As Michael Billig notes, Bergson is describing a conflict between empathy and laughter.[19]

The "absence of feeling" characteristic of laughter is tied to a larger purpose—the social disapproval of automatic and unreflective behavior. "It is the part of laughter to reprove . . . absentmindedness," to wake the offending person from his "dream." Societies use humor as a mode of behavioral correction, a way of humiliating someone who isn't in line with what the situation demands. Here Bergson again echoes Freud: the pleasure of the comic is not exclusively "aesthetic or altogether disinterested." On the contrary, "in laughter we always find an unavowed intention to humiliate, and consequently to correct our neighbor."[20] Feeling has returned but now as something negative, a desire to humiliate and correct. Similar to Freud, Bergson's analysis of humor's affect is complicated, requiring an unemotional, rigid appraisal of a person or event, even as it is driven by a social desire to correct a wrong. And, of course, those who are laughed at are often feeling intensely too, not joy or laughter, but embarrassment or humiliation. Bergson is useful not only for his nuanced understanding of affect and humor but for his emphasis on the sociality of humor. Like affect, laughter is relational and social, representing "the circulation of power through feeling and emotion."[21]

JAZZ HAS ALWAYS HAD A SENSE OF HUMOR

Contrary to its reputation for seriousness, jazz musicians have displayed a strong sense of humor—being silly as well as humorously critical of themselves and the larger society. In a brief article reflecting on the controversy that erupted over a 2014 *New Yorker* parody of Sonny Rollins, Jason Gubbels reminds us that "Fats Waller, Spike Jones, Dizzy Gillespie, the Art Ensemble of Chicago, and any number of '70s fusion acts never shied away from playing the clown(s)."[22] In his essay on the humor of jazz artists, Charles Hiroshi Garrett argues that humor, in different forms, has been an "integral part of African American expressive culture," fundamentally shaping its practices and aesthetic goals. Jazz humor, expressed through music, lyrics, or stage behavior, was many things: "a mask for social critique, a display of comic artistry, a mode of communication, a fount of pleasure, and sometimes all of these at once."[23] For example, early jazz artists defined themselves, in part, by poking fun at and rebelling against middle- and upper-class respectability (something that later jazz artists would take up, often, as with bassist and composer Charles Mingus, inflected with racial critique).

The beginnings of recorded jazz are flush with musical humor. One of the most famous jazz recordings ever, the Original Dixieland Jazz Band's "Livery Stable Blues" (1917), features the instrumentalists raucously imitating barnyard animals. A little over a decade later, jazz was featured often in live and animated musical shorts, using the music's "primitive" origins in Black culture as a source of humor and absurdity, often depicting it as the music of the African jungle.[24] Humor was an integral part of Louis Armstrong's music and stage performances from the beginning.[25] Recordings he made with his Hot Five and Hot Seven often feature humorous titles ("Yes! I'm in the Barrel," "I'm Gonne Gitcha," "Who'sit," "Big Fat Ma and Skinny Pa") and ribald lyrics ("Heebie Jeebies," "Georgia Grind"). Although scholars have focused on Armstrong's musical innovations, his use of humor was arguably just as influential on future musicians. Singer Cab Calloway and trumpeter (and sometime singer) Dizzy Gillespie are two well-known inheritors of Armstrong's approach to humor in jazz, but many other musicians infused their performance with comedy. Pianist Dorothy Donegan was a virtuoso with a wild, anarchic style that was often as funny as it was dazzling.[26] Guitarist and singer Slim Gaillard built a career on comically eccentric songs, often featuring Vout, his invented hipster language. Because of their perceived "unseriousness," both Donegan and Gaillard have long remained peripheral to jazz history. A more recent example is singer, songwriter, and pianist Mose Allison. A jazz player with strong blues inclinations, Allison became best known for recordings of his original compositions. Songs such as "Your Mind Is on Vacation," "Your Molecular Structure," and "Middle Class White Boy" are hip and witty, cleverly manipulating lyrical tropes of blues and Tin Pan Alley popular music to speak to contemporary American norms. In "Your Molecular Structure," Allison expresses romantic infatuation using the technical, very unsexy language of biological science: "Your molecular structure is really something swell / a high-frequency modulated Jezebel / thermodynamically you're getting to me." These musicians—and many similar ones from before and after—have not fit into the understood hierarchy that places "serious art above everyday humor." Garrett concludes that recognizing the role that humor has played—and continues to play—in jazz helps expand our notions of what constitutes the music: "Jazz has contained, and still holds, greater possibilities for creative musical expression than are commonly acknowledged."[27]

As Gubbels, Garrett, and others note, jazz—at least since the 1960s—has emphasized seriousness over humor, the result of complex historical developments that changed the music's place in American culture. Jazz has moved from nightclubs to dance halls, then theaters, concert halls, and, more recently, universities and dedicated performance spaces. The institutionalization of jazz in schools, universities, and nonprofits such as Jazz at Lincoln Center and SFJazz has made seriousness more important: jazz must compete with other arts for the institutional support of private donors and foundations.[28] It is against this backdrop that many musicians have sought to infuse their playing with more humor. Garrett points to Horace Silver as one important example. His 1999 release, *Jazz...Has...a Sense of Humor*, is an explicit call to reenergize jazz with "some fun and laughter." "It's important, I think, just as important," Silver tells an All about Jazz interviewer, "that the world have music to give us some happiness and joy, to uplift them. They need some comedy to uplift them too. I'm a great lover of comedians."[29]

If jazz musicians, fans, and critics struggle over the place of humor in the music, the larger public has embraced it. In the vast, interconnected web of media that constitutes the terrain of American popular culture, jazz is almost always part of a joke. Many times that joke is a pretext for something else—jazz is just a vehicle to get to the real punch line. Other times, jazz music and culture are the target. But even here, the jokes range from mild to harsh, gentle ribbings to vicious takedowns. In the rest of the chapter, I will explore the ways humor, past and present, shapes the way Americans engage with jazz. But even innocent jokes contain seeds of something murkier; most humor relies on some degree of ridicule for what others take as meaningful and sincere. And when that seed sprouts, the humor that emerges is often a species of hate.

JAZZ AS THE VEHICLE FOR HUMOR

The gentle humor of *Parks and Recreation*—jazz plus jazz equals jazz—represents one pole of jazz mockery. There are other examples where the humor is gentle or where the real target is something else. In his work, comedian and writer H. Jon Benjamin uses jazz as a vehicle to explore his recurrent failings as a person. A comedian, actor, and writer with a deadpan, ironic style, Benjamin has become best known as a voice actor on several popular animated series for adults (*Bob's Burgers, Family Guy,* and *Archer*). In his 2015 recording, *Well, I Should Have . . . * (*Learned to Play Piano)*, the comic attempts to play piano along with real jazz musicians.[30] It is immediately evident that he is a terrible pianist with no jazz skills. Using the moniker Jazz Daredevil, Benjamin joins a trio of real musicians—saxophonist Scott Kreitzer, bassist David Finck, and drummer Jonathan Peretz—to play a standard, "It Had to Be You," and a four-part work titled "I Can't Play Piano." The record also features comedy skits. The first, "Deal with the Devil," with Kristen Schaal and Aziz Ansari, has Benjamin failing to sell his soul to the devil in exchange for jazz piano skills. Another skit, "Soft Jazzercise," features Benjamin narrating a mock meditative exercise to Erik Satie's first *Gymnopédie*. These skits and comic songs clearly contextualize Benjamin's musical performances as absurd.

In an accompanying video for the project available online, the comedian says, "I don't play piano at all, and I'm not a huge fan of jazz. I never was. And that's why I thought it was funny to make a jazz album."[31] After listening and watching Benjamin pluck random notes on the piano (his rhythm is often passable), it becomes clear that the target here is not jazz. In the video released with the album, the musicians act perplexed and annoyed, a *What is this idiot doing?* expression on their faces. Benjamin doesn't revel in his ineptitude; he just dourly and dutifully plods on—he shows no excitement about the project; he knows it is a failure. Here, jazz is a vehicle for the comedian's humor of abjection. The comic has little to say about jazz, except that it is difficult to play and requires skill and training. Against a backdrop of accomplishment, Benjamin presents himself as a useless and humiliated object. The comedy of Benjamin's jazz project is an extension of a larger comic persona. His 2018 book, *Failure Is an Option: An Attempted Memoir,* is structured around a life of failures.[32] Chapter titles include "How I Failed at Pretty Much Everything as a Kid (the Foundations of Failure)," "The Teen Years (or How I Failed Hosting a Bar Mitzvah Party)," and "*Dee Har* (or How I Failed to Move to France)." In an interview with NPR's Mary Louise Kelly, Benjamin acknowledges that he represents a contradiction—he is quite successful in real life. But he believes that his stories of failure represent his sense of reality: "I think the stories that I tell, or at least all the relatable ones, are kind of about failures, you know, that I hold my own, that are part of who I am, my nature as a failure as opposed to my more evident success as an actor or voiceover artist. So I spend most of my time in that world."[33]

Benjamin's humor starts from a point of respect. By putting himself next to highly skilled musicians, Benjamin is implicitly recognizing that jazz is a serious and valuable activity. But a lot of jazz humor begins before that, with a questioning of the music's value. In its kindest form, this humorous investigation begins from perplexity: What even is jazz, and why do its fans talk in such convoluted ways about it?

THE MANY FUNNY MEANINGS OF JAZZ

Printed evidence suggests that the term *jazz* first entered the American lexicon separate from any kind of music. A 1913 column in the *San Francisco Bulletin* by Ernest J. Hopkins argues that *jazz* is a word that "can be defined but not synonymized": "this remarkable and satisfactory-sounding word, however, means something like life, vigor, energy, effervescence of spirit, joy, pep, magnetism, verve, virility, ebulliency, courage, happiness—oh, what's the use—JAZZ."[34] His playful fascination continues:

> You can go on flinging the new word all over the world, like a boy with a new jack-knife. It is "jazz" when you run for your train; "jaz" when you soak the umpire; "jazz" when you demand a raise; "jaz" when you hike thirty-five miles of a Sunday; "jazz" when you simply sit around and beam so that all who look beam on you. Anything that takes manliness or effort or energy or activity or strength of soul is "jaz."[35]

In Hopkins's tongue-in-cheek take on this new word, *jazz* describes just about anything, from running for a train to demanding a raise. Just a few years later, with the success of the Original Dixieland Jazz Band, the word became permanently yoked to the New Orleans–style small-group music that had spread around the country.[36] The earlier ambiguities around the word were now fused to the separate question of defining the new and wildly popular music. To capture these sounds, writers reached for unwieldy metaphors. In a 1917 *New York Sun* article, Walter Kingsley writes that "jazz music is the delirium tremens of syncopation... an attempt to reproduce the marvelous syncopation of the African jungle."[37] The struggle continued, with writers often falling back on extravagant figures of speech. In his 1957 *Book of Jazz*, Leonard Feather suggests that "the attempts to define jazz have frequently reached an *ignotum per ignotius* dead end." For Feather, the question of describing this great music remains nearly impossible: "The task of imbuing in the layman, with expositive words, a sensitive understanding of the dry, ascetic beauty of a Miles Davis improvisation is as hazardous an undertaking as an effort to explain English grammatical construction by playing a trumpet solo. Many have tried to explain jazz in words; all have failed."[38] Recent writers have similarly struggled. In an early part of the companion book to Ken Burns's 2000 PBS series *Jazz*, Geoffrey C. Ward and Burns describe jazz as "America's music—born out of a million American negotiations, between having and not having; between happy and sad, country and city; between Black and white and men and women; between the Old Africa and the Old Europe—which could only have happened in an entirely New World." Like Hopkins, Ward and Burns make jazz about nearly everything—possessions, emotions, identity, nation, and the world.[39]

This long-standing linguistic struggle has been ripe for mockery. In the short story "The King of Jazz," published in 1977 by the *New Yorker*, Donald Barthelme writes about a trombonist, Hokie Mokie, who believes that, after hearing that his rival Spicy MacLammermoor is dead, he is now the king of jazz.[40] At the beginning of the story, Mokie plays his trombone out of the window to "reassure" himself of his new title. Two people passing the window hear the music. One immediately recognizes the player: "Sounds like Hokie Mokie to me. Those few but perfectly selected notes have the real epiphanic glow." Mokie soon encounters a new rival, a visiting Japanese trombonist named Hideo Yamaguchi. At a gig, and after debating what tune to play, the two battle each other on the bandstand. Two listeners (the same ones?) hear the music. The first asks, "What's that sound coming in from the side there?" The other responds in epic, purple prose:

> You mean that sound that sounds like the cutting edge of life? That sounds like polar bears crossing Arctic ice pans? That sounds like a herd of musk ox in full flight? That sounds like male walruses diving to the bottom of the sea? That sounds like fumaroles smoking on

the slopes of Mt. Katmai? That sounds like the wild turkey walking through the deep, soft forest? That sounds like beavers chewing trees in an Appalachian marsh? That sounds like an oyster fungus growing on an aspen trunk? That sounds like a mule deer wandering a montane of the Sierra Nevada? That sounds like prairie dogs kissing? That sounds like witchgrass tumbling or a river meandering? That sounds like manatees munching seaweed at Cape Sable? That sounds like coatimundis moving in packs across the face of Arkansas? That sounds like—[41]

The other listener suddenly realizes who it is: "Good God, it's Hokie! Even with a cup mute on, he's blowing Hideo right off the stand!" On the bandstand, Yamaguchi is struggling to keep up, at one point reaching for a sword on his belt, the shame leading him to attempt hara-kiri. With the Japanese rival vanquished, Mokie once again takes his crown as the king of jazz.[42]

In this very short story, Barthelme playfully skewers many aspects of jazz culture—fans' detailed and obscure knowledge, the masculine bandstand cutting contests, the cult of genius—but he seems especially focused on the language of jazz appreciation and culture. Mokie's admirers deploy extravagant metaphors in an attempt to capture his inimitable greatness, his "epiphanic glow." One listener describes Mokie as playing in the "English sunrise" manner, "with lots of rays coming out of it, some red rays, some blue rays, some green rays, some green stemming from a violet center, some olive stemming from a tan center."[43] A little later these attempts to describe Mokie's sound take on absurd proportions, with each comparison straying further and further from the music. At first, the comparisons seem plausible if distant—a forceful jazz solo might have the thunderous power of a herd of musk ox. But as the list grows the comparisons grow sillier. It is hard to understand how a virtuoso trombone solo could sound like prairie dogs kissing or manatees munching seaweed. If it weren't for the other listener's recognition ("Good God, it's Hokie!"), the list may have continued indefinitely. Barthelme is clearly aiming at a larger issue: the inadequacy of language to express musical experience. But in focusing on jazz, he is also referencing a long history of similar attempts to describe the music's greatness to others.[44]

Even if these examples, as I have been arguing, do not appear hostile to the music, its musicians, or its listeners, it is not always clear who or what we are actually laughing at. For Freud, the affective power of jokes comes not from what he called their "joke-work"—the formal techniques employed—but from the underlying emotional or psychological impulses driving them, their "tendentious" or "hostile" purposes. As Billig writes, summarizing Freud, "We laugh more at tendentious jokes than we do at non-tendentious ones, but we convince ourselves that we are laughing at the cleverness of the joke-work. In this we deceive ourselves, for it is the tendentiousness that provides the greater impulse to laughter."[45] Although they seem, on the surface, to be *using* jazz to get at something else—such as our very human inability to find the right words to describe the things we like—an ambiguity remains. There is a sense that, perhaps, we are indeed laughing at the stupidity of the music. The parodies and jokes, then, become a way to obliquely "validate the expression of [our] forbidden feeling[s]" toward jazz.[46] In this sense, the examples I have examined, and many similar ones, offer us a "both-and" situation: both affirming jazz and expressing a latent sense that, just maybe, jazz is really a scam, a music that doesn't deserve its accolades.

LAUGHING AT JAZZ FROM THE INSIDE: SETTING BOUNDARIES

Despite the music's current reputation for seriousness, a great deal of jazz humor comes from within the jazz community. The music has a long history of laughing at itself.[47] In a 2019 article in Jazz History Online, website creator, writer, and editor Thomas Cunniffe provides a brief history of jazz in stand-up comedy.[48] Cunniffe begins his survey with the jazz-inspired comics of the 1950s and '60s such as Mort Sahl, Stan Freberg, and Lenny Bruce. Other figures such as Woody Allen and Bill Cosby were noted jazz fans who derived inspiration from the music's improvisational aesthetics. Although not a core part of their routines, jazz did make appearances. Freberg's 1956 parody recording of the Platters' hit "The Great Pretender" features a hip pianist devoted to the work of Erroll Garner and George Shearing who is perplexed that all he should do is play the same few unembellished chords over and over again. Thinking he should play more, the pianist begins interpolating boogie-woogie and jazz figures, only to draw rebukes from the singer, who has to interrupt his performance to chide the pianist.

A more obscure example, also referenced by Cunniffe, is George Crater, a character created by the writer and comic Ed Sherman in the late 1950s and early '60s. In the character of Crater, Sherman wrote a column for *DownBeat* titled "Out of My Head." Also in character, he hosted a regular radio show on New York City radio station WNCN and recorded a 1960 comedy album titled *Out of My Head* for the esteemed jazz label Riverside Records.[49] Sherman's character is clearly influenced by Lenny Bruce in his delivery and outsider critique of American hypocrisy (Sherman—as Crater—interviewed Bruce for *DownBeat* in 1960). On his album, Crater demonstrates a deep knowledge of the jazz world, making jokes about musicians, fans, and the larger music industry.

The LP opens with "Wind-Up Dolls," which would become Sherman-Crater's best-known shtick. He sets things up with an announcement: "I've come up with an invention that is going to scare the music business. Like the whole music business is destroyed when this invention hits the street." What is this invention? It is a set of jazz windup dolls. His first one is a four-inch-tall Miles Davis dressed in a fine Italian silk suit and beautiful Italian shoes, carrying a shiny trumpet. When you wind it, "it turns its back on you." Should this one be successful, he has plans for others: a Thelonious Monk doll in a little red wagon that, after you wind it up, disappears; a Charles Mingus doll that punches a critic; a Dizzy Gillespie doll with trumpet that comes with a "bend it yourself tool-kit," and an Ornette Coleman one that "forgets the chords." Crater imagines a jazz scene where the dolls replace the live musicians, infuriating the union. These jokes are unabashedly for the jazz insider. Each windup doll references a well-known, if exaggerated and stereotyped, characteristic of the musician. Davis was noted for his sharp dressing and penchant for expensive suits but also for his aloof demeanor onstage, often turning his back on the audience. Crater's joke about Monk references the famous album cover of *Monk's Music* that shows the pianist sitting in a child's red wagon. Crater also alludes to the pianist's reputation for unreliability, a result of his sometimes unpredictable behavior on- and offstage. The other dolls evoke similar stereotypes: Mingus's frequent angry outbursts at musicians, fans, and critics; Coleman's reputation as a jazz charlatan; and Gillespie's iconic bent trumpet.

Crater's humor sweeps in the broader world of jazz critics, media, and audiences. In one bit, he mocks the pretentions of reviewers who fill their prose with absurd metaphors, overgeneralizations, and half-baked sociologisms. Adopting the tone of a pompous critic, Crater recites an imaginary record review: "Although he sounds much like Jelly Roll Morton, Dizzy Gillespie, although animalistically beautiful, unfortunately suffers from a past environment which contributes greatly to his playing on this record which by all means because of such sociological reasons Nina Simone could not have possibly sung 'Bess You Is My Woman' or 'I Loves You Porgy' for that matter. And all the world is a stage, you know. All right: five stars."[50]

Out of My Head is aimed squarely at a jazz audience. While some of Crater's jokes are still relevant, many of them—especially the famous windup doll bit—land awkwardly today. The tropes the comedian works with—the anger and aggression of Davis and Mingus, for example—evoke racist stereotypes of "angry Black men." But more than this, the jokes start from a place of white hipness, and Crater, channeling Lenny Bruce, situates himself as a critic of a regressive mainstream culture. Although the jazz world was diverse, the record-buying market was overwhelmingly white. What is missing is what Amiri Baraka would point out just a few years later in "Jazz and the White Critic": a blindness to the struggles of Black musicians in a white-dominated world. What Crater finds funny about Davis, Mingus, Coleman, and others is more accurately read as responses to racist violence and trauma.

A much more recent example of insider jazz humor is Larry Goldings's videos and interviews as the Austrian pianist Hans Groiner. Wearing an awkward blond wig, Groiner is featured in several videos speaking sincerely, pompously, and utterly cluelessly about jazz. His primary goal is to fix the music, to correct its confusing rhythms, melodies, and harmonies. In Goldings's first Groiner video, posted in 2007, the fake pianist talks about his interest in jazz: "I heard the first jazz . . . when I was seven. I did not like it. For the most part, I still do not like it." The rest of the four-minute video has Groiner analyze and then "correct" Thelonious Monk's tune "Well You Needn't." In the opening two bars, Groiner changes Monk's dissonant half-step chord alternations (F–G♭) and makes them two major chords one step apart

(F–G). He also changes the melody to fit the "corrected" harmonies, changing E♭ (the sixth of G♭) to D (the fifth of G). He makes a similar alteration to the next two bars, ending the first eight measures by deleting Monk's tritone-inflected closing phrase (B–C–F) and replacing it with the blandly consonant 5–6–1 (C–D–F) of F major. Groiner also removes all syncopation, making everything fall on the beat. Groiner believes his music "breathes calmness and serenity." "And when I combine it with the music of Monk," he says, "this to me is what Monk was trying to do." The rest of the video has Groiner walking and posing in a backyard garden.[51] By making his character Austrian, Goldings also gets to mock European cluelessness. We don't know much about Groiner, so it is, again, not clear who or what is the real target. Is Groiner a classical musician who reveres his country's rich musical legacy and looks down on jazz and other popular musics? Or is he a fan of jazz who is simply incapable of understanding the music and its culture? Goldings gets to have it both ways.

In all these examples, race inevitably plays a significant if oblique part. Most of the time it is hinted at. Sometimes the intersection of humor, race, and jazz is made explicit. In 1931, the all-white Casa Loma Orchestra recorded two tracks, "White Jazz" and "Black Jazz," clearly meant as parodies. But it is the first, with its stiff, hectic groove, that is the primary target. "White jazz" is meant to evoke the popular sweet bands of the time such as the orchestras led by Paul Whiteman and Guy Lombardo. In 1982, Mose Allison recorded "Middle Class White Boy," a satire of white baby-boomer rebellion. The character narrating the song is trying to rebel with facial hair ("the Mountain Man and the Fu Manchu"), religion ("went halfway around the world to find the right guru"), and antisocial behavior ("I even got in trouble / I left town on the run"). Allison's "hero" is trying and failing to "just have some fun" and be cool. The humor of white jazz insiders such as Crater, Goldings, Allison, and others, is often playful and knowing. These are "hip" men who understand the Black vernacular and can speak authoritatively about important Black and white jazz musicians. And although they are often more sensitive to issues of race, these insider jazz jokes nonetheless tread perilously close to racially inflected mockery. These moments of jazz humor inevitably point to the real racial tensions that have historically shaped and often divided the jazz community.

JAZZ IS STUPID

Jazz comes up unexpectedly in "The Target," the eighth episode from the ninth season of NBC's *The Office*. One of the storylines features Angela Kinsey (Angela Martin), who, having discovered that her husband is having an affair with coworker Oscar Martinez (Oscar Nunez), organizes a "hit" on him, a single kneecapping by an inept thug named Trevor. The plot goes awry, and a tearful Angela, coming to grips with her husband's homosexuality and the betrayal of her office friend, says to former lover and coconspirator Dwight Schrute (Rainn Wilson), "I feel so stupid. I sit next to [Oscar] every day." "You're not stupid," Dwight consoles. "Jazz is stupid." A weeping Angela agrees. "Jazz is stupid. I mean, just play the right notes!"

The reference to jazz comes out of nowhere, with no connection to anything that has happened in the episode. Some of the humor comes from its randomness—the hapless Angela is upset and confused about her husband's homosexuality. In fact, Angela blames Oscar for her husband's "gayness." Dwight, equally hapless in the situation, reminds Angela that, although they don't understand "gayness," they are not stupid. Really stupid things do exist in the world—jazz, for example—and her situation is not one of them. But when Angela agrees with Dwight ("Just play the right notes!"), jazz becomes not just an absurd way to comfort someone but a target of ridicule itself. Perhaps some viewers would find humor in the two characters' inability to appreciate the music, but I think the joke works precisely because it emanates from these two characters: dumb as they are, Angela and Dwight both see clearly that jazz is pointless, lacking even a melody to follow. We laugh because, although they don't see much correctly, they understand the obvious truth that jazz is stupid.

Although it is brief, only a passing jab, this moment demonstrates another, more direct and aggressive strain of jazz humor. It is a hostile joke—we laugh *with* Angela and Dwight at the self-important and self-delusional jazz fan. For Freud, jokes are defined not by their technique but by the structure of their audience. In contrast to his notions of humor (an internal psychological process of reflection) and the comic (an interpretation of an external person or object), the joke requires three people: the teller, the hearer, and the object of the joke. "No one," Freud writes, "can be content with having made a joke for himself alone. An urge to tell the joke to someone is inextricably bound up with the joke-work; indeed, this urge is so strong that often enough it is carried through in disregard of serious misgivings." The humorous and the comic can be enjoyed by oneself; "a joke, on the contrary, must be told to someone else." This three-part structure is basic also to the joke's psychological work, the discharge of psychical energy that would, under other circumstances, be repressed. The teller and the hearer expend their energy differently—joke tellers cannot laugh while telling the joke, but they require the laughter of the audience to get the full psychological benefit. This structure creates a momentary community. With "innocent jokes," ones that "reinforce" insightful observations on life, the teller and hearer are united in a moment of pleasure reminiscent of the unrestricted, often nonsensical, play of childhood. But in the case of "tendentious" or "hostile jokes," the community created is one of shared aggressiveness, even hate: aggressive jokes "turn the hearer, who was indifferent to begin with, into a co-hater or co-despiser, and creates for the enemy a host of opponents where at first there was only one."[52] When Dwight and Angela expose jazz as stupid, they feel empowered, saying aloud something that is not allowed to be said. As an audience—as hearers of this joke—our laughter brings us into this community of truth; we become "co-haters" and "co-despisers" of jazz. The situation is very close to Freud's tripartite scheme: Dwight is the teller; Angela and the viewer are the audience; jazz is the object.

Yet the show's overarching ironic mode puts distance between the viewer and Angela and Dwight. "Jazz is stupid" is a sentiment that we are allowed to both embrace and still keep at a distance. We can agree with them but also laugh at them because we are pretty sure Angela and Dwight have little idea what they are talking about. The show just barely hints at a racial subtext here. Angela and Dwight represent conservative, white middle-class America. We know from earlier episodes that Dwight is ignorant, prone to prejudicial and racist comments (for example, anti-Semitism in "Diversity Day," the second episode from the first season), even if he knows in a general way that racism is bad. In the larger context of the show, Angela and Dwight's "jazz is stupid" has it both ways: skewering the music's elitist reputation while demonstrating an ignorance of an "important" music born and developed in Black America. As Simon Frith astutely notes, the charge of stupidity is a common mode of cultural censure. Calling jazz, or any art, stupid asserts that it is not just bad but "somehow demeaning, that it demeans us through our involvement," Frith writes. "Stupid music... is offensive because it seems to deny what we're capable of, humanly, rationally, ethically, aesthetically."[53]

On his 2007 stand-up album, *Impersonal*, comic Paul F. Tompkins offers his own version of "jazz is stupid." "Jazz music," Tompkins says, "is all about making the common man feel dumb. It's just a bunch of dudes playing solos at the same time. It's like a genre of music that is *defying* you to like it." He imagines the musicians saying, "Maybe you're too dumb, dummy. It's the notes we're *not* playin'." No normal person goes out to hear this music, he says, unless "it was an accident, like maybe you lost a bet or you fell down some stairs and you woke up in a jazz club." For Tompkins, the worst thing about jazz is how the musicians seem so enamored of their own insider hipness. Why does everyone get a solo? And why do all the musicians laugh when the bass player plays particular notes?

> That leaves you in the audience saying [*in a high-pitched voice*], "I don't get your jazz joke. What is happening? You've played many notes this evening, none particularly hilarious; why is that note so sidesplitting, jazzbos?"
>
> It's not *funny*. Because if something is inherently funny, it is relatable after the fact. I don't wanna hear this "you had to be there" nonsense, right? I can't rearrange my whole schedule around when funny things are gonna happen to you.
>
> You can't relate this to someone else, even if you understood it. You can't go into your job the next day and say, "Oh, uh, last night, we saw the funniest jazz fellow. Um, at one point, instead of going *bearlp*, he went *bear-rl-b*."
>
> Oh, that's a hot one, eh? Oh, my brain has many wrinkles.[54]

Not only do jazz musicians seem to deliberately keep their music obscure, they have no sense of what is funny. As a comic, Tompkins knows funny: no one in the audience can go home and tell the funny musical jazz joke the next day.

Sometimes described as an "alternative comic," Tompkins sports a mustache and frequently dresses in three-piece suits, presenting himself as a throwback to an earlier era (Tompkins helped run a show at the Los Angeles nightclub Largo that was structured as an old-time radio program). In keeping with this image, his humor mostly satirizes contemporary norms and preoccupations. Along with the jazz piece, *Impersonal* features bits on beautiful Hollywood women claiming to be tomboys as kids ("you don't hear Brad Pitt saying he was a sissy"), on wealth ("sometimes I eat money"), on daylight savings time ("it is just an hour adjustment twice a year"), on a fancy balloon store ("where are your elegant balloons?"), and on hipsters and their pets ("maybe even animals would like some alone time... maybe they don't want to come with you on all your jackass errands."). Tompkins's humor mixes absurdity and satire to puncture our obsession with trends and our inflated sense of self-importance. Tompkins avoids any overt reference to race or Blackness. Yet, that absence is telling: Is he critiquing Black vernacular musical practices? Or is he mocking the white adopters, the white hipsters, who have taken on these vernacular practices? Even more than *The Office*, Tompkins's joke works in an ambiguous space, never specifying the real target. The ambiguity only highlights the racial implications of jazz mockery.[55]

Humor as a deflection of more troubling kinds of attacks—those driven by racism, misogyny, or homophobia—has strong echoes in the history of American popular music. For example, the antidisco fervor of the 1970s and early '80s echoes the humor of Tompkins and other purveyors of "jazz is stupid." Unlike jazz, disco never had an elite cultural reputation. On the contrary, it was a music of the masses, a showy culture of nightclubs. For the haters, disco was an embarrassingly vacuous culture, its soundtrack a mindless, repetitive thumping of drums with saccharine strings. The attacks on disco's shallowness and inauthenticity reflected much deeper anxieties about the cultural standing of lower- and working-class Americans, about Blackness and Latinidad in mainstream American culture, and about homosexuality. For some listeners, the popularity of the music among the working class and the queer and Black communities made disco a symbol of all that was tasteless and déclassé in American culture. Historian Gillian Frank argues that disco's association with gay men was particularly strong. "The commercial success of disco music," he writes, "triggered a fearful and homophobic reaction from rock fans because it was considered to be a quintessentially gay genre of music."[56] When that homophobic fear of disco manifested, it often did so in the language of humor. Disc jockey Steve Dahl, organizer of the notorious Disco Demolition Night in July 1979 at Comiskey Park in Chicago, mocked disco on the air, lisping the word in an effeminate manner, "verbally attacking disco by drawing upon a shared vocabulary of derision and insult that revealed widely held antigay attitudes."[57] Dahl's attacks set the tone for many in the antidisco movement. A Los Angeles radio station released an antidisco record with songs like "Disco's What I Hate," "Disco Defecation," and "Death to Disco."[58] The underlying racism and homophobia of these attacks was deflected by humor and the familiar stance of it's-just-a-joke.

Mocking and ridiculing music, whether it be disco or jazz, is sometimes done just to get a laugh, but often the ridicule serves a purpose—not in the Freudian sense of an unconscious release of aggression, but in a self-aware attempt to unveil a cultural practice that is foolish. Satire is the general term for this kind of motivated ridicule. Satire, as many scholars have argued, makes a social judgment, one that implies a recognized and desired standard of behavior or values. It does this by exposing a variety of human follies: vanity, greed, selfishness, narrow-mindedness, and stupidity. Satire may use humor and irony, but it does not require either to make its point. Above all, satire is meant to be public, to unmask for all to see what is and, by implication, what should be. In this way, satire is often political—a way to call people with power to account.

Tompkins's comedic takedown of jazz is satire: he is trying to deflate the music's undeserved cultural status. Jazz musicians, Tompkins suggests, are frauds, passing off nonsense as serious and smart music. And while some in Tompkins's audience might find this view challenging, he is putting into words what many others already feel. But the satirical assaults on the music that have come from *within* the jazz community pack a special punch: in these cases, the audience is fiercely committed to the music and view it as serious and culturally important. Here the satirical unveiling goes right to the heart of deeply held values about what jazz is and what it means.

One excellent example is the video series *Jazz Robots*, created by guitarist Joe Hundertmark and posted online in 2010. To make the videos, Hundertmark used a program called Xtranormal, a web-based software that animates text. The software uses templates, in this case a group of robots who speak in affectless "computer" voices against a grimy, brown, futuristic industrial landscape. Because templates are used, there are many videos of the same robots having wildly different conversations. Rather than animation as traditionally understood, these creations are much more akin to internet memes where the same image is combined with different text.[59] The humor of these videos comes, in large part, from the juxtaposition of emotion-laden words with the expressionless voices of cartoon robots, what Henri Bergson calls "the mechanical element which resembles a piece of clockwork wound up once for all and capable of working automatically."[60] The robots' deadpan voices and stiff reactions run counter to the flux and flow of lived experience.

In the first *Jazz Robots* video, the two robots talk about a recent gig. The first robot remarks on how well the show went, how the other robot was "so killing": "That thing you did during that one jam, when it went up high, and you did that thing, it was the most killing thing I have ever heard." The second robot responds in kind: "Thank you so much, man. However, you were the one who was killing. You are such a bad motherfucker. When we hit the coda, and you started with that one thing [*robot scats*], wow, it was super killing, man." They talk about practicing ("I have been in the shed"), original compositions ("I really like your tunes. That one tune, with the thing going up and the really cool melody"), swinging ("You swing so hard"), and having a private "session."[61]

Aside from the deadpan robots scatting and swearing, the real bite of the satire comes from the deployment of jazz lingo—*motherfucker, swinging, the shed, a session*. For viewers with the background, these are all part of the jazz lingo. They are a real part of the music, especially among younger musicians enculturating to the jazz world.[62] Putting this jargon in the words of deadpan robots highlights their artificiality and pretentiousness—why not speak plainly about what you like and find musically exciting and beautiful? As his YouTube and social media accounts demonstrate, Hundertmark is himself an accomplished musician skilled in variety of genres, including jazz. He is no doubt speaking from personal experience and observation. At this level, *Jazz Robots* is funny for the ways it accurately captures a subculture with its own peculiar, often absurd ways of talking.

Jazz critic Nate Chinen has a word for the real-life version of the jazz robots: the *jazzbro*. Riffing on the old slang of the *jazzbo*, an exuberant jazz fan, the jazzbro combines a love of jazz with elitism and machismo:

> A jazzbro—not to be confused with a jazzbo, its older taxonomical cousin—is a self-styled jazz aficionado, overwhelmingly male and usually a musician in training himself, who expresses a handful of determinative social behaviors. Among these are a migratory pattern from the practice room, where they often nest alone, to the jazz club, where they travel in packs; a compulsion to signal the awareness of any mildly startling musical detail, with muttered exclamations like the aforementioned "*Woooo*"; the emphatic adjectival use of the word "killing," as in "that solo was *killing*"; and the exploitation of jazz knowledge as a private commodity selectively put on public display.[63]

Echoing the satire of jazz robots, Chinen here explicitly adds the masculinist posturing, sometimes edging into misogyny. Jazzbros are not "jazz nerds," a subgroup that looks inward; jazzbros are sociable and voluble. They make their specialized knowledge known at jazz performances. Chinen frames his discussion in the context of a performance of a gender-mixed band, led by the drummer Allison Miller. Watching Miller's group, Boom Tic Boom, at a club outside New York City, Chinen overhears a young man behind him say, "Check that shit out.... She's *such* a badass." In this context, the exclamation echoes the perennial backhanded compliment "You don't play like a girl," which so many women jazz musicians have endured. But the jazzbro is oblivious of what Chinen describes as his "irrefutable dudeness."

Throughout the piece, Chinen suggests that the jazzbro is a largely white phenomenon. He mentions writer Norman Mailer as a spiritual forefather and the white musicians of Chicago's Austin High Gang as early exemplars. And given the much smaller presence of Black and other musicians of color in jazz conservatories, it is safe to assume that most of Chinen's musicians "migrating" from the practice room to the club are white.[64]

Chinen's jazzbros, then, in their behaviors also evoke a tradition of whites adopting Black style. The words used by the jazzbro robots—*shedding, swinging*, even superlatives such as *motherfucker*—were created in African American communities and represent Black vernacular speech. White jazz musicians have long adopted this language—the classic example is white clarinetist and saxophonist Mezz Mezzrow's 1946 autobiography *Really the Blues*—but it has always been a complicated and fraught borrowing. Hearing the jazz robots, in their stiff, electronic voices, deploy such language is a reminder of how awkward any appropriation really is. The jazz lingo may be elitist and pretentious, but it can also be a kind of racial mimicry, what scholar Barbara Savage calls aural blackface, a long-standing practice of adopting Black vernacular speech patterns to represent or signify Black Americans.[65] It expresses, however unintentionally, white supremacy—white culture is given but Black culture is for the taking.

Taking all this into account—the affectless robots discussing their passion, the excessive jargon of the milieu, and the white appropriation of Black culture—*Jazz Robots* turns the very serious into the absurd. In *Laughter*, Henri Bergson notes, "all that is serious in life comes from our freedom." When something questions our sense of freedom, it transforms it into comedy: "What, then, is requisite to transform all this into comedy? Merely to fancy that our seeming freedom conceals the strings of a dancing-Jack, and that we are, as the poet says, 'humble marionettes / The wires of which are pulled by fate.'"[66] *Jazz Robots* is mocking not simply the surface absurdities of one kind of jazz culture but a deeper anxiety about the very nature of expressive freedom in an art form rooted in racial appropriation. It is comic, Bergson notes, to fall into a ready-made category. Are these jazzbros really developing an authentic jazz voice, or are they just aping a culture they admire? Are they free, creative agents or just prisoners of a game of racial appropriation they do not, or cannot, fully understand?[67]

Far more sour are the defunct blog *Jazz Is the Worst* and its associated Twitter account, @JazzIsTheWorst (collectively, JazzIsTheWorst), active from 2013 to 2017. In the profile page, the anonymous poster provides this description: "I hate jazz, you should too." There has been a lot of speculation about the author, with some suggesting that it is Ambrose Akinmusire, a highly touted jazz trumpet player.[68] Other people have also thought the creator was a jazz musician.[69] The blog posts target the posturing and elitism of musicians; the aging, middle-class white audience; and the overpriced and empty venues that host the music. A December 2014 post, "How to Become a Successful Jazz Musician in 2015," has some advice for aspiring artists. "Becoming a famous jazz musician today," the author warns, "is harder than it's ever been before" because jazz is "less popular and more widely hated than ever before." But don't fret: the author has a half-dozen "simple tips" that can help. The list that follows is a bitterly ironic take on the posturing and self-fashioning the jazz world rewards: "alienate your audience," dismiss listeners who "don't get it" as being "not smart enough," take "selfies with famous people," remember that "it doesn't hurt to be a girl," follow "the soulful path," and hire a publicist. Accompanying the list are publicity photos of younger musicians with older, established ones: saxophonist Steve Lehman with Nicholas Payton; pianist Vijay Iyer with Chick Corea and Nicholas Payton (Iyer seems to be a favorite target of the author); saxophonist Melissa Aldana with George Coleman; saxophonist Grace Kelly with Phil Woods; and bassist esperanza spalding with Joe Lovano.[70] The Twitter posts, in their brevity, are even sharper, taking aim at jazz education ("Jazz Fact #65: There are more instructional books on 'How to Play Jazz' than there are people who can actually play Jazz"), cultural events ("If Jazz had sex with *American Idol* their child would look like #JazzAtTheWhiteHouse"), industry ("Jazz News: 'New jazz club set record by opening and subsequently going out of business within 30 minutes'"), and jazz styles ("Free Jazz: For when you're just too lazy to read a lead-sheet, write a tune, or rehearse at all").[71] The posts are often mean spirited, attacking musicians directly (such as saxophonist Kamasi Washington).[72] And while there are misogynistic gestures ("it doesn't hurt to be a girl," referenced above), the posts avoid the kind of aggression or broad social generalizations that would edge things toward hate in its strongest form. JazzIsTheWorst is often personal, but it never demands an offender's extinction or total elimination. It is classically satirical in the way it seeks to expose, through irony and humor, the foibles of others.

Partly because of its insider references and self-aware tone, JazzIsTheWorst was most popular among jazz musicians themselves, as Margret Grebowicz points out. Despite the acidity, its commentary was widely circulated by professional musicians in the jazz world, providing a way for them to reflect on their community. "In the hands of the players themselves," Grebowicz writes, "the pronouncement that jazz is in fact 'the worst' has become something like a form of resistance, precisely when the music itself has ceased to be resistant enough."[73] The jazz community's embrace of JazzIsTheWorst reinforces the satirical nature of the project: offering judgment on the faults of jazz people and institutions, unmasking a world sheltered by unthinking truisms. JazzIsTheWorst also, implicitly, suggests that the jazz world could be better—more authentic, more honest, more true to the value of its dedicated creators. For Grebowicz, the Twitter account is also a way of reckoning with how digital culture has created a "crisis of community" for American jazz. Drawing on the ideas of Jean-Luc Nancy and Derrida, Grebowicz argues that the new digital side of the jazz world, particularly social media, has damaged the in-person "deep relationality" that makes jazz improvisation vital and meaningful. "Internet sociality [is] an atrophied sociality that forecloses the interstitial nature of being-with and thus precludes community."[74] For Grebowicz, JazzIsTheWorst is more than just a joke; it is a symptom of deeper problems in a jazz world fractured by the digital era.

The most notorious recent example of jazz satire is the 2014 parody of Sonny Rollins published in the *New Yorker*. Written by comedy writer Django Gold and titled "Sonny Rollins: In His Own Words," the brief piece purports to be an autobiographical account of the saxophonist. Starting with his first exposure to the saxophone ("I thought it was fun. I later learned that these guys' parents had forced them into it"), the essay revisits many of the clichés of jazz autobiography: the haunting of nightclubs, the attention to dress and being cool, the recording, and the traveling. In each case, Gold flips expectations: the nightclubs were filled with clueless patrons, the musicians' fancy suits were wasted in the dingy club basements, long jam sessions were tiresome for everyone involved. And about the music itself—the driving force of it all—the pseudo-Rollins calls it the "stupidest thing anyone ever came up with. The bands start a song, but then everything falls apart and the musicians just play whatever they want for as long as they can stand it." Rather than celebrating the ups and downs of his musical journey, Gold's Rollins is demoralized: "Once you get stuck in a rut, it's difficult to pull yourself out, even if you hate every minute of it." Ruing his choices, he thinks he would have preferred to be an "accountant or a process server" because at least "they make good money." Despite a prolific career and critical acclaim, Gold's Rollins thinks it was all "idiotic." "I hate music," he concludes. "I wasted my life."[75]

The response to Gold's piece was ferocious. Jazz critic Howard Mandel and trumpeter Nicholas Payton both posted extensive, passionate essays on the piece.[76] In a more reflective mood, Sonny Rollins himself responded in an interview with Bret Primack posted on YouTube.[77] The magazine received enough reactions from confused or troubled readers that the editors soon appended a note at the beginning of the piece: "This article, which is part of our 'Shouts & Murmurs' humor blog, is a work of satire." Part of the confusion was caused by the photograph that accompanied the online piece: it was a professional head shot rather than a small cartoon illustration typical of *Shouts and Murmurs* essays. Further complicating things, the *New Yorker* had published critic Stanley Crouch's essay celebrating Rollins in 2005. What is especially potent here is the mixture of affect with race: the fiery reaction that focused directly on the centrality of Blackness to jazz culture.

From one perspective the parody failed because it didn't uphold certain social agreements about jokes, what Dennis Howitt and Kwame Owusu-Bempah call maxims or general principles of good conduct. The parody was not appropriately and clearly "signaled... using a standard format or formula."[78] Along with the photograph, the title gave no hint of parody—there was no joke embedded in it, no clear irony or absurdity. Furthermore, the *New Yorker* has a long tradition of profiling musicians, including an important history of profiling jazz musicians. But the parody also failed because it didn't have a clear intertextual partner—a real text that the parody is remaking. Recent scholarship on parody has explained it as primarily defined by intertextuality: "an imitation (allusion, if not direct quotation or misquotation) of some other text or texts even if only by using stylistic devices which are typical of the text(s) in question."[79] Howard Mandel makes this argument: Gold's parody was technically deficient, deploying the techniques of humor—incongruity, absurdity, substitution—in a clumsy or incompetent fashion. What Gold was asking the reader to do was unclear. Was Gold mocking hagiographic jazz oral histories? Did he have in mind a certain style, such as that used in *DownBeat* or the *New Yorker*? Or was Gold trying to point up the incongruity between what the real Sonny Rollins—an undeniable genius—would say and what this fake Rollins says about his career and music? Unlike Barthelme's "King of Jazz," it is unclear what exactly Gold is making fun of. Some readers would get it, but others, even if they understood it was parody, could not conjure up the other text, its point of comparison.

In his criticism of the parody, Nicholas Payton focuses not on the violation of the maxims of joking (he agrees that it was satire) but on the very act of using Rollins to ridicule jazz. "Charlie Parker died to play this music. Bud Powell died to play this music," Payton writes. Jazz—Payton prefers Black American Music—is a music that tells a story of survival; it represents triumph over oppression. Gold's parody reduces and emasculates Rollins: "Theodore Walter 'Sonny' Rollins is no mouse. He is a man." For Payton, Gold is mocking not just jazz but Black struggle generally. Seen this way, Gold's essay is part of a long history of humor supporting white supremacy: "You've done enough over the past 500 years. Black life in a world of White oppression and supremacy is satirical enough."[80] This history, Payton argues, is personal and real, a history of tangible pain. Things of such a serious nature should not be joked about. As Matthew D. Morrison points out, there is already a legacy of violence "embedded in the commercialization" of Black musical practices, starting with nineteenth-century blackface minstrelsy. White performers "freely express themselves through the consumption and performance of commodified Black aesthetics without carrying the burden of being black under white supremacist structures." Making fun of Sonny Rollins is an extension of this "free" engagement and consumption. From this view, the mockery—however well intentioned—is yet another moment of symbolic violence in the long history of white engagement with Blackness.[81]

But Payton's criticism rests on more than a split between caring and not caring about jazz. What Payton brings to the surface—that the parody is really a neo-minstrel attack on Black culture—is something that other satirists have acknowledged when reflecting on jazz parody and satire. In 2013, writer Amy Rose Spiegel authored a piece published on *BuzzFeed* titled "What's the Deal with Jazz?" The brief article, typical for *BuzzFeed*, featured short, snarky criticisms illustrated with web images (photos, cartoons, animated GIFs). For example, at the end of the piece, Spiegel writes, "And how can anyone truly take scatting seriously? Are you people for real?" The illustration was a video featuring a clip of actor and pianist Jeff Goldblum trying to scat (melodically improvise with nonsense syllables).[82] Not long after it was posted, Spiegel deleted her article. After talking to friends, she recognized that her piece, in the name of a quick joke, perpetuated racist stereotypes, that her "jazz and the white critic" dismissal of the music was ignorant and racially charged. In other words, Spiegel realized her hating on was awfully close to hating.[83]

Context and history are key: Payton explicitly situates the Rollins parody in a long history of white mockery and ridicule of Black people and their accomplishments. Gold, by imaginatively speaking for Rollins, is practicing a kind of minstrelsy, putting on a figurative "Black mask" to speak for the great saxophonist. Barthelme's "King of Jazz," in contrast, leaves the race of Hokie ambiguous. Gold's piece is an act of ventriloquism—he speaks for a Black artist in a way that confused a lot of readers. If you see minstrelsy here, you see something that is steeped in an affective history of shame and ridicule. Those feelings will almost certainly block any amusement. In Payton's view, Gold's piece is not just another jab at Black music but another example of white hatred of Blackness, of white supremacy lightened with a laugh. It was a tendentious joke that used humor to demean not just a person but an entire group of people. This would make it a strong form of hating. With Payton's critique in mind, George Crater's jokes from the 1960s seem equally as offensive—a Miles Davis windup doll that turns its back on the audience. I don't think Payton is saying you can't laugh at jazz; what matters is who is doing the joking and who is supposed to laugh. As scholar Jerry Palmer observes, the determination of humor and its allowability—whether the humorist should have permission to ridicule—is one of power relations. Whites have long given themselves permission to laugh at Black culture. Payton's blog post denies that permission, a way to force Gold, and those who laugh with him, to see how some humor can't be brushed off as "only joking." Humor can play an active role in the perpetuation of racism.

Although these satirical examples all appear to be narrowly focused on jazz musicians and the sounds they make, they all, at different levels of clarity, evoke race, specifically Blackness. Each of these satirical attacks rests on a fundamental ambiguity: Where does the self-importance of jazz come from? Is it the result of white musicians' appropriation of Black cultural practices, elevating it, and themselves, to a position of cultural superiority? Or does it come from Black musicians themselves, the founders of the music and creators of the tropes we associate with jazz (coolness, hipness, nightclubs, sunglasses, and berets)? The comedians never specify the target clearly. In some cases, as with *Jazz Robots*, the target seems to be the stereotypical white jazz-school musician, Chinen's jazzbro. But in other cases—as with Paul F. Tompkins or @JazzIsTheWorst—the target could be Black or white (or someone else). This ambiguity gives all these satires a racial charge rooted in that foundational American entertainment, blackface minstrelsy. Each example dances around the minstrel issue to some degree: Is jazz, or some forms of it, a kind of neo-minstrelsy? Are white jazz musicians metaphorically donning blackface when they perform? Are the satirists themselves donning blackface? Are *they* the minstrels in this equation?

◉

In *Laughter*, Bergson argues that generalization and abstraction are essential to humor. Laughter deals with classes of people, not individuals. "Comedy," Bergson writes, "depicts characters we have already come across and shall meet with again.... It aims at placing types before our eyes."[84] As a means of social generalization, humor also serves a corrective function, pointing out behaviors that are inflexible or mechanical and at odds with how life should be lived. That purpose, however, often relies on humiliation. Humor's disciplinary function combined with its negative affects—shame and embarrassment—can often put it in the vicinity of the strongest forms of hate. As I argued in chapter 1, hate abstracts disliked behaviors into generalized characteristics, a set of "intolerable traits" belonging to an individual or group.[85]

Humor represents an especially complicated affective engagement with jazz. Amusement or mirth, as psychologists and philosophers argue, requires a kind of emotional distance, an ability to focus on conceptual categories and their incongruities. But as Freud noted, that surface disengagement hides a deeper, displaced affect. Humor is a way of transforming anger, aggression, and contempt into laughter. Laughing at jazz can be playful, but it also can be aggressive, seeking to strike a blow against pretension, elitism, and obscurity. The precarious position jazz occupies in American popular music along with its inextricable connection to Black history and culture makes laughing at it a fraught exercise. The legacy of blackface minstrelsy and the continuing appropriation and exploitation of Black music by a dominant white culture makes ridiculing jazz always part of a much bigger conversation about the white adoption of Black cultural practices. Love of jazz can mingle with other, negative feelings. It may not be hate in the strongest sense of the word, but the most biting attacks on the music represent a kind of hating on that treads a very thin line between critique and nihilistic snark.[86] As Ken Willis notes, humor is always about power, and "as power is unevenly distributed throughout society, it becomes highly significant to the success of a joke who is telling what kind of joke to whom at what time and in what place."[87] Laughing at jazz is never "only a joke"; it is always about social positioning, a statement about the kinds of people we do and do not value.

◎ 4 ◎

The Musicians Suck

CONTEMPT AND DISGUST IN THE HISTORICAL RECEPTION OF JAZZ

> *Righteous indignation can be one of the cruelest and most vindictive of aggressive pleasures.*
>
> JOAN RIVIERE, "HATE, GREED, AND AGGRESSION"

> *If only you'd been straighter*
> *Said, "Honey, I'm a hater.*
> *If you want to know what floats my boat,*
> *Then ask what gets my goat."*
>
> RACHAEL AND VILRAY, "HATE IS THE BASIS (OF LOVE)"

For many jazz musicians, past and present, the real rewards of playing are affective, the desire to create shared emotional experiences, what Nichole Rustin-Paschal calls "richly imagined feelings of community, wellbeing, and selfhood." These affective experiences were, and remain, special "because [they] articulated emotions and feelings that mainstream society diminished."[1] If, as Lawrence Grossberg writes, affect is "the agency and locus of the investment within reality," what is the place and character of *negative* investments in our reality?[2] Where do they come from, and who or what are they directed at? This chapter looks at the strongest negative affects, feelings such as contempt and disgust, and their place in jazz history.

Jazz communities are defined by identity (race, gender, social class), by place (city or country), and by a generalized sense of belonging to a shared history or tradition. But, as Ken Prouty notes, "claims to an authoritative knowledge of jazz are deeply contested among and within various communities."[3] In this chapter, I will focus on the negative affects of contempt and disgust, examining the ways these feelings have shaped two central dynamics in the music's history: the changing place of women in the music, and the changing nature of jazz practice itself. Criticism by writers, fans, and musicians toward others in the jazz world is common. As I argued in chapter 2, taste judgments, including criticisms of musical choices and techniques, are baked into art worlds, integral to the pleasure and meaning of popular music. But the examples of negative affects I explore are particular to jazz history and culture, especially in the United States. The domination of jazz by men, in nearly all its aspects, has led to many criticisms of women in jazz. These criticisms are part of a larger sexism and misogyny that has pervaded different jazz cultures.

The reception of new musical styles has been another occasion for the expression of hostility. The rhetorical policing of the genre has often slipped from mere dislike to something much stronger: contempt and disgust. According to philosopher Michelle Mason, contempt is an attitude, an affective stance toward another person; it is a form of negative regard indicating a lack of respect. The contemptible person is one who "ranks low in worth as a person in virtue of falling short of some legitimate interpersonal ideal of a person." The object of contempt causes unpleasant feelings and a sense of pain in their presence.[4] Contempt is also a globalist emotion, in that it is focused on the whole person and not on a specific act. It is not simply that the contemptible person has done bad things, but that these bad things indicate some deeper failure to meet general ethical or moral standards.[5] With its social rejection, contempt comes close to hate in its strongest meaning—the desire to permanently remove an undesirable or offensive person or thing.

Disgust, however, can be even stronger than contempt. Rooted in the sensations of eating (like "taste," discussed in chapter 2), disgust embraces other senses such as smell, touch, sight, and hearing. It is "a moral and social sentiment," and "it plays a motivating and confirming role in moral judgment in a particular way that has little if any connection with ideas of oral incorporation."[6] If contempt is a devaluation of another person, disgust is a whole-sale rejection. Both ideas fuse affect with moral judgments. The examples of jazz contempt and disgust I will consider—the sexism and misogyny of the jazz world, the racism that simmers in some corners of the genre, and the policing of the music's boundaries, deciding who is or is not playing jazz—do not necessarily indicate hate in its strongest sense, but they come awfully close to it.

The aggressive hostility that circulates within parts of the jazz world originates in a deep love for the music. Passion for a musical genre or work is not just a representation of a taste or aesthetic preference but a much deeper claim about sincerity. Expressions of anger or aggression by certain people toward others often start with a sense of betrayal—a betrayal of talents, values, or norms.[7] The notion that love and hate are twins has been a constant in the historical writing on emotion from Descartes to Freud, and it remains a commonplace in our understanding of these affects. In the *Cultural Politics of Emotion*, Sara Ahmed argues that hate is a "negative attachment to another that one wishes to expel, an attachment that is sustained through the expulsion of the other from bodily and social proximity."[8] This negative attachment is part of hate's paradoxical structure: the hater needs the despised object in order to define the object of genuine love, even as that hated object must be rejected, pushed away, even destroyed.

Such intense negative affects also compel us to give justifications: if I really, truly find this example of jazz repulsive or offensive, there must be a strong reason for it. These justifications, although often based on musical details or judgments of authenticity, are, at a deeper level, expressive of foundational values. Jazz love and hate often form a loop—affect generating justification, and justification called forth by affect. Given the Janus-faced nature of affective investment in jazz, it is not surprising that writers and musicians, those with the strongest affective investments, would write with such intensity about their feelings, both positive and negative. Throughout the music's history, jazz critics and musicians, in the service of celebrating the music, have frequently leveled the most contemptuous evaluations of other jazz musicians, performances, and recordings.[9]

Critics, more so than musicians, are culturally positioned in a way that makes these tensions acute. As writers, they function across different social fields—journalism, art creation, and commerce—that require different behaviors. As journalists they report on new releases and artists, providing both an accounting of the present and a sense of historical change. As members of an art-making world, they act as promoters and translators to a larger public. But they also function in the commercial ecology that seeks to profit from music by selling it to consumers. By advising readers on what is and is not worthy of their money and time, critics play an integral role in generating profits for those with capital. Jazz writers have wrestled with this ambiguous position, and they have offered different ways of understanding their work as news reporters, cultural historians, aesthetic judges, and advertisers. The influential critic Dan Morgenstern sees his work as evaluative—deciding good and bad—but always with a sensitive accounting for context. True criticism, he argues, is more than "a reflection of the writer's personal opinion," it is "a bridge between artist and audience," an act that "enhances appreciation and understanding and facilitates the development of perception and taste." Even so, Morgenstern believes that the "true" role of the critic—embodied in the work of great past critics such as André Hodeir and Martin Williams—"is to lead the listener to the best the art has to offer," to help them "distinguish between the timeless and the ephemeral, and a sense of the place of jazz in the artistic and social scheme of things."[10] Here Morgenstern attempts to synthesize the often competing aspects of the critic's job: to bridge artist and audience and enhance understanding, but also to help listeners develop perception and taste and identify the "best"—the timeless—from the bad or mediocre—the ephemeral. But is evaluation—deciding the "best"—necessary to the work of connecting artists and audience? Is it necessary to identify the timeless works of jazz in order to help audiences understand the social and historical importance of a jazz performer? Morgenstern avoids these questions, fusing the critic's social function with an aesthetic mandate.

Jazz critics, historian John Gennari writes, "are the inheritors of a calling that since the 1930s . . . has been crucial to the history of jazz. . . . As proselytizers, intermediaries, gatekeepers, translators, rhetoricians, conceptualizers, producers, and analysts of jazz, jazz critics have been undeniably powerful voices—some would say too powerful—in the music's public discourse."[11] Writers such as Morgenstern, Stanley Crouch, Leonard Feather, Ira Gitler, Ralph Gleason, John Hammond, Nat Hentoff, André Hodeir, A. B. Spellman, Greg Tate, and Martin Williams have been important evangelists for the music, developing a "superstructure" unique to the jazz world, one that combined intellectual engagement, aesthetic appreciation, and the instigation and promotion of musical recordings and performances.[12] In many cases, they have supplemented their writing with real-life music industry work, seeking out talent for record labels, promoting particular artists, and staging concerts. But such passionate engagement with the music has also generated a substantial body of hostile writing. Attacks on particular jazz musicians or styles sometimes show contempt or even disgust: they seek, implicitly or explicitly, the silencing of the offending sounds as well as the people who made them. And given the historically central place of jazz in African American life and the preponderance of white critics, such attacks are inevitably entangled in racial discourse.[13]

Although their perspectives and motivations are often different from critics, jazz musicians also evaluate one another's work. Musicians, perhaps not surprisingly, have strong opinions—often, they are the harshest critics of all—but their desire to publicly communicate those opinions varies widely. Some are careful in their assessments, especially negative ones, while others are more outspoken. One's position in the jazz industry—career stability, for example—likely has something to do with this, but it also may be driven by personality. *DownBeat*'s long-standing feature "The Blindfold Test," started by Leonard Feather in 1946 (originally in *Metronome* magazine), represents an especially valuable archive of musicians' praise and criticism. Its format has remained virtually the same: a *DownBeat* writer plays six or seven recordings for a guest musician without identifying them. The participant is then asked to rate each recording one to five stars (five being the best). After the rating, the writer identifies what was played.[14] When he began it, Feather thought this exercise would combat racial and gender bias in the jazz community by combining expertise—the jazz musicians themselves—with objectivity—the blindfold.[15] The tests offer a remarkable archive of jazz historical criticism from the "inside"—musician to musician.

For the participant, the test poses a dilemma: Do you honestly evaluate what you hear? What if you insult or diminish a legend? From this angle, it is fascinating to read prominent musicians apologize for misidentifying or even criticizing celebrated musicians. In an August 10, 2018, blindfold test conducted by journalist Dan Ouellette, Vijay Iyer responds to a piano trio recording this way:

> I don't know who this is, and I have zero guesses. I like the composition, the opening scene, the figures, the written stuff. That's the role of a pianist in a trio. It's the contrapuntal and harmonic [elements] that make it intriguing about what was going to happen next. But then in the solo section, it seemed like the solos were over changes without getting a handle on the tune or making it have its own shape. The eighth notes on the left and the soloing on the right sounds like a lot of other pianists. I would have liked to hear more handling of the full range of the piano and its sound. In particular, I would like to hear more detailed interaction with the drums because that, to me, is the heart of the music. That's what the core of the interaction should be. Here I felt the drums were more ornamental. [*Ouellette identifies the recording.*] Oh, it was Fred? Then I'm definitely not qualified to say anything more. He's a master pianist. I like the composition, and I will check it out again.[16]

Iyer's critique is mild but still tough. He likes the "composition" but feels the solos did not get "a handle on the tune." He goes on to critique the pianist's style as not individual enough ("sounds like a lot of other pianists") and his soloing as lacking range and sufficient interaction with the drums, which are "the heart of the music." Once he is told that the recording is by Fred Hersch, a highly respected jazz veteran, Iyer immediately discounts his criticism, saying he is "definitely not qualified to say anything more." Although he doesn't recant his critique—he emphasizes that he did like the composition—the pianist admits that he should listen to, and perhaps reevaluate, the recording on a second listen. Iyer's response is especially interesting because Hersch is known for a highly personal, even idiosyncratic approach to jazz piano, a style that is often described as classically influenced and highly lyrical.[17] Once Iyer realizes that he has been listening to Hersch, he needs to recalibrate his judgment. My point here is not to say that Iyer messed up or that there is no such thing as objective listening (although that may be true); it is simply to show an example of the nature of internal jazz criticism directed toward other musicians. Hersch himself is a frequent and outspoken critic, unafraid to find fault with music he feels is subpar.[18] A critical culture is a core part of the jazz world, and Iyer's comments reflect that.

Developing an individual "voice" in jazz involves not just individual practice but a critical assessment and synthesis of the musicians around you. Who you are is as much who you are not.

Criticism, even when aimed at musical choices, can sometimes turn very personal. In an April 2019 interview with Rachel Olding of the *Sydney Morning Herald*, saxophonist Branford Marsalis criticizes current jazz musicians as too obsessed with complex structures and harmonies. Their music, he tells Olding, has become "rigid" and improvisation "mostly over-rehearsed regurgitation." Summing up, Marsalis says this: "[I'm often asked] the question, 'Jazz is so unpopular, why do you think that is?' And the answer is simple: the musicians suck."[19] More than disliking certain choices, Marsalis goes big: these musicians "suck." Marsalis has never been shy in expressing his strong opinions, and there is definitely a sense of the winking provocateur in such a pronouncement. Still, the words show contempt. Marsalis is an idiosyncratic voice, and his frankness seems a family trait (his brother Wynton is also notoriously opinionated). But his rhetoric reflects his own complicated position in the jazz world: with one foot in the jazz neoclassicism of the 1980s and another in the mainstream pop world—he played with Sting for a period in the 1980s and led the house band for NBC's *The Tonight Show* in the mid-1990s—Marsalis carved out an unusual and successful professional career straddling distinct, if overlapping, musical cultures.

Internal criticism is fundamental to jazz, and it reflects not just a shared culture but a shared set of tensions rooted in the music's history. Is this jazz authentic improvisation? Does it feature improvisational dialogue? Is this jazz full of overly complicated compositions and arrangements? Does the music embrace the traditional craft of the jazz masters? And behind these concerns are even larger tensions between institutionalized jazz education and a dynamic commercial marketplace, a marketplace that seems unpredictable, embracing some artists but not others. The frequent focus on technique—determining what is proper jazz practice—suggests disagreement but also common ground, a contentious but definable cultural field. But that critical culture, when it intersects with race and gender, can transform criticism into something much stronger and aggressive, a movement toward hate.

DON'T PLAY LIKE A GIRL: SEXISM, MISOGYNY, AND HOMOPHOBIA

The different cultures of jazz have been, and many believe still are, pervaded by hostility toward women. "From the violent gangster milieu of jazz's early sporting life environs," John Gennari writes, "to the urbane, stylized machismo of the jazz-inflected New Frontier; to Wynton Marsalis and Stanley Crouch's tendentious feminization of the 1960s counterculture, jazz culture has been dominated by masculinist voices."[20] Following philosopher Kate Mann, the hostility to women in jazz is a combination of sexism—essentialist ideas about the nature of women—and misogyny—actions designed to police the norms and expectations of a man's world. By distinguishing ideas from actions, Manne challenges what she calls a naive understanding of sexism and misogyny, one that blurs the two terms, reifying the hatred of women as merely a set of beliefs confined to individuals and bounded by an often "inscrutable" personal psychology. Against this popular notion, Manne argues that misogyny is "primarily a property of social environments in which women are liable to encounter hostility due to the enforcement and policing of patriarchal norms and expectations.... Misogyny's essence lies in its social function, not its psychological nature."[21]

For most of its existence, the jazz world—despite its diversity of opinions and practices—has kept women from playing the music (or, when they do, from earning financial rewards and artistic acclaim), writing about the music, and becoming part of the jazz business. Buttressing these actions is a sexist ideology that insists that women are biologically or culturally unable to play and improvise at the level of men. An extension of this idea insists that women simply don't like or cannot enjoy sophisticated and lengthy improvisations.

These sexist ideas change and develop over time, but the core belief remains consistent: women are incapable, either culturally, psychologically, or biologically, from understanding and mastering the music. From jazz's earliest days, female musicians were discouraged from playing, shut out from gigs, harassed, mocked, and artistically dismissed. Although singing and piano playing were acceptable musical activities for women in the nineteenth and early twentieth centuries, playing popular music such as jazz was not. And regardless of style, women were strongly discouraged from playing instruments such as brass and reeds that involved contortions of the face.

Despite this, women did indeed play jazz. As Kristin McGee demonstrates, images of women jazz performers were ubiquitous in the first half of the twentieth century, many captured on film and later television. The question McGee asks us to consider is not why no women were playing jazz but why women were written out of jazz history.[22] Despite their marginalization, as mainstream jazz culture solidified, women jazz musicians played and sought out work in male, female, and mixed groups. But as drummer Viola Smith recounts in Judy Chaikin's 2011 documentary *The Girls in the Band*, "it was difficult for the individual [female] musicians to get booked by the male bands." Later in the documentary, Black trumpeter Clora Bryant explains that "there was just an unwritten law that they wouldn't hire the women."[23] The denial of jobs to women, although rooted in sexist ideas, was, as Manne reminds us, a set of actions by bandleaders and managers. These men, some sexist, some not, would not hire women, thus perpetuating a misogynistic culture.

In addition to not getting jobs, women musicians were harassed on and off the bandstand. The women interviewed by Chaikin recount example after example of hostility. Saxophonist Peggy Gilbert remembers the obstacles she faced in getting hired by a male band: "I was substituting for a man one time, and they called me and asked me if I could jump in, and I said, 'Certainly.' So I did." Afterward the bandleader wanted to keep her in the group, but "all the men in the band got together and talked the leader out of it," she says. They told him that having "a girl around" creates problems: "We can't talk the way we want to talk, and we can't do things we want to do . . . and besides, [women] can't play very well," Gilbert recalls. These professional hurdles were complicated by a set of expectations for women onstage: that they be attractive and sexually appealing to male audience members.

Chaikin's documentary is indebted to recent scholarship on women jazz musicians that has recovered and celebrated innovative artists who have largely been ignored in jazz historiography.[24] The research has also brought to light the persistent sexism and misogyny of different jazz communities. In *Swing Shift: "All-Girl" Bands of the 1940s*, Sherrie Tucker presents, in fine-grained detail, the challenges and triumphs of the era's all-women bands and how they "played the changes" of a turbulent era in American social life.[25] Although a few women made it into the male bands, female groups were the primary vehicle for professional women musicians of the era. These bands were nearly always presented as visual spectacles meant to reaffirm accepted ideas of femininity. Women musicians were often trailed by perceptions that they were sexually deviant (lesbians) or loose (prostitutes).[26] With so many bands depleted because of the draft, women musicians suddenly found themselves with more opportunities (although still largely with all-women outfits). But with these commercial opportunities came new demands on their playing and presentation: playing for troops meant portraying themselves as the girls next door, the women the G.I.s were fighting for.[27]

In the segregated music world, all-girl nonwhite bands faced all the same difficulties in addition to the indignities of racial discrimination. Things were especially hard traveling and working in the South, where Jim Crow restrictions and harassment by the police were inescapable. The intersection of Jim Crow culture and gender expectations made the situation for African American women especially volatile: Black female musicians, just by performing, were undermining deeply held beliefs of white supremacy and pure white womanhood. These women thus faced a particularly toxic mixture of racism and misogyny. In her biography of pianist, composer, and arranger Mary Lou Williams, Tammy Kernodle documents Williams's nearly constant fight "against the racism that said she was inferior because of her color, against the sexism that said her place was not on stage or on record but in the kitchen, [and] against the professional jealousy that had robbed her of her proper place in jazz history and had stunted her professional advancement."[28] Despite some measure of respect and financial stability late in life—the result of a university teaching appointment—Williams fought a constant battle against sexism, misogyny, and racism, the three intertwining in complex and painful ways.

Although the place of women in jazz has improved dramatically, particularly since the turn of the twenty-first century, sexist ideas and misogynistic practices remain pervasive in the jazz community.[29] Even when praising women musicians, male musicians often fall back on stereotypes. In *The Girls in the Band*, Herbie Hancock praises drummer Terri Lyne Carrington as not just a great drummer "for a girl" but as a drummer "at that upper level." Carrington, Hancock continues, doesn't have to have that "testosterone" in her sound; she can bring in some "feminine aspect[s]" to her playing. Hancock's framing of female success in jazz is still defined by sexist notions of gender. This assessment shows just how *structural* gender associations are in jazz. Basic musical components continue to have strongly gendered associations. Drums are the sound of testosterone or masculine virility. Carrington, to be a drummer, must somehow also redefine drumming, allowing for femininity.

The emphasis on masculinity as a positive, even required jazz trait has made all kinds of effeminate behavior suspect. Accusations of effeminacy carry not just sexist implications but homophobic ones too. Mirroring broader societal attitudes, the jazz community has been, for a good part of its existence, hostile not just to homosexual musicians but to queer musicians more broadly. In this, jazz is not alone: other Black forms of popular music, notably disco in the 1970s and '80s, were widely and very publicly attacked for their associations with "deviant" sexuality, particularly homosexuality.[30] For some critics, queer musicians simply don't exist in jazz, past or present. In his 1984 book, *Jazz: America's Classical Music,* Grover Sales makes the preposterous argument that there were almost no gay musicians in jazz history.[31] Recent scholarship, for example on queer subcultures in 1920s jazz or on artists such as Billy Strayhorn, show that there were indeed many LGBTQI+ musicians.[32] But as Sherrie Tucker reminds us, simply finding queer bodies is not enough; scholars must look more broadly at jazz cultures, "interrogat[ing] the historicity of straightness, not to mention the historical and cultural specificity of the closet."[33]

In his moving autobiography, *Good Things Happen Slowly: A Life in and out of Jazz,* pianist Fred Hersch writes about his closeted life in the jazz world of the late 1970s and '80s. Fearing that his homosexuality would be discovered by fellow musicians, he went to great, sometimes agonizing, lengths to hide his identity as a gay man. He recalls a panicked rush around his apartment in the early 1980s to clear any signs of his gay life before the arrival of saxophone legend Stan Getz. But being in the closet was not just about protecting professional relationships or the fear of losing gigs or musician friends; it was also about shielding one's musical aesthetics from accusations of effeminacy. Critics have often likened Hersch to pianist Bill Evans because both have a pronounced lyrical side to their playing, particularly in their lush and romantic approach to ballads. Although flattered by the comparison to the late master, Hersch was worried that these adjectives—"beautiful, lyrical, elegant, or romantic"—would somehow "out" him as gay or, at the least, pigeonhole him as a weaker, less muscular jazz player: "The problem for me was that all those terms had traditionally been associated with male homosexuality in a restrictive and demeaning way. It was one thing for a straight man such as Evans—or Chet Baker or Miles Davis—to be praised for playing beautifully. But for a gay man to be described that way, it was almost like saying, *Of course he plays beautifully—he's gay!*"[34] Hersch, who has battled HIV/AIDS for several decades, was one of the first jazz musicians to come out in the early 1990s. But as Hersch points out, that means that for much of the music's history, musicians that were queer—for example, composer-arrangers Billy Strayhorn and Ralph Burns, vibraphonist Gary Burton, and singer Andy Bey—had to live closeted or semiclosed lives to protect themselves and their musical careers (a situation arguably more challenging for lesbians, trans people, and others in the larger queer community). The homophobia of the jazz world was often less obvious than the misogyny, but both were tied to a normative "straight" masculinity that could be boastful and aggressive.

One of the most prominent recent examples of jazz's deep-seated sexism comes from an interview that pianist Ethan Iverson conducted in 2017 with Robert Glasper for Iverson's highly regarded blog, *Do the M@th*.[35] During their conversation, the two pianists talk about their influences, the nature of the genre today, and the ever-evolving music industry. Glasper blends Black musical styles in strikingly innovative ways that challenge a white-dominated industry's ideas about genre and Black musical practice.[36] In the interview with Iverson, Glasper speaks about his reasons for infusing jazz with hip-hop and R&B, explaining that it allows him to be true to his musical roots. Glasper has played these styles professionally, having spent several years touring with neo-soul singer Bilal Oliver. But this fusion also helps bring jazz out of the "museum," as Glasper calls it, making the music "current and cool again" and accessible to new audiences.

Glasper continues by referencing the genre-bending band Iverson founded, the Bad Plus. "I've had people tell me about your music. Like women you would think never listen to jazz: Young, fine, Euro chicks ask me, 'I heard this band, the Bad Plus, do you know them?'" Iverson responds that reaching these audiences is "one of the reasons to play, really." Glasper then picks this up, turning to female responses to these updated jazz sounds. Playing groove-focused music such as hip-hop and R&B, Glasper says, has a particularly strong effect on audiences, especially women: "Women love that. They don't like a whole lot of soloing. When you hit that one groove and stay there, it's like musical clitoris. You're there, you stay on that groove, and the women's eyes close and they start to sway, going into a trance." Glasper then abruptly shifts his metaphor: groove music is like "providing a house" where the listener provides the furniture. The music can be a "soundtrack" with space for the audience to fill in.

Glasper's comments and Iverson's tacit support of them (not helped by a follow-up blog post defending the interview from "liberal self-policing") quickly circulated around the internet, evoking strong reactions on social media.[37] In a digital story on NPR's website, Michelle Mercer summarizes the controversy and its effect among women musicians: "Glasper's comments came as a shock to exactly zero people who've spent time in the jazz world." Although seemingly directed at audiences, Glasper's comments also hit at women jazz musicians, many of whom became interested in the music as listeners before they were players. "I've heard variations on the 'women can't really follow jazz' theme ever since I first started hitting jazz clubs and loving extremely long solos. To be a female jazz fan and critic is to live with a frustrating irreconcilability: I have an intellectual passion for creative, complex music, and sometimes, the musicians who make that music doubt my ability to appreciate its creativity and complexity."[38] Glasper appears to give little agency to female listeners and seems oblivious to the idea that there would be female musicians reading the interview. Most egregious, however, is Glasper's conflation of female engagement with female reproductive anatomy, an unambiguously sexist statement.

This incident points to the broader misogyny that permeates the jazz world. Glasper and Iverson's conversation reaffirms an old belief that jazz is a masculine endeavor. It is not difficult to see how this view can dissuade or intimidate women musicians, critics, and fans. As Kate Manne argues, misogyny is not primarily a "psychological matter—but rather ... [a] social-political phenomenon with psychological, structural, and institutional manifestations."[39] Although it may be tempting to dismiss this incident as an isolated example, the interview is a reminder that sexist ideas and misogynistic actions are social phenomena. Glasper is in dialogue with another musician, not venting in private.

Many are trying to change the culture. Certainly the presence of more women musicians is one important factor. Younger musicians such as Melissa Aldana, Lakecia Benjamin, Kris Davis, Nicole Glover, Mary Halvorson, Samara Joy, Ava Mendoza, Linda May Han Oh, Cécile McLorin Salvant, esperanza spalding, and Alexa Tarantino have developed successful, high-profile careers. Still, the presence of more women musicians does not necessarily change a misogynistic culture. To do that requires something more. In 2019, drummer Terri Lyne Carrington founded the Berklee Institute of Jazz and Gender Justice, housed in the Berklee College of Music in Boston. The institute's motto—Jazz without Patriarchy—makes clear that its mission is broader than simply recruiting more female musicians; it aims to correct and modify "the way jazz is perceived and presented, so the future of jazz looks different than its past without rendering invisible many of the art form's creative contributors." To effect such a "cultural shift," the institute provides college-level classes and ensembles, scholarships, and public programs aimed at "all gender identities and expressions."[40] In 2022, the institute published *New Standards: 101 Lead Sheets by Women Composers*, a collection of original jazz compositions spanning the music's history.[41]

CONTEMPT AND DISGUST IN THE RECEPTION OF NEW JAZZ STYLES

One of the most obvious instigators of hostility in jazz has been the emergence of new approaches to performance. These moments of challenge and redefinition are nearly always the result of larger social forces that generate a crisis. The antipathy toward new styles, whether swing, bebop, fusion, or smooth jazz, has been, at the root, a concern with boundaries. As David Ake, Charles Hiroshi Garrett, and Daniel Goldmark write in their collection, *Jazz/Not Jazz: The Music and Its Boundaries*, "The lines some people draw between 'jazz' and 'not jazz' can be at once fiercely guarded and very difficult to discern."[42] This combination of protectiveness and ambiguity—joined with the social stakes involved, most obviously the place of Blackness in American culture—has given these debates a special intensity. To hate a new style of jazz always involves a larger claim about the genre, what belongs and what does not. For Sara Ahmed, hate is an affect defined by a concern with boundaries:

> Hate is involved in the very negotiation of boundaries between selves and others, and between communities, where "others" are brought into the sphere of my or our existence as a threat. This other, who may stand for or stand by others, presses against me, threatening my existence. The proximity of the other's touch is felt as a negation.[43]

The boundaries in question, although presented as musical, are always about a complex web of historical and cultural ideas, ideas about race, politics, history, art, and commerce.

The battle between the jazz "revivalists" and "modernists" in the 1930s and '40s—the former celebrating small-group New Orleans–style jazz, the latter boosting modern swing, and then bebop—is one important example of how discussions of musical boundaries can quickly escalate into hyperbole. Statements of taste rapidly turned into statements of aggression and contempt, not just toward the music but toward the people who made and listened to it. It was, Bernard Gendron writes, a "war primarily of words, indeed a profusion and superabundance of words."[44] That war of words encompassed many themes—technique versus feeling, folk culture versus mass culture, and Leftist politics versus right. But running through everything was the "pressing anxieties of racial contact." The combatants were largely white; their heroes and villains were often Black.[45]

Although many of the participants flirted with self-righteous anger, revivalist Rudi Blesh and modernist Leonard Feather frequently indulged in the most intense rhetorical fireworks. In his 1946 history of jazz, *Shining Trumpets*, Blesh attacks swing with a visceral sense of disgust and rage:

> Hot swing during the last fifteen years, and particularly in the last five, has been simplified to a half-dozen screaming brass and bleating reed riffs. It is easy to prove that any swing is completely anti-jazz,

completely anti–New Orleans, opposed to the real musical values which jazz represents. Of still greater importance and significance, is the fact that riff-swing is anti-music. There is scarcely a canon of art or common good taste which it does not violate. Establishing no new art form, developing no older one, it is nihilistic, cynically destructive, reactionary.[46]

Blesh not only sees no value in "commercial swing," he loathes it. He views swing as a threat not just to the "real" jazz he loves but to society as a whole. "Swing," he continues, "is a form of rabble rousing that elicits for itself and its exponents the same blind idolatry the demagogue or the dictator receives from the mob."[47] The implication of this judgment is clear: like recently defeated fascist "demagogues and dictators," swing must also be destroyed.

For his part, modernist Leonard Feather happily returns the favor. In the September 1945 issue of *Metronome*, Feather compares his moldy fig opponents to American Nazis: "Just as the fascists tend to divide group against group and distinguish between Negroes, Jews, Italians, and 'real Americans,' so do the moldy figs try to categorize New Orleans, Chicago, swing music and 'the real jazz.'" And just like the American fascists who "tried to foist their views on the public through the vermin press of *Social Justice*, the *Broom*, and *X-Ray*, so have the Figs [*sic*] yapped their heads off in the *Jazz Record*, *Jazz Session* and *Record Changer*." These arrogant critics, frustrated that the general public does not accept their "idiotic views," turn their hatred toward others, such as Feather himself.[48]

We can see a similar kind of anger and aggression surrounding the reception of avant-garde jazz, alternatively called "free jazz" or "the new thing" by the jazz press, in the early 1960s. Because the avant-garde movement was so diverse, representing a variety of approaches to rethinking jazz musical practices, writers often focused their criticism on specific musicians. One notorious example is John Tynan's 1961 review of a John Coltrane and Eric Dolphy concert at Hollywood's Renaissance Club. Tynan, *DownBeat*'s West Coast critic, is horrified by the "musical nonsense ... being peddled in the name of jazz." Although he finds the rhythm section (drummer Elvin Jones, bassist Reggie Workman, and pianist McCoy Tyner) "good," their playing could not redeem the "nihilistic exercises of the two horns." Coltrane and Dolphy arrogantly defy musical standards, turning what is supposed to be a collective experience into solipsistic "anarchy." In the name of innovation, Coltrane and Dolphy create not jazz as it should be but something else, what Tynan calls "antijazz." Tynan frames his attack with a tongue-in-cheek proviso: he may just be a stodgy reactionary incapable of understanding the innovations he is hearing. His disclaimers, however, only serve to highlight his attacks. As a critic and as a fan, Tynan feels an obligation to speak his mind. What he hears is not simply bad, but actively oppositional to all that is musically good.[49]

Tynan's attack is largely formalistic. He has nothing to say about the musicians' beliefs or behaviors. The reactions to saxophonist Ornette Coleman, on the other hand, were often very personal. His musical experimentations were regarded by some as direct affronts. What kind of individual makes such offensive music? As David Ake notes, Coleman "did not dress like his bop contemporaries," avoiding the sharp suits that defined musicians such as Miles Davis. He was vegetarian in an era when that was unusual, and he criticized the machismo that defined the mainstream jazz scene. "Coleman," Ake writes, "presented an alternative model of the male jazz musician. His music and demeanor worked to downplay the prevalent phallocentric aspects of jazz performance, destabilizing positions of masculinity and prestige in the jazz community."[50] And while not every Coleman hater was driven by masculine insecurity, the explosive reactions to his presence on the New York jazz scene show how formal aesthetic critiques always fell short. Coleman's music generated such intense affect that critics struggled to make sense of it. The formal criticisms—no chord changes, out-of-tune instruments—aren't sufficient to explain such intense negative feelings. The explanation for the venom directed at Coleman and others only makes sense if these critics, consciously or unconsciously, are reacting to some deeper violation of social norms and values.[51]

The reaction to jazz-rock fusion in the 1970s generated another moment of intense, often vitriolic debate. As before, criticism of musical choices often turned personal, with attacks on particular musicians and their fans. Fusion, as Kevin Fellezs notes, was a catch-all term that embraced widely different musical approaches. What united these diverse musicians—Black and white, American and European, men and women—was a desire to trouble boundaries "by staying between them, creating an informal, even feral, set of musical practices and aesthetics."

Fusion artists such as Herbie Hancock, John McLaughlin, and Tony Williams situated their music in "a 'broken middle,' an overlapping yet liminal space of contested, and never settled, priorities between two or more musical traditions."[52] For those who were committed to keeping clear genre boundaries, such artists were an affront to the jazz tradition. Miles Davis's "electric" period, beginning with *Bitches Brew*, released in 1970, and continuing until his death in 1991, remains a source of heated debate.[53] Some of these records—*Bitches Brew*, for example—have been canonized, but others from that era have only recently been reevaluated, their position as "good" or "landmark" jazz records still uncertain. In a 2007 article in the *Guardian* titled "The Most Hated Album in Jazz," author Paul Tingen describes the early reception of Davis's 1972 album *On the Corner*.[54] The original *DownBeat* review described the record as lazy and repetitive: "Take some *chunka-chunka-chunka* rhythm, lots of little background percussion, diddle-around sounds, some electronic mutations, add simple tune lines that sound a great deal alike and play some spacy solos. You've got the 'groovin'' formula, and you stick with it interminably to create your 'magic.' But is it magic or just repetitious boredom?" (The reviewer, Will Smith, grudgingly praised Davis's solos as "mostly fine.")[55] Although the jazz press largely followed *DownBeat*'s lead, Tingen's claim—*On the Corner* as the most hated album in jazz—certainly overstates the case: many other Miles Davis records, from the early 1970s onward, have had very mixed, sometimes hostile reviews. But Davis's work in the "broken middle" of fusion and jazz-pop remains an important part of the jazz-hating story.

By the late 1970s, a less experimental fusion of jazz with R&B and soul was proving especially successful. George Benson's 1976 record *Breezin'* was a watershed moment, reaching number one on the R&B and pop charts and going platinum (it would eventually reach triple-platinum status). Although not the first of its kind, Benson's mixture of jazz-influenced improvisation with pop and R&B demonstrated the great commercial possibility of this kind of fusion. The groups and artists that followed such as Spyro Gyra, Grover Washington Jr., Chuck Mangione, and Earl Klugh plied the same territory but also opened the field to other variants, some more pop than R&B. Soprano saxophonist Kenny Gorelick—commercially known as Kenny G—began his career playing in the jazz-R&B style of Benson and others, but eventually developed more of a pop sound that emphasized less driving rhythms and blues playing. By the mid-1980s, especially after the release of his massive hit "Songbird" (from 1986's *Duotones*), Kenny G became one of the best-selling artists in what was now called smooth jazz.

Kenny G's success made him the highest-profile musician in smooth jazz and also the target of outsized antipathy.[56] "As a surrogate for the supposed evils of crossover success," writes Brian Wright, "the specter of Kenny G has haunted jazz discourse for nearly four decades."[57] One of the most notorious takedowns of Kenny G remains Pat Metheny's blog posts on the saxophonist. Metheny's first post appeared June 5, 2000, in the message board of his personal website and came as a response to a question from an anonymous poster: "Pat, could you tell us your opinion about Kenny G? It appears you were quoted as being less than enthusiastic about him and his music. I would say that most of the serious music listeners in the world would not find your opinion surprising or unlikely—but you were vocal about it for the first time. You are generally supportive of other musicians it seems."[58] As with the reactions to bebop in the 1940s and Coleman's free jazz in the '50s, Metheny's critique is also about boundaries—between jazz and pop, art and kitsch, authentic expression and commercial pandering. Implicit in his discussion is another boundary, the one between Black musicians and their white appropriators. This last one, not surprisingly, is the most fraught, not the least because Metheny himself is a white musician who has incorporated and appropriated Black vernacular musical practices into his own music making.

Metheny's discussion begins with an acknowledgment: "Kenny G is not a musician I really had much of an opinion about at all until recently." Before this current moment, Metheny had no *affective* engagement with Kenny G. The saxophonist did not *impinge* or *impress* himself on Metheny; he was simply another musician in the commercial-music world, one that Metheny had little to do with as a performer or listener. To Metheny, Kenny G was a moderately competent musician: his melodic and harmonic vocabulary was limited, and he consistently played sharp. Metheny understands that many musicians resent his great commercial success; after all, there are much more talented musicians who never achieve fame or financial success. But Metheny won't be taken in by this kind of "production argument": Kenny G plays a kind of soothing pop music that is generically remote from the world of "professional improvising musicians" like himself. He does, however, feel obliged to criticize the saxophonist as a *jazz* musician, one who is ostensibly upholding a tradition of improvisation. By those standards, Kenny G simply doesn't measure up.

But then Metheny pivots, turning to a recent album featuring Kenny G playing on top of Louis Armstrong's 1967 recording of "What a Wonderful World." The track appears alongside other jazz, bossa nova, and pop standards on the 1999 release *Classics in the Key of G*—a tribute, Kenny G explains in his liner notes, to the "great musicians who came before me."[59] Here we have a discursive account of the moment of affect—the moment when something ignored becomes unignorable. Metheny's language turns fiery, aggressive, and "disordered." "With this single move," Metheny writes, "Kenny G became one of the few people on earth I can say that I really can't use at all." The recording was an act of "musical necrophilia" that "defiled" an icon. Metheny, though, is just getting started: "But when Kenny G decided it was appropriate for him to defile the music of the man who is probably the greatest jazz musician that has ever lived by spewing his lame-ass, jive, pseudo bluesy, out-of-tune, noodling, wimped out, fucked up laying all over one of the great Louis's tracks ... he did something I would not have imagined possible."[60] Metheny's sense of outrage is situated in religious terms: Kenny G has shit on the grave of a hallowed figure, a sacred musician in the jazz firmament.

Some of Metheny's antipathy is certainly related to his own proximity to smooth jazz, Kenny G's generic home; Metheny's reaction, in part, being a product of how he sees himself and his own crossover career.[61] As Charles Carson observes, *smooth jazz* is a "slippery and contested term," one that defines not just certain musical sounds—a "cleanly produced amalgam of R&B, funk, soul, and jazz"—but an approach to marketing and branding as well as a social ideal, a set of values and expectations by listeners as to what these sounds mean.[62] The significant financial success of smooth jazz, particularly in the 1980s and '90s, made the style a frequent target of jazz musicians and critics.[63] Metheny's work, particularly with his Pat Metheny Group, was commercially successful and sometimes labeled smooth jazz. Recordings such as 1978's "Phase Dance" were popular on adult-oriented radio stations at the time.[64] Also, Metheny doesn't point out that the recording Kenny G is desecrating is not from the canonical early part of

Armstrong's career in the mid- to late 1920s but from late in his career, the 1960s, when Armstrong was recording more mainstream pop fare such as Disney songs. Like Metheny himself, Armstrong fluidly crossed between jazz and pop worlds, enjoying great commercial success (and often critical disparagement).

But seeing Metheny's attack as merely a psychological defense mechanism ignores the tremendous positive affect Metheny feels for jazz and its traditions. His aggression is, in large part, the result of his unwavering investment in that heritage.[65] By playing around with a jazz icon, Kenny G is violating a sacred figure in the jazz canon. He is an inauthentic interloper in the jazz world, one who lacks the knowledge and authority to be a genuine participant.[66] For example, in the documentary *Listening to Kenny G*, the saxophonist is unable to name one of the figures (Thelonious Monk) and misidentifies another (it is guitarist Charlie Christian, not saxophonist Dexter Gordon) in a painting celebrating the creators of bebop.[67] The fact that the painting hangs on the wall of his home studio suggests that, despite his assertions to the contrary, he doesn't really know, or care to know, jazz history. In addition, Kenny G never "paid his dues" through the kinds of musical apprenticeships common in the mainstream jazz world, for example by playing in the band of an older master.[68] As Kelsey Klotz notes, Gorelick's blasé engagement with Black jazz history is enabled by white privilege. Unlike Black musicians, who are often expected to know about and speak for Blackness, Gorelick can choose to engage when he wants and in his own way. "Choosing ignorance (choosing not to know)," Klotz writes, "represents a performance of whiteness."[69]

Metheny's affective investment in "real" jazz and his loathing of Kenny G's record "with" Armstrong represent more than the rejection of particular musical sounds or even a broader aesthetic. They are the result of a historically specific meeting of social and economic forces. In the late 1990s and early 2000s, the development and widespread adoption of shareable music files such as MP3s produced a crisis in the music industry, as sharing sites such as Napster exploded in popularity. Despite massive pushback from record labels, digital consumption of music was the future, and the music industry, which had been buoyed for years by massive profits from CD sales, nearly collapsed.[70] At the same time, the radio industry was going through another round of consolidation. The success of smooth jazz rested at the nexus of radio formats and CD sales, and the reshaping of the music industry destroyed that profitable arrangement. Of course, consumer tastes changed too, along with the demographic paying (or not paying!) for music.[71] The year 2000 also saw the release of Ken Burns's ten-part PBS documentary *Jazz*. The scale of the project and the largely positive press coverage dominated discussions in the jazz world for several years. Significantly, Burns's series organized its expansive history around two figures, Duke Ellington and Louis Armstrong. The participation of more aesthetically conservative jazz musicians and writers such as Wynton Marsalis and Stanley Crouch made the series a heritage project, where issues of preservation and continuity superseded jazz's modernist impulse to always make things new.

At this time, Metheny sat uncomfortably in the middle of these larger forces. His musical career was driven, in part, by his crossover appeal to audiences beyond the narrow world of jazz fans. His music, especially with the Pat Metheny Group, found its way onto smooth jazz radio stations. But Metheny also recorded albums that were more unambiguously in the mainstream jazz world. In 2000 the guitarist was performing and recording with a trio featuring bassist Larry Grenadier and drummer Bill Stewart. The music fits clearly into the mainstream of jazz at the time: adventurous music that featured extensive group and individual improvisation. Around the same time, Metheny also recorded with the Pat Metheny Group, releasing *Imaginary Day* in 1997 and *Speaking of Now* in 2002, projects with a clearer pop profile.

Metheny's contempt is not, as he claims, merely an objective reaction to transparently bad art. A few important claims he makes are either exaggerated or inaccurate. In his analysis of Kenny G, Robert Walser reminds us that, in fact, the saxophonist has impressive technique on a difficult instrument, skills he worked assiduously on through regular, extended practice. Metheny's antipathy emerges from something else, what Tony Whyton describes as "the underlying value judgements of a particular social order."[72] In his analysis, Walser notes that Kenny G represents a certain "sensibility" at odds with the mainstream jazz community.[73] That sensibility is connected to a particular social alignment around the cultural site of jazz at the turn of the millennium. The guitarist's aesthetic contains a fundamental tension: Metheny's position on Louis Armstrong represents what Jerome Harris calls a "canonical" approach to defining jazz while his overall career represents a "process" approach. In the canonical approach, jazz is defined by "a specific African American originated genealogy," whereas in the process understanding, jazz "is viewed as the result of certain African American originated processes and aesthetics" that can be developed and extended. This latter view is more open to experimentation and adaptation, particularly with popular forms (something Metheny has embraced).[74] Also evident is a related tension in how to define authentic Black musical practice: Kenny G's playing, and by extension, the larger world of smooth jazz indebted to him, is "too simple, too effete, too commercial [and] too 'white.'" But by attacking Kenny G's music as "too white," Charles Carson argues, Metheny is continuing a historical conversation in which mostly white critics, scholars, and musicians act as adjudicators of Black authenticity. Metheny's attack on Kenny G, although ostensibly defending Black achievement, ends up reifying a specific, white-identified notion of Blackness that dismisses not only Kenny G but, more subtly, an entire world of "crossover" artists redefining Blackness by bringing jazz into dialogue with a range of commercial genres.[75]

The tension in Metheny's position, along with the profound changes to the music industry in the late 1990s, helps explain his contempt. For Metheny, Kenny G is not just a bad artist making bad art, but a stand-in for all the cultural forces that demean jazz and its traditions. In this way, Metheny's contempt and disgust generalizes and reifies Kenny G. Metheny condenses the uncertainties of a historical moment, one defined by massive upheaval in the music industry, into a very personal attack on a single, representative musician. He is trying to clearly mark self and other during a moment of crisis and rapid change. Metheny has always had one foot in the aggressive, masculinist world of mainstream postbop jazz and the other in the crossover world of smooth jazz. These worlds, though in reality overlapping, are often presented by critics and fans as oppositional, what Walser calls a "searching" versus a "finding" sensibility.[76] In hating Kenny G, Metheny can maintain the fiction of a musical field that is clearly defined and stable, aesthetically and commercially.

STANLEY CROUCH, MILES DAVIS, AND "ANGRY BLACK MEN"

In the mid-1980s jazz regained some cultural ground with the rise of a group of Black musicians dubbed the Young Lions. Led by trumpeter Wynton Marsalis, musicians such as Roy Hargrove, Terence Blanchard, Christian McBride, and others rejected (at least initially) the many fusion experiments of the 1970s, returning to acoustic small-group jazz largely in a bop and postbop idiom. The significant press attention to these musicians, particularly Marsalis, provoked another debate about the nature of jazz. Was this movement retrograde, a rejection of jazz's modernist, progressive tradition? Or was it a salvage effort, meant to reclaim real jazz from irrelevancy on one hand and empty commercialism (that is, jazz-rock fusion) on the other? The debate reached a climax in 1988 with the establishment of the Jazz at Lincoln Center Orchestra under the direction of Marsalis, who—not surprisingly—offered a vigorous defense of his conservative programming.[77]

Another figure at the center of these debates was the critic, poet, novelist, and essayist Stanley Crouch, one of the sharpest but also polemical observers writing about African American life across the cultural landscape. Drawing on his own experiences as a jazz musician, he became one of the most visible commentators on jazz from the mid-1970s until his death in the fall of 2020.[78] He is prominently featured throughout Ken Burns's *Jazz* series (and acted as a senior creative consultant). In his writings and talks on jazz, Crouch takes an aggressively conservative pose on historically thorny questions about how to define and value the music. He was especially consistent in his rejections of any understanding of the music that reduced the profound aesthetic experience of jazz into "aural sociology in rhythm and tune."[79] But in a well-known essay on Miles Davis, "*On the Corner*: The Sellout of Miles Davis," Crouch fuses this ideological orientation with a rhetorical anger that spreads beyond Davis's 1980s incarnation to sweep up a large part of Black culture of the era.[80]

Crouch begins his essay with a snapshot of Miles Davis, a picture of aesthetic bankruptcy driven by a desire to appear relevant. Formerly a paradigm of Black style and achievement, Davis has now "fallen from grace," "turned butt to the beautiful in order to genuflect before the commercial." This is obvious in his appearance: "Once given to exquisite dress, Davis now comes on the bandstand draped in the expensive bad taste of rock 'n' roll." As for the music, Crouch is equally direct: "terrible performances and terrible recording." More than a caricature playing "decadent" music, Davis is a "remarkable licker of monied boots," a "pimp," and a coward hiding behind "the murky fluid of his octopus fear of being old hat." Davis's musical choices reflect a deeper and pervasive corruption, a "shriveled" soul. Crouch finds Davis contemptible; his musical and lifestyle choices have morally compromised him. He doesn't deserve any respect.

But Crouch's rhetoric goes beyond contempt, moving into disgust, a "response to persons that engage in activities that remind us of our animal natures," especially our basest sexual nature.[81] Crouch describes Davis's stage demeanor:

> [He] walks about the stage, touches foreheads with the saxophonist as they play a duet, bends over and remains in that ridiculous position for long stretches as he blows at the floor, invites his female percussionist to come, midriff bare, down a ramp and do a jungle-movie dance as she accompanies herself with a talking drum, sticks out his tongue at his photographers, leads the din of electronic clichés with arm signals, and trumpets the many facets of his own force with amplification that blurts forth a sound so decadent that it can no longer disguise the shriveling of its maker's soul.[82]

Davis's lewd movements are part of a larger bacchanale of debased sexuality. Crouch seems especially concerned with the trumpeter's bodily movement, as if Davis and his musical circus will breach the proscenium and embrace the critic himself. This fear of contagion is a key feature of disgust. Davis's behavior, though, is part of a larger social decay, and Crouch brings in that "Minneapolis vulgarian" and "borderline drag queen" Prince, as Davis's bedfellow. Crouch's contempt for 1980s Davis begins with a criticism of his musical choices but quickly swells into a conservative broadside against vulgarity. Crouch is disgusted by a Black popular culture that celebrates gender bending and other gross violations of sexual propriety.

He follows this opening salvo with a long, detailed career summary, an attempt to capture both Davis's "large and complex" aesthetic achievements and his current debasement playing electrified pop. Crouch's narrative, even as it traces Davis's accomplishments, is seeded with the musical and personal characteristics that will lead to his later disgrace. When 'Round about Midnight was released in 1957, Davis was on the verge of stardom, but he was also "destined to sink down in a way no one—himself least of all—could have imagined."[83]

Crouch is particularly critical of what he perceives as the trumpeter's embrace of a minstrel persona—his adoption of "glowering, sullen, even contemptuous nineteenth-century minstrel characters known as Jasper Jack and Zip Coon."[84] Although rooted in a rejection of Armstrong's entertainment ethos, Davis's onstage behavior—such as turning his back or leaving the stage—and his offstage aloofness strike Crouch as merely recycled minstrel tropes and not legitimate social protests against racial degradation.

But Davis's sellout is more than his adoption of an explicitly sexualized stage presence or a minstrel-like image. It is the distortion of an earlier masculine eroticism, one that fed his music rather than sapping its vitality.[85] Davis's commercial prostitution represents a profound loss of sexual potency, the enervation of a once strong, erotically defiant Black male body. As Sara Ahmed points out, hate is obsessively concerned with bodies, their nature and especially their proximity to one another.[86] Crouch is disgusted by the trumpeter's debased body and the ways it threatens rightly sexualized bodies both on and off the stage.

But Davis is not the only target, and Crouch's analysis soon swallows up most of the significant cultural developments of the 1980s. His aesthetic evaluations fuse musical critique with a much broader political and social diagnosis of Black American culture of the '80s and '90s. The defining developments of that era—deindustrialization, white flight from urban centers, escalating rates of incarceration for Black men—were continuations from previous decades. And although there were economic and social gains for African Americans, Reaganism gave new fuel to old racist ideas that struggling Black people were themselves the cause of their own drug use, poverty, and violence. This idea, although deeply rooted in American racist thinking, was given cover by the findings of the 1965 Moynihan Report (officially titled *The Negro Family: The Case for National Action*), a sociological study that blamed dysfunctional families for the problems afflicting segments of Black America. The report, authored by then assistant secretary of labor Daniel Patrick Moynihan, provided the foundation for a broad set of ideas that media scholar Jimmie Reeves calls "cultural Moynihanism."[87] This new "culturally based" racism fused with a broader public suspicion of social welfare initiatives, leading to the reduction and elimination of many programs aimed at inner-city African Americans.[88]

Crouch's contempt for 1980s Miles Davis was really a hatred for an entire segment of the era's African American culture, a culture that spanned art, social life, and politics. The intensity of this attack was rooted in a struggle over the basic identity of American Blackness. The "blaxploitation" culture disparaged by Crouch and exemplified by Davis's mobile, abject body was threatening to erase another, earlier way of being Black. Crouch's analysis of Davis is then both an attack on and an act of love for an identity and way of being under threat. As Ahmed puts it, "In hating another, [the] subject is also loving itself; hate structures the emotional life of narcissism as a fantastic investment in the continuation of the image of the self in the faces that together make up the 'we.'"[89]

But Davis is not exactly a victim here. The trumpeter was similarly outspoken and polemical, offering frank, sometimes insulting opinions on the value of other musicians and cultural figures. The trumpeter, a boxing aficionado, never pulled a punch (the many eulogies of Crouch after his death in 2020 also describe him with boxing metaphors).[90] One of the more infamous examples is Davis's 1964 blindfold test in *DownBeat*, his third with Leonard Feather (the first two took place in 1955 and 1958). Feather plays Davis a wide range of current jazz records, including releases by Les McCann and the Jazz Crusaders, Clark Terry, trombonist Rod Levitt, Duke Ellington, Sonny Rollins, Stan Getz and João Gilberto, Eric Dolphy, and Cecil Taylor. Although given no information about the records, Davis easily identifies most of the key musicians. His reactions are widely divergent, praising some performances ("As for [João] Gilberto, he could read a newspaper and sound good! I'll give that one five stars") and castigating others. About Les McCann and the Jazz Crusaders' version of Davis's own "All Blues," the trumpeter says, "That ain't nothin'," criticizing it as neither a good blues nor a good modal (scale-based) performance: "The trombone ain't supposed to sound like that. This is 1964, not 1924. Maybe if the piano player had played it himself, something would have happened. *Rate* it? How can I rate that?" Most surprising are Davis's assessments of recordings by Ellington, Terry, Dolphy, and Taylor. With Ellington and Terry, Davis critiques the record label's choices more than the artists themselves. After listening to "Caravan" from *Money Jungle* by Ellington, Charles Mingus, and Max Roach, Davis says, "That's ridiculous. You see the way they [the record label] can fuck up music?" The trio is a mismatch: "Duke can't play with them, and they can't play with Duke." This disaster was the fault of producers and executives who don't understand what works musically and what doesn't. But after listening to Dolphy and Taylor, Davis's attacks become specific, questioning their basic musicianship and sense of musical taste. On Dolphy, Davis says, "That's got to be Eric Dolphy—nobody else could sound that bad! The next time I see him I'm going to step on his foot. . . . He's a sad motherfucker." Davis is equally contemptuous of Taylor. On hearing the record, Davis is immediately dismayed: "Take it off! That's some sad shit!" Taylor's music is "nothing," the pianist completely lacking the right "touch" with the piano.[91]

Through their writings and interviews, Crouch and Davis demonstrate important and revealing aspects of socially mediated affect: their public expressions of strong feeling, positive or negative, seem to blur the lines between some kind of private emotional truth and public social judgment, between "real" feeling and rhetorical, socially "performed" feeling. Both self-consciously present themselves as "angry Black men," a racist trope that has roots deep in American history.[92] In her study of Mingus, Nichole Rustin-Paschal provides a nuanced analysis of this "anger," a set of feelings rooted in a complex mixture of social, personal, and artistic stress. Mingus's anger was real—the result of a history of racism—but also a performance, "a thumb in the eye of the poseurs, rubberneckers, and frauds that saw in the jazzman's art a spectacle for their enjoyment."[93] Mingus's anger was made a "fetish," a reified characteristic that erased a specific history. But this anger also had a critical ability to expose "the metalanguage of race, the double-voiced discourse . . . serving the voice of black oppression and the voice of black liberation."[94]

Mingus and Davis, and I would argue Crouch too, are in part self-consciously performing anger and its associated affects of contempt and disgust. This anger was a justifiable response to the racist tropes perpetrated by white critics. But these men also took hold of the anger, bending it toward their own needs. As a performance, the rhetoric of contempt echoes a broader pattern in African American language and culture.⁹⁵ Mingus, Davis, and Crouch prod us, poking at our complacency, demanding that we pierce through liberal pieties and get to the heart of America's race problem.

The intensity of the feelings expressed by these musicians points to a much larger conversation about the character and place of Black cultural production in the construction of Black humanity, a conversation as vital today as it was in the 1950s and '60s. Drawing on the ideas of Sylvia Wynter, Katherine McKittrick argues that "making black culture reinvents black humanity," ways of life destroyed through transatlantic slavery and colonialism. Black culture, including expressive forms such as music, affirms "black humanness" through an "'alienated reality' that is rooted in antiblack plantocratic histories, practices, and geographies."⁹⁶ Black creative practices such as visual art, music, literature, theater, and poetry "provide intellectual spaces that define black humanity outside colonial scripts."⁹⁷

For musicologist Samuel Floyd, "cultural memory"—the "repository of meanings that comprise the subjective knowledge of a people, its immanent thoughts, its structures, and its practices"—is the basic mechanism for the project of reconstructing Black humanity because it provides a link not just to the recent past but to the distant one before the Middle Passage. Music, Floyd writes, is one of the most important forms of Black cultural memory.⁹⁸ It is such a powerful force because it is so flexible: "African Americans," Guthrie P. Ramsey writes, "have continually (re)articulated, questioned, abandoned, played with, and reinforced their ethnic identities through vernacular musical practices and many other activities."⁹⁹ Given the centrality of music to the shaping of African American identity and humanity, it becomes easier to understand the intensity of Crouch's attack. Hating the late-period Miles Davis is an argument with heavy political, social, and existential significance. It is about the very nature and place of Blackness in a white (and white supremacist) world.

◉

Criticism is an integral part of jazz, and it functions to both bind a community together as well as mark out its boundaries, determining which musicians belong and which ones do not. As Ken Prouty notes, arguments about the canon—what belongs and what doesn't—are not "corrections" of jazz history but an inextricable part of it.[100] But with contempt and disgust, judgments of taste shift into a different register. Although taste judgments are often supported by racist or sexist beliefs, the language of taste discrimination often obscures these underlying forces. The contemptuous rhetoric I have discussed here—accusing other people of stupidity, desecration, and sexual perversion—represent only the most explicit attacks. In much jazz criticism these negative affects and prejudices are more subterranean, shaping taste discriminations in less visible ways.

Stanley Crouch's attack on Miles Davis is not just an aesthetic rejection but a sexist and homophobic one too. The disparagement of women and queer people in jazz, whether as musicians, fans, industry professionals, or wives and partners, is widespread, part of a long and ignoble history, and one that is not unique to jazz. Crouch's hyperbolic criticisms, however, are complicated by the music's social and historical position as a crucial voice of Black American life. Jazz has represented and embodied a profound challenge to racist notions of American identity. But can critiques such as Crouch's be effective or even justified when they display such contempt and disgust? Can hating certain kinds of jazz ever be part of a useful cultural critique? In chapter 5, I briefly tackle these issues, exploring some of the arguments for and against hating as a mode of cultural engagement.

● 5 ●
The Ethics of Hating Jazz

My discussion of jazz hate has touched on ethical issues but not confronted them directly. If hating something reifies it, making it an abstract and depersonalized object, is it ever justified to hate a specific kind of music? Although many of the jazz haters I have looked at have been racist and sexist, none of them can compare to the kind of jazz hate promulgated by totalitarian governments, such as in Nazi Germany or Stalinist Russia. Surely that kind of hatred is the strongest kind, a hatred in proximity to mass murder. But as scholars Michael Kater and Frederick Starr show in their studies of jazz under Hitler and Stalin, the music held a surprisingly ambivalent place in these totalitarian societies.[1] Attitudes toward jazz and other popular musics were often affectively mild, with politicians and bureaucrats dispassionately focused on how to instrumentalize people's tastes to forward ideological, political, or even military goals.[2]

In the case of the Nazis, although the rhetoric was violent, intended to generate repulsion toward the "degenerate" musics of Jews, Blacks, Roma, and other "non-Aryans," the actual policies regarding the music and its performance were carefully calculated.[3] Borrowing the language of psychologist Robert Sternberg, the Nazi hatred of jazz was a mixture of two elements—a "negation of intimacy" intended to generate disgust, and "passion-less" bureaucratically administered policies that tolerated, and even promoted, the genre when it was useful.[4] This kind of hate was not defined by strong affects such as anger, aggression, or contempt. Jazz as a degenerate Negro, Bolshevik, or Jewish music certainly made up a large part of Nazi ideology, one that played a direct role in initiating and supporting horrifying genocidal violence, but the Nazi hatred of the music was complicated both in definition and practice.

Jazz was treated in a similarly complicated way in the Soviet Union and its client states.[5] First widely heard in the early 1920s, jazz in different forms was a part of twentieth-century Soviet life, heard in many cities, regions, and states across its vast expanse of political control and influence. Just as the Soviet leaders changed over time, so did the reception of the music. But even during the most oppressive regimes, such as Stalin's rule, the position of jazz shifted, moving between "prohibition, censorship, and sponsorship," Martin Lücke writes. The genre's ups and downs tracked larger material and ideological changes in Soviet life. Initially accepted as an avant-garde people's music, jazz came under severe censure with the upheavals of 1928 and 1929, condemned as "sonic idiocy in the bourgeois-capitalist world."[6] Writer Maxim Gorky's essay "On the Music of the Gross," published in *Pravda* in 1928, became a touchstone for all future condemnations of the music.[7] Jazz, for Gorky, was social and moral degeneracy in sound. Its frank sexuality was a path toward bourgeois decadence and collapse. But in just a few years, by 1932, jazz was rehabilitated, recognized as an authentic music of the proletariat. This ushered in what was later to be called the Red Age of Jazz. Soviet musicians played it in public and on state radio. With the purges of the Great Terror (1936–1938), things had shifted again. Jazz and its musicians once again became targets for repression and violence, although the real focus, Lücke writes, was less the music per se than the idea of musicians as purveyors of foreign influence.[8]

During the war years, the climate for jazz again become more hospitable, particularly so when the US became an ally. There were many Russian-staffed jazz orchestras playing for troops across the war's battlefields. But when the war ended, things turned against jazz, part of the Soviet retrenchment from the West. Despite this, jazz continued to survive through the 1940s and '50s, and curious and dedicated fans could seek out isolated live performances as well as recordings. Reception of the music continued seesawing in the post-Stalinist period, caught, as before, between recognizing the music as a folk or proletarian music of the oppressed (Negroes) and as a symbol that embodied the worst of Western capitalist values. Despite the turbulence of its official reception, Soviet musicians and fans continued to support the music, forming bands, finding places to play, and building audiences.[9]

As with the other kinds of jazz hatred I have discussed, the Nazi and Soviet attacks on jazz were complicated, neither fitting neatly into a commonsense notion of hate as an intensely "negative and difficult emotion" often characterized by "rage, resentment, or unconcern."[10] In both cases, state policy was often reasoned and calculated, not driven by an overwhelming emotional experience. In *The Nature of Hate*, Sternberg argues that hate can be emotionally "cool," felt as a set of long-term commitments to eliminating or annihilating something undesirable.[11] But, as the history shows, in both cases government rhetoric was at odds with behavior both public and private. Jazz may have been condemned rhetorically, but it was not rejected in any widespread way in day-to-day musical life.

HATING AS A PROGRESSIVE ACT

Today, *hate* is a provocation. The word has an intensely negative valence in our culture, in part because it is so closely aligned with right-wing, neo-Confederate, and neofascist movements. Because of its "pathologization," Jakob Norberg writes, hate "has declined in reputation." "Social scientists, journalists, perhaps the general public," he continues, "associate hate with intolerance, xenophobia, racism, anti-Semitism, and homophobia."[12] Some writers, however, have argued that hating is not necessarily morally repugnant or unjustified, and that it is pleasurable, even socially useful. Scholars Lara Langer Cohen and Brian Connolly, borrowing from nineteenth-century essayist William Hazlitt, argue that hate is fundamental to human psychology and social life. Hate can, of course, be a very dangerous thing, but its pathologization has "ceded" its radical potential to the far right, those "who feel their power threatened." Hating, the writers counter, can be an "affect of radical political organizing," an activity that can create "affirmingly social experience[s]." "In a conflict-averse culture," they write, "it forges strong solidarities." They make a further distinction between *hating* and *hating on*: the first is reserved for "obviously abhorrent objects," people and things clearly "injurious to human survival and flourishing." Hating on, in contrast, is an action focused on the "repugnance of minor [things]," such as celebrity chefs or wellness gurus. Like affect more generally, hating on is discursive, contingent, and relational, and this makes it dynamic, adaptable to changing conditions. Unlike love, which seeks mastery over the beloved, "hating on acknowledges that the individual is most often arrayed in combative relation to the world." This combative relation is driven not by nihilism but by passionate engagement with what the world could or should be like. For example, hating on is hard to monetize—Facebook has a Like button and not a Dislike button. How do advertisers sell you things that you hate? Cohen and Connolly do recognize some limits: hating is "differently legible—and acceptable—when read across different bodies." In other words, it is safer for some citizens to hate (white and middle class) than others (Black or brown and lower class). For the latter, hating is read by white society as being "out of control," a threat to the social and moral order. Hating has its risks, but Cohen and Connolly argue, it is foolish to ignore its progressive potential. They end their essay with a brief analysis of Lucas Moodysson's 2013 Swedish-language film, *We Are the Best!* In the movie, three teenage girls find common ground by forming a punk band. One of their songs, "Hate the Sport," angrily satirizes a world that cares more about soccer than about the degradations of the earth and its people. Cohen and Connolly see in the film an example of hating's "joyous ethics of solidarity" and, in the song, hating's "political possibilities."[13]

Rock musician Mike Krol's first album, *I Hate Jazz*, is a good example of what hating on jazz looks like. Krol, who describes his music as "American Lo-Fi Power Pop," self-released *I Hate Jazz* in 2011, followed by *Trust Fund* two years later.[14] After signing with a label, he released his third record, *Turkey*, in 2015 and his fourth, *Power Chords*, in 2019. Krol's musical identity has remained relatively consistent: punk-meets-garage songs with catchy melodies over noisy, lo-fi production, heavy on distorted guitars and drums. The songs on *I Hate Jazz* are short—seven of the eight clock in at or under two minutes—and focus on the angst and alienation of growing up and the struggles of connecting to friends. Other than its title, there is no mention of jazz in any of the songs. The album's name is both an absurdist joke (who titles a record something that has nothing to do with the songs?) and a statement of independence from convention. Noting this combination of humor and defiant individualism, the *Village Voice*'s Brad Cohan writes that "Krol embraces his being part of just one [music] scene: his own."[15]

Krol has little investment in actually hating jazz or even finding out more about it. In an April 2019 feature for the French online magazine *Still in Rock*, after discussing Krol's *Power Chords* album, the interviewer asks Krol, "Do you really hate jazz? Even Sun Ra?" "Yes," Krol responds. "Don't know any Sun Ra, but if it's jazz, then yes, I hate Sun Ra."[16] There is little affect behind his hating—it is a simple and proudly uninformed rejection. Sun Ra—the jazz outsider par excellence—would be a natural aesthetic fit for a musician described as "anti-everything."[17] But to Krol that is not the point. Cohen and Connolly describe this perfectly: "Loving traffics in mastery; it asks for a passionate pursuit of more knowledge about an object ('Have you heard the bootleg live version of that song?'). But hating is constituted by an arbitrary rejection based on partial knowledge ('That song fucking sucks'). In its refusal to accumulate more knowledge, hating challenges the dominance of the subject-supposed-to-know."[18] Krol's jazz hating is a pure statement of rejection. In his interview with the *Village Voice*, Krol says he is "just trying to do the opposite of what everyone else is doing. If everyone is gonna draw an alien head, a peace sign, and a weed leaf on their cover, I'm gonna wear a police outfit and say, 'Fuck you. I'm a cop.' That's a joke, but in a sense, the idea is, whatever is cool, I want to do the opposite."[19] Krol is certainly rejecting jazz, but that is not his main purpose: it is primarily a way of defining a cultural space at odds with the mainstream. Liking Krol and supporting his music is an act of social affirmation. You can even buy a bright orange *I Hate Jazz* T-shirt inspired by the album art: I HATE JAZZ appears in blue type on the front, and on the back is the message THIS ALBUM WAS RECORDED DURING THE WORST WEEK IN MIKE KROL'S LIFE. In 2021, musician fans of Krol from his Discord server released a tribute album titled *We Hate Jazz*.[20] In a culture that celebrates positivity, hating on jazz "forges strong solidarities." "There are few pleasures keener," Cohen and Connolly write, "than discovering that someone shares the feelings of hate you have nursed alone."[21]

Krol illustrates very well the paradoxically affirmative nature of hating on. But is this a moral position, one with benefits beyond a small group of music fans? Philosophers have offered justifications of hate as both moral and constructive. Berit Brogaard, drawing on the work of Peter Strawson, argues that hate can be a "reactive attitude," a response to the bad actions of "morally responsible agent(s)." Reactive attitudes are morally justified because they have a regulating function in communities; they "uphold the moral norms that govern our interactions and conduct." Certain kinds of hating, what Brogaard calls "critical" hating, are reactive and thus have a socially useful function. In contrast, "dehumanizing hate," where the hater sees no humanity in the target of their hate, is always wrong.[22] In critical hate, the hater acknowledges the basic humanity of the wrongdoer by insisting that the person could and should have done better.[23]

Other scholars have also embraced negative affects as useful tools in political and social struggle. In her famous essay "Killing Rage: Militant Resistance," bell hooks argues that Black rage, once recognized and harnessed, "can act as a catalyst inspiring courageous action."[24] Drawing on hooks and political theorist Wendy Brown, Niza Yanay distinguishes between objective hatred, exemplified by feelings of rage at injustice, and ideological hatred, an emotional-discursive experience built on fear and mobilized by hegemonic power. Like reactive hatred, objective hatred is focused on unjust and cruel actions and is solid ground for political and social action.[25] Marxist philosopher Georg

Lukács takes this idea to an extreme, arguing infamously for "holy hate" as "vital to a properly politicized, active cognitive engagement" with a corrupt capitalist world. "Rather than exclude hate from the range of politically acceptable affects," Jakob Norberg writes, "Lukács offers us a structured account of its legitimate and illegitimate uses based on a Marxist class analysis."[26] For Lukács, hatred is not only justified but necessary for transformative political change.

Literary scholar Sianne Ngai presents an intriguing argument for the political and aesthetic possibilities of the related notion of disgust. For Ngai, disgust "is urgent and specific"; it demands "concurrence" and a movement to uphold boundaries. The affective certainty of disgust stands in contrast to a dominant progressive ideology of "tolerance," a celebration of heterogeneity that has roots in theoretical notions of desire. The desire for "tolerance" is not sexual or psychoanalytic, but "the vaguely affective idiom" that searches for "fluidity, slippage, and semantic multiplicity," any "perceived transgression of the symbolic status quo." Although this concept has radical potential—celebrating difference can undermine implicit and explicit structures of power—it has also been subsumed into consumerism and neoliberal capitalism, severely limiting its radical potential.[27]

In contrast, disgust "is never ambivalent about its object." Disgust "policies the boundaries" between subject and object, in an attempt to keep the repulsive object away. Unlike desire, which can be "vague, amorphous, and even idiosyncratic," disgust is immediate and definite. Although she makes a point not to claim special transformative powers for disgust, Ngai argues that disgust in "its centrifugality, agonism, urgency, and above all refusal of the indifferently tolerable . . . offers an entirely different set of aesthetic and critical possibilities from the one offered by desire." Disgust, unlike the desire of "tolerance," is not "concordant, ideologically as well as aesthetically, with the aesthetic, cultural, and political pluralisms that have come to define the postmodern."[28] From this perspective, Stanley Crouch's and Pat Metheny's expressions of disgust provide new and creative ways of engaging with the music, ways that don't simply mimic the pieties of either postmodernity or neoliberalism. By insisting on boundaries, what appears to be a conservative rejection of difference is actually a productive act of contestation, one that demands a response and justification.

So, can hating *music* ever be an ethical or politically progressive act? Can it provide a kind of "joyous ethics of solidarity" that pushes us toward a better world? The arguments for a progressive notion of hate and disgust I've outlined have a compelling logic. But in practice, as can be seen in Metheny's attack on Kenny G or Crouch's on Miles Davis, the underlying intentions of the hater are obscured by caustic and aggressive rhetoric, rhetoric that rapidly generalizes from the actions and beliefs of an individual to the actions and beliefs of groups. The hate moves from being reactive or critical to dangerous and ideological. If, as Christopher Small argues, making music (or "musicking," as he calls it) is a way to explore, affirm, and celebrate human relationships, then music that is hated is not just an isolated attack on a musical performance but an attack on an entire community.[29] For Metheny, that is everyone who supports and rewards a bad actor such as Kenny G; for Crouch, it is the entire infrastructure that supports blaxploitation culture. We cannot and should not separate out the linguistic expression of contempt or disgust from an individual's internal cognitive-affective experience. As part of the "surface" of our social relationships, the ways we encounter each other, language is an inextricable part of our affective engagement with the world.[30] Metheny and Crouch might very well assert the basic humanity of their targets, but their rhetoric pushes toward abstraction, generalization, and perhaps dehumanization. Critical hate may theoretically exist, but I cannot find it in the world of jazz hating.

The different varieties of jazz hate I have examined are a part of many jazz communities. But in their most extreme forms these attacks are corrosive to the music and its culture. This destructiveness comes, paradoxically, from the hater's intense affective engagement with the music, the way the music "presses" on them, the way it demands participation. As psychoanalysts have long argued, love and hate originate together in the very foundation of our subjectivity and remain entwined in all our interactions with the world around us. Like love, hate is sentimental, an affective orientation focused on the truth of feeling as a way to assure oneself of an authentic experience in a disenchanted world. But however sentimental hate might be, it is not a sign of a vibrant jazz world. As political theorist C. Fred Alford argues, hatred may appear vitalizing, uniting like-minded others into a community, but in the end it is a lie, corrosive to both self and other. "The lie of hatred," Alford writes, "is that it can connect a person with others as love does." But "hatred," he argues, "is not the opposite of love," only an imitation of it, love "in the realm of malevolence."[31]

One of the most compelling arguments against the pleasures of hate remains William Hazlitt's 1826 essay "On the Pleasure of Hating," the starting point for Lara Langer Cohen and Brian Connolly's 2015 "Theses on Hating." As Cohen and Connolly note, Hazlitt astutely and sympathetically explains the human affinity for hate, the tendency of all the good and beautiful in the world "to turn to meanness, spite, [and] cowardice."[32] But Hazlitt's essay is not a celebration of hating. On the contrary, it is a warning. For Hazlitt, hating is a basic feature of human life: "Nature seems (the more we look into it) made up of antipathies: without something to hate, we should lose the very spring of thought and action.... The white streak in our fortunes is brightened (or just rendered visible) by making all around it as dark as possible." We seem conditioned to turn the best things in life into sources of bitterness and bile, to derive pleasure from our antipathies. "There is a secret affinity, a *hankering* after, evil in the human mind," Hazlitt writes. "Pure good soon grows insipid, wants variety and spirit." Hazlitt turns to the things in his life that are most meaningful—friendship and art—and realizes how often these things turn sour. Friendship, even when it thrives, is often fed by gossip and cruelty to other people. Most troubling, Hazlitt notices how even his intense love for certain books and art lose their attraction, affection turning into hate or disgust. Remembering a beautiful Titian pastoral scene, Hazlitt wonders why even this, one of the most beautiful things he knows of, cannot ward off feelings of bitterness, contempt, and anger: "Why do I not call up this image of gentle sweetness, and place it as a perpetual barrier between mischance and me?—It is because pleasure asks a greater effort of the mind to support it than pain; and we turn after a little idle dalliance from what we love to what we hate!"[33]

Reading through the essay it becomes clear that the title is ironic. Hate may be pleasurable—we may derive some perverse energy from it—but it is, in the end, "a poisonous mineral" that "eats into the heart" of things: it turns religion "to rankling spleen and bigotry" and "makes patriotism an excuse for carrying fire, pestilence and famine into other lands." The essay ends bleakly, with Hazlitt, a political radical, in despair over the failures of the 1820 democratic revolution in Spain. Whether in public or private life, humans seem doomed to wallow in the false pleasures of hating. Hazlitt concludes with a bitter capitulation to these pleasures: "Have I not reason to hate and to despise myself? Indeed I do; and chiefly for not having hated and despised the world enough."[34]

Hating, Hazlitt reminds us, may be a condition of human nature, and it may even be a source of pleasure, but it is nihilistic and damaging to human connection. Cohen and Connolly's "hating on" culture might support a community, but it does so at a cost for both the hater and the hated. Pat Metheny's rant against Kenny G offers an undeniable pleasure for like-minded fans, the guitarist saying in public what so many jazz fans and musicians might say only in private. But can the jazz world thrive, can it generate beauty, community, and racial justice, if it needs to define itself through such contempt and disgust? Evaluating and criticizing the music will always be a part of the jazz world, but the future of the music will depend on the nature of that criticism, the ways it fends off the dangerous pleasures of hating.

WHO STILL CARES ABOUT JAZZ? AFFECT AND THE ALGORITHM

So what is the nature of jazz hating today? What kind of affective charge does the music have for today's listeners? The 1950s represented a kind of high-water mark for the cultural relevance of jazz, a period when the music commanded the affective attention of substantial, if declining, numbers of listeners and critics. By the early '60s, however, the center of popular music had definitively moved toward rock and soul, new genres positioned by many musicians, fans, and critics as oppositional to mainstream pop of the '50s and its jazz-based musical practices such as the use of horns, melodic chromaticism, extended seventh-chord harmonies, and swing rhythms. As I argued above, '60s jazz, although fractured into substyles such as cool and hard bop, was still an important site of affective engagement—to love or hate jazz was a meaningful way to argue about the culture. By the '70s, with a few prominent exceptions (Herbie Hancock and the Headhunters, Weather Report, George Benson), jazz had slipped to the cultural periphery. In this environment, hating jazz did not have the same cultural resonance:

What did it mean to hate something that was selling so few records and rarely heard on the radio? With the emergence of the so-called Young Lions in the '80s and '90s, jazz moved closer to the center of the cultural conversation again, making the music a recognized site of affective investment and cultural contestation. But this was only a brief respite, and the music quickly receded to the periphery of American musical culture.

Any accounting of jazz in today's musical culture involves understanding the radical changes wrought by digital technologies, especially the internet. The upending of the music industry at the turn of the twenty-first century, combined with the growth of big data, analytics, and digital algorithms, changed the ways music operates in our social lives, the ways it functions as sites of affective engagement. As David Wright observes, these technologies alter "the contemporary *experience* of tasting, not least because the language of liking, disliking and sharing is so ubiquitous online and because the stuff of taste—music, films, television and books—is a significant part of how these digital media technologies are lived and used."[35] The dustup over *La La Land* represents a kind of cultural lag: critics' concern with the music's cinematic representation was operating with outdated modes of analysis, the rules of the taste game having changed. The flurry of writing about *La La Land* focused a lot on whether jazz is liked or hated. That conversation echoes a broader, long-standing discourse engaged in by arts institutions and jazz musicians. Since the mid-1990s, several national surveys have tried to account for American musical tastes. Although these surveys are interesting, they do not capture the ways affective engagement in music—or in the arts more generally—has been reshaped by our digital lives.[36] Music has become more accessible even as it is mediated by algorithms and artificial intelligence. But focusing on whether jazz is loved or even liked speaks past the immediate conjuncture, the new "structures of feelings" that shape our networked lives. "Today," write Michael Hardt and Antonio Negri, "we see networks everywhere we look—military organizations, social movements, business formations, migration patterns, communication systems, physiological structures, linguistic relations, neural transmitters, and even personal relationships.... Network has become a common form that tends to define our ways of understanding the world and acting in it."[37] The question now is, in a networked age, how do digital media "orchestrate our sensibilities" (to adapt Highmore's phrase)?[38] How are investments in culture directed or mediated by data and algorithms?

Polling, although a mostly predigital technique, takes on new importance in the age of the internet and big data. Perhaps not surprisingly, jazz, according to many polls, is not Americans' favorite music. And while it does have an audience—even a dedicated one—its commercial viability is tenuous, at least as measured by record sales and radio and internet play. This story—jazz as a declining music—is a familiar one. The response from arts institutions, radio stations, critics, and musicians has been an old one too: how to attract new listeners who will appreciate this often intricate and historically important (African) American music.[39] That response, I believe, is a misreading of the data and a grafting of an old problem onto a very different, digitally mediated cultural landscape. Jazz is liked well enough. The issue is not appreciation but one of affective engagement, an engagement scrambled by the paradoxes of the digital era: overabundance of music controlled by obscure algorithms and an opaque tech industry.

The most extensive survey of the place of jazz in American life remains the 1995 report by Scott DeVeaux, *Jazz in America: Who's Listening?* Using data from the 1992 Survey of Public Participation in the Arts (SPPA), sponsored by the National Endowment for the Arts, DeVeaux tracks positive engagement with jazz: how many Americans like jazz, attended jazz concerts, listened to jazz radio, or performed the music themselves. Although the study is inconclusive and incomplete, DeVeaux is hopeful: "For those who cherish jazz as a uniquely American form of artistic expression ... these figures cannot help but encourage a feeling of optimism. The audience for jazz is modest, but diverse and expanding.... For the foreseeable future, the music will continue to be heard."[40]

In 2005, Lee Mizell, Brett Crawford, and Caryn Anderson authored a similar but much broader study, *Music Preferences in the U.S.: 1982–2002*, again sponsored by the National Endowment for the Arts. The goal of the study was "to describe music preferences in the U.S. and how they have changed over time" as well as "the relationship between key demographic characteristics and music preferences." The authors again use SPPA data as the foundation for their analysis. Although they don't say so explicitly, they are clearly working with the same open definition of jazz that DeVeaux uses in his earlier analysis. The SPPA does not provide parameters for the genre, so participants could interpret jazz broadly to cover a wide variety of musical approaches, including big-band swing, the music of vocalists such as Harry Connick Jr., smooth jazz, and instrumental R&B. But even with this caveat in mind, Mizell, Crawford, and Anderson's study demonstrates clearly that jazz is still "liked." According to the authors, "jazz is the fifth most popular music genre in the United States." Over the twenty years of the study, 27 percent of adults consistently responded that they listened to jazz. Taking into account population growth, that steady 27 percent means that the jazz audience expanded by 34 percent, an increase of 15 million adult listeners (from 44 million to 59 million).[41] The rest of the analysis tracks closely with DeVeaux's: jazz has a strong appeal to nonwhite listeners, it is favored strongly by men, and participation is correlated with higher education levels. Looking at DeVeaux's 1995 report and Mizell, Crawford, and Anderson's 2005 study, jazz is doing... well, fine. It has a stable and enthusiastic audience. It is not growing like rap and hip-hop, but it is not declining either, like folk music. Looking at a table from the 2005 study (see p. 142) that summarizes how musical preferences have changed over two decades, it is easy to see jazz's middling location.

Jazz, the data suggests, is not actively disliked, even if its proportion of the national audience isn't growing. Based on its rise or fall in popularity, jazz appears to have no significant positive or negative affective hold on the adult listening population. Significant too is the still-strong connection between nonwhite audiences and liking and participating in jazz. A taste preference for jazz remains strongly connected to America's Black musical heritage. The place of jazz in the culture is strong, even if it is not central to American popular musical life. The study may be more of a mixed bag than DeVeaux's analysis from ten years earlier, but it still isn't bad news.

Ten years later, many jazz writers are not so optimistic. In a 2015 article for the online publication *JazzLine News*, David La Rosa finds bad news in *Nielsen Music U.S. Report* for 2014. La Rosa notes that "jazz and classical represent just 1.4% of total U.S. music consumption a piece." Unlike classical music, however, jazz saw declines in the purchase of physical and digital albums. In 2011, jazz "represented 2.8% of all music sold," about 11 million units, but three years later, jazz represented just 2 percent of all music sales. Just as worrying for La Rosa, jazz saw

Summary of changes in music preference over time

Music genre	Change in popularity	Magnitude of change (percentage points)	Estimated change in audience size (millions of adults)
Big band/wwing	Declined	−9	−4
Bluegrass	Declined	−4	2
Blues/R&B	Increased	3	19
Choral/glee club[a]	Declined	−5	−7
Classical/chamber music	No change		13
Classic rock/oldies	Increased	13	44
Country/western	Declined	−18	−11
Dance music/electronica	New category in 2002		
Ethnic/national tradition[a]	Declined	−4	−4
Folk	Declined	−10	−10
Hymns/gospel	Declined	−9	−2
Jazz	No change		15
Latin/Spanish/salsa[a]	No change		6
Mood/easy listening	Declined	−19	−18
Musicals/operetta	Declined	−6	−3
New Age/world music[a]	Declined	−3	−2
Opera	No change		6
Parade/marching band[a]	Declined	−6	−9
Rap/hip-hop[a]	Increased	6	15
Reggae[a]	Declined	−3	−2
Rock/heavy metal	New category in 2002		

Source: Lee Mizell, Brett Crawford, and Caryn Anderson, *Music Preferences in the U.S.: 1982–2002*, prepared for the National Endowment for the Arts (June 2005), vi, https://files.eric.ed.gov/fulltext/ED511715.pdf. Data is from 1982, 1992, and 2002 Surveys of Public Participation in the Arts.
[a] Data available for 1992 and 2002 only.

declines in digital album purchases between 2011 and 2012, and, despite the massive growth of streaming services such as Spotify, jazz represents just 0.3 percent of streams. For La Rosa it appears that jazz is becoming America's least popular genre.[42] But La Rosa is focusing on sales and streaming, and as DeVeaux's study demonstrates, engagement with jazz is broader than that. Many of the comments to La Rosa's article point out that jazz remains attractive for music students, and jazz programs in secondary schools and colleges are well attended.

Jazz critics echo this discourse: to expand the audience, the music needs more than acceptance; it needs passionate, engaged fans. How can jazz musicians and critics inspire greater emotional engagement with the music? In his 1997 book *Blue: The Murder of Jazz*, Eric Nisenson offers one answer: jazz must embrace its inherent progressive and experimental core. Jazz, he argues, is grounded in a pragmatic existentialism, motivated by the recognition that life is about choices made in the here and now. This attitude grew naturally from the condition of its inventors, African Americans, who were faced with constraints, often violent, on who and what they could be: "To black people, freedom and self-definition, principles so close to the heart of existentialism, are obsessions because they have been denied their rights as citizens and been stereotyped as a people for so long." The existentialist character of jazz has made it a music constitutionally about "natural innovation and progress." "Jazz," Nisenson writes, "is constantly in a state of becoming, pushed forward by the currents of the river that is our life and culture." But the rise and domination of jazz by neoclassicists, represented most prominently by trumpeter Wynton Marsalis, have cut the music off from its best tendencies, putting it in a straitjacket and starving it of its need to change.[43]

The straitjacketing of jazz not only stymies musical innovation, it enervates the music, weakening its affective impact, according to Nisenson. "Jazz is such a visceral art form in that we feel what a musician is feeling or what he or she is expressing while he or she is in the act of creating. Because of its visceral power, jazz can shape our lives profoundly, opening us up to the sensibility of others, making us more compassionate, humanizing us." But reclaiming the music's existentialist character does have specific parameters. He laments that free jazz has "gone too far outside the envelope" and that fusion "has made too many compromises" to pop music. Although he critiques traditionalists like Marsalis, he invokes his own idea of the jazz tradition to ground the argument. In the end, Nisenson articulates a familiar modernist position: jazz must respond to contemporary life by always "making it new." Jazz, he argues, is a great art of individualists, a music "based on the musician's inner life," emerging "from the deepest part of his or her soul." Jazz is a music of the "individual against a society that attempts to make it conform to its strictures." To keep jazz fresh, musicians must embrace internationalism, fusing existing jazz with musical styles from around the world. This has become more feasible, Nisenson argues, because of the communication revolutions of the digital age.[44]

Musicians, too, have spoken similarly about this issue. Robert Glasper represents one important and commercially viable way of responding to the issue of affective engagement with jazz.[45] Exemplified in his successful series of *Black Radio* recordings (*Black Radio* in 2012, *Black Radio 2* in 2013, and *Black Radio III* in 2022), the pianist "infuses improvisational sensibilities into an array of contemporary black music traditions, from R&B and neo-soul to funk and hip-hop."[46] But as interviews show, Glasper has wrestled with how to integrate these genres with a traditional notion of jazz craft. Even though he understands that jazz is not at the center of the culture, that it doesn't speak to many listeners today, he is committed to a jazz aesthetic that values training and tradition. At the same time, he celebrates popular taste for the ways it speaks to American, and especially African American, life today. Glasper sits self-consciously at the fluid intersection of popular taste, traditional jazz aesthetics, and American Blackness. In his own way—and shaped by the specificities of our time—Glasper is tackling some of same complicated questions that have preoccupied Black musicians and critics for the past fifty years: how to define Black culture vis-à-vis American culture. On one hand, Glasper, echoing writers such as Amiri Baraka, is reaching for an ideal of a unified Black music, a "changing same." But in his commitment to the jazz tradition, he is also articulating a version of Albert Murray's omni-Americans. For Murray, Black music *is* American music. American identity is "mulatto" from the start.[47]

In interviews, Glasper speaks often on the overlap between commercial viability and social relevance: "You always have to stay relevant. If what you're playing sounds like 1960 at its best, or at its worst, you're not going to have a lot of younger people hanging around." Jazz, he argues, has become a "museum" music, embalmed in an outdated aesthetic.[48] In a 2012 interview with Guy Raz, Glasper laments the nostalgia that dominates the genre: "We kind of killed the alive to praise the dead. And I don't think that the jazz community embraces newer artists anymore. We get mad that new audiences don't want to come watch us play, you know? But it's like, you know, we keep sending our grandfather out to the playground."[49] Talking with Samantha Hunter of Okayplayer, Glasper makes clear that jazz is still central to his musical identity and represents a set of tools and aesthetic values that he relies on, regardless of what he is playing or who he is playing with:

I'm definitely more than just jazz [but] I'm a jazz musician at my core. I go by the old definition. Back in the day, in the '60s, when you heard that somebody was a jazz musician, you were excited, because you knew they could play other things. A lot of those Motown albums you hear are all jazz musicians because that's when the music was black. Jazz was super black, which means it was super soulful, which means it translated through other genres of music, so that's why all the Motown albums used jazz musicians. So for me, being a jazz musician really means giving you the tools to play everything else. Because, even to be a *bad* jazz musician, you kind of gotta do better than everybody else. Because you have to master your instrument pretty much just to play the music correctly, just to play the melodies and to actually improvise even on a mediocre level, you're pretty much better than most musicians in any other genre when it comes to just mastering your instrument.[50]

The language of quality and craft is a nod to a transcendental idea of the aesthetic and a rejection of the vagaries of commercial taste. There are standards, he implies, and they exist across time and place. But he also recognizes that other genres require study and practice—just because you are a jazz musician doesn't mean you can play hip-hop well: "That's why I tell people all of the time if you really want to cross over stop playing hip-hop with jazz bands. Stop playing R&B with jazz bands. Stop playing hip-hop with gospel bands. If you want to play real hip-hop, and get your hip-hop chops up, play with a hip-hop band. That's what you need to do. Do that." Jazz, Glasper argues, has lost its practical connection to the wide range of Black vernacular musical practices, thus losing its affective grip on listeners.[51]

The pianist also harshly judges music and musicians who lack a certain body of musical skills. Commercial radio stations, driven by financial imperatives and the whims of its listeners, "just play the same five horrible songs. You know, it's all about what's hot now. And what is hot now, especially when it comes to African American music, they choose the dumbest stuff to play sometimes." These "hits" are dumb for their lyrics—"The guys are talking about the same [things], and the women are talking about the same things that don't mean anything, you know, degrading each other"—but also for their music—"It's just bad, and the music's bad." These commercial pressures lower the quality of everything, leading to copycats and creative stasis: "So now, artists are coming out trying to do that exact same thing. And that's not cool because we're going to lose a lot of great artists because artists think you have to do this certain thing to be heard on the radio."[52] Here Glasper articulates the tension between embracing shifting musical tastes while insisting on musical standards that are defined and applicable across genres. Despite his early twenty-first-century context and centering of Blackness, Glasper echoes a much older discourse in American popular music, one that predates jazz: how to serve popular taste and retain standards of musical excellence. And at the center of this dilemma is the role of feeling: Glasper recognizes that the problem with jazz is not that it is hated, it is that it is affectively inert. At their foundation, Glasper's musical projects such as the *Black Radio* series are about jazz and feeling in the context of race: How do you reactivate the music's affective urgency while also centering Blackness?

But DeVeaux's, Nisenson's, and Glasper's concerns with the relevance of jazz are not quite aligned with the nature of our new culture of digital music. From one perspective, jazz is actually doing quite well simply because it has no strong affective pull. A 2013 poll conducted by Public Policy Polling (PPP), a Democratic-leaning political polling company based in North Carolina, offers an interesting contrast to the SPPA surveys, demonstrating the way affect works in a digital environment. PPP is best known for its highly regarded polls about voting and other political behaviors, but it occasionally seeks more lighthearted information, such as voters' musical tastes. In 2013, the company surveyed 571 voters via automated telephone interviews, asking questions about the favorability of genres and artists as well as political affiliations. It is difficult to assess the validity of the poll, since the questions are neither very thoughtful nor specific. Along with questions about musical genres and artists, the pollsters also asked what name Snoop Dogg should go by, whether Justin Timberlake should stick to acting or music, and which pop star should be president. But despite the silliness, the message for jazz is still positive: 71 percent of respondents had a favorable opinion of jazz, 20 percent had an unfavorable opinion, and 9 percent weren't sure. Only 6 percent of respondents rated jazz as their favorite genre. Many of those polled, however, were unfamiliar with certain artists (more than 50 percent of respondents did not know who Morrissey and Skrillex were). The main takeaway from the survey—and the headline of the PPP press release—was that everyone, Republican and Democrat, hated Justin Bieber. Jazz haters are no match for Bieber haters. Jazz, the PPP poll suggests, is definitely not hated. In fact, it is liked well enough.[53]

In the still-dominant discourse—represented by DeVeaux's analysis of the SPPA data, Nisenson's lament of the lost experimentation of jazz, and Glasper's urge to connect to contemporary Black music—the issue is to make people care about jazz. But as the PPP poll suggests, not caring about jazz can be a positive attribute in the digital attention economy, allowing the music to move seamlessly across platforms. Following Dale Chapman, the low affect of jazz also facilitates its deployment as a mode of neoliberal capital accumulation.[54] Since nearly everyone can get on board with jazz—it's America's classical music!—jazz can support—or mask—corporate priorities that have little do with the needs and desires of the people that make and listen to the music. The stakes of loving and hating jazz have changed the ways the music flows through our lives. These changes have not made the Blackness of jazz any less important to its reception, but they have changed the larger ecology of how racial representations and racialized affect circulate.

THE FUTURE OF JAZZ HATING AND JAZZ LOVING

In Irish writer Roddy Doyle's short story "Jimmy Jazz"—another installment in Doyle's Barrytown trilogy chronicling Dublin's Rabbitte family—the main character is forty-nine-year-old Jimmy Rabbitte, a rocker who says he "fuckin' hate[s] jazz." His wife, Aoife, loves it. Jimmy tries to pretend that he doesn't hate it, but he really can't: "He hated jazz. Hated it, and he always had. He'd decided way back, when he was seventeen—he remembered the day—that he hated it, and he hadn't budged since. He wasn't a bigot; he was just right. Jazz was shite." Jimmy traces his hate to an incident from his teenage years, when a sexual encounter he'd attempted with an eager girlfriend had been thwarted by the Charlie Parker music her father was listening to in another room.[55]

But readers who are familiar with Doyle's first Barrytown book, *The Commitments* (1987), also know that Jimmy learned his jazz hate from a professional soul trumpeter turned preacher named Joey "the Lips" Fagan. Answering a want ad placed by Jimmy, Joey joins the new band—named the Commitments—and becomes their musical and spiritual mentor. After regular rehearsals, Joey notices that Dean, the band's young saxophonist, has been improving rapidly, and his soloing is starting to have more jazz influences. Joey tells Jimmy that he's worried about Dean. "He told me he's been listening to jazz," Joey says. But Jimmy doesn't understand the problem. "Jazz," Joey explains, "is the antithesis of soul." It is "intellectual," "anti-people," and "abstract." Dean, it seems, has been listening to Charlie Parker, a musician who sold out his soulful Black birthright to play "polyrhythms" for "hip honky brats and intellectuals." Dean, Joey fears, is going to become a "Jazz Purist." As an arid intellectual exercise, jazz kills soul. Joey's fears turn out to be exaggerated; Dean reassures Jimmy he is committed to the band and will play jazz on his own time.[56]

Now, years later, Jimmy remains unmoved in his feelings toward the music. So when Aoife buys him tickets to hear pianist Keith Jarrett, Jimmy thinks his wife is being spiteful. He notes to himself that she won't even be attending. Jimmy thinks the tickets are part of some cruel test of his love and patience. He decides to take his friend Outspan—the former guitarist and fellow jazz hater from the Commitments—but has doubts after reading about Jarrett's prickly attitude toward audience noise. Outspan has lung cancer, and the threat of a disruptive coughing fit is very real.

With great trepidation, Jimmy and Outspan go to the concert. Outspan is perplexed by Jarrett's appearance—"He isn't black. . . . He's supposed to be fuckin' black"—and Jimmy tries to quiet him; he can't risk Jarrett walking out on everybody because of his friend.[57] But all of Jimmy's anxiety vanishes as soon as the music starts:

> It was incredible. It was like he—Jarrett—didn't know what was happening, didn't know what note was going to follow the last one. Like he was composing the piece Jimmy was hearing but throwing it away at the same time. He'd no sheet music in front of him, and his eyes were shut. He stood up and stamped his foot. He sat. He stood again and

looked into the piano—he was the kid again—wondering what it was like inside, what happened when he hit the keys. Jimmy could hear it now; the man was grunting. There was long moments when Jimmy forgot he was listening to music.[58]

Jimmy is "amazed and frightened" that "something so brilliant" would vanish when the performance was over. The sense of danger in Jarrett's performance, the sense that decisions were being made on the fly, was "a bit terrifying." Even Outspan is impressed ("a bit of a prick" but "fuckin' unbelievable"). Jarrett's performance involved his entire body—feet moving, body swaying. At moments, Jimmy "forgot he was listening to music." He engages with jazz at an entirely affective level. He forgets himself and the concert hall; all the annoying associations, personal and social, recede. Jimmy just simply feels the event—its excitement, danger, and euphoria.[59]

On one hand, Jimmy's experience seems to be what so many jazz lovers think should happen when jazz haters really listen. They will feel its greatness and its power. Jimmy even did his homework, reading up on Jarrett and his music. He is what Seb from *La La Land* dreams of: Jimmy just gets it now. He has heard the real thing and been open to its power. But there is a different way of understanding what is happening, one that doesn't require the language of aesthetic transcendence. Jimmy's experience is rooted in his current situation: his love for his wife, his love for music, and his friendship with Outspan. His affective response to Jarrett is mediated through this context. In Ben Highmore's terms, the experience was an "orchestration of sensibilities," of the macro (Jimmy's life at the time) with the micro (the sounds and movements of Jarrett). From this vantage, Doyle's story provides an important lesson for the future of the music. Turning a jazz hater into a jazz lover (or even a Jarrett lover) is not simply about education and exposure. It is about a conjuncture—a meeting of feeling and context. Any assessment of the future of jazz in American life has to engage with the complexities of affect, the way socially mediated feelings direct our attention, investments, and judgments. Our affective experiences of music are shaped by and through the messy and conflicted social worlds we inhabit, worlds riven by class, gender, and especially racial divisions.

In his analysis of the SPPA data, DeVeaux concludes that jazz advocates—despite having succeeded in modestly increasing the music's audience—have a "peculiar challenge" for the future: "to marshal the prestige and financial resources of the arts and educational establishment on its behalf without endangering its appeal to a youthful, pop-oriented audience." It is useful to reframe DeVeaux's challenge in affective terms: What can be done to make the music more intense, more urgent for new listeners accustomed to contemporary genres such as pop, electronic dance music, hip-hop, R&B, and rock? Accomplishing this, however, requires more than the education and marketing efforts of the "arts and educational establishment." Affect, as I have been arguing, comes not just from the sounds but also from the context. As Ingrid Monson notes, jazz has paid a "high price" in its transformation into a largely institutionalized music: the shrinking market for the music and the departure of a significant part of its African American audience.[60] For jazz to have an impact—to grab listeners' attention—it needs to fit into a complex web of artistic, technological, economic, and social developments. Hip-hop is one obvious point of contact, and many young, critically acclaimed artists are active in this area, such as Glasper, Lakecia Benjamin, Theo Croker, Nubya Garcia, Makaya McCraven, Kassa Overall, and Brandee Younger. But there are many other paths that take the traditions and practices of jazz in new directions, fusing with other musical genres or rethinking traditional jazz practices. In his recent collection of essays on contemporary jazz, critic Phil Freeman outlines four "key zones" of jazz practice centered in certain cities but extending well beyond municipal boundaries: a London scene that draws heavily on the immigrant and postcolonial experience; a Los Angeles "spiritual, Afrocentric" scene; a Chicago avant-garde community rooted in the players and institutions of the Association for the Advancement of Creative Musicians; and a New York scene composed of several parallel worlds (traditionalists playing standards in a bop and postbop style; R&B- and hip-hop-oriented musicians working across genres and commercial milieus; and a group focused on "complex, frequently through-composed music," with connections to the world of classical New Music).[61] Although no generalized typology can really capture all the ways jazz is being made around the world, Freeman's description is a very good attempt.

Although not an organization known for its attention to the jazz and improvised music scene, even the Recording Academy has recognized the ways jazz has changed in the past two decades. The academy introduced a new category for the 2024 Grammy Awards: Best Alternative Jazz Album.[62] The term is not widely used among jazz musicians and critics, but the category does usefully capture the many streams of jazz fusions happening now. The 2024 nominees—albums by Arooj Aftab, Vijay Iyer, and Shahzad Ismaily; Louis Cole; Kurt Elling and Charlie Hunter; Cory Henry; and Meshell Ndegeocello—represent widely divergent approaches to jazz practice, from the improvised, avant-electronic Pakistani and Indian sounds of Aftab, Iyer, and Ismaily to the gospel and R&B fusions of Henry and the eclectic mixture of soul, funk, and rock of Ndegeocello (who won the award). These musical fusions and partnerships are not new to jazz, for the history of the music has been defined by them: think of the Caribbean influences on New Orleans musicians in the early twentieth century, bebop's embrace of Cuban and Puerto Rican musicians in the 1940s, and the fusions with African and South Asian musics and musicians in the '50s, '60s, and '70s. But the range of practices and their global scope are new, reflecting a much more connected world. They offer the possibilities for new affective engagements in new contexts with new audiences.

The music's long-standing relationship with social justice, specifically Black civil rights, offers another avenue for infusing jazz practices with urgency and intensity. As Katherine McKittrick writes, building on Sylvia Wynter, Black music "is not only an invention that subverts and undoes commonsense workings of racism; music, music-making, and music-listening, together, demonstrate the subversive politics of shared stories, communal activities, and collaborative possibilities wherein 'one *must participate* in knowing.'"[63] The murder of George Floyd brought new attention to Black Lives Matter, a movement that had been trying for years to get Americans to do something about police brutality toward African Americans and other people of color. Although many jazz musicians have been using their music for political activism, the aftermath of Floyd's murder saw a perhaps too-brief reckoning with the racism embedded in institutions across the arts and education communities. Even organizations devoted to Black music, such as SFJazz, issued statements acknowledging the ways they had "fallen short" of their goal "to be a leading figure in supporting Black, Indigenous, and people of color."[64] Since so much jazz education and performance happens in academic institutions, from high schools and universities to conservatories such as Berklee and Juilliard, infusing jazz practice with political praxis faces the additional hurdle of the inherent conservatism of large bureaucratic organizations.[65] For example, the number of Black teachers, students, and administrators remains unsettling low. But how the events of 2020 shape jazz will depend on the ways younger musicians find political urgency in the music. How will that broader affective political engagement shape not just their music but their understanding of and participation in the jazz world, from the stage to the classroom?

Despite its ups and downs, jazz has been resilient, and it will survive. The future of the music is, of course, in the hands of the musicians, critics, and fans, but how it reaches and connects to audiences depends on many factors outside any one person, group, or institution's control. The task, then, is not simply to advocate for it, but to more fully understand its affective power in all its social aspects. Public performance, commercial support, and education can certainly play a role, but any assessment of its present and future requires something more, an understanding of how jazz might be made to move us, whether that is toward passionate engagement and love or vociferous rejection and hate.

Acknowledgments

Although researched and written over the past several years, this book is really the product of decades of engagement with jazz as both a performer and a scholar. My first in-depth exposure to the music—its history, culture, and musical building blocks—came in high school from Bob Sinicrope, a brilliant teacher who shaped not only my musical and intellectual life but that of hundreds of other students, many of whom have made careers in music. In college I played drums in the Columbia University jazz orchestra directed by Don Sickler. There I met more fantastic musicians and students of jazz: Gary Wang, Arthur Mintz, Daniel Srebnick, John Wriggle, and Andrew Rosenblum. All of them opened my eyes and ears to new artists, recordings, and approaches to improvisation. It was in college that my focus changed from performing to research. Of the many great professors I had, two—Eric Foner and Barbara J. Fields—profoundly shaped my approach to American history and culture. As an undergraduate student, I was fortunate to work closely with both, and their capacious knowledge as well as kindness and support showed me how to conduct rigorous and ethical historical research.

It was at UCLA's musicology department that I found a welcoming place for a jazz drummer with a history degree. Rather than seeing my mostly informal academic musical training as a deficit, the faculty saw it as a strength. They took a chance on me, and I am forever grateful for their open-mindedness. The guiding force of my graduate experience was Rob Walser. His insistence on a close attention to musical sounds, along with his view of music as an extension of social life, in all its complexities and contradictions, forms the core of my approach to musicology. He has remained an important part of my intellectual life, providing invaluable critical perspectives on my research and writing. Also foundational was the brilliant Susan McClary. Her astonishing knowledge of Western musical practice and her broad humanistic approach to music's relationship to gender, sexuality, and the body deeply influenced my own thinking. She remains a source of guidance and inspiration. The other faculty at the time, many of whom served on my dissertation committee, were sources of vibrant conversation and intellectual challenge: Robert Fink, Raymond Knapp, Elisabeth Le Guin, Tamara Levitz, Mitchell Morris, and Christopher Waterman. Thanks also to my former graduate school colleagues: Kate Bartel, Steve Baur, Dale Chapman, Daniel Goldmark, Gordon Haramaki, Loren Kajikawa, James Kennaway, Erik Leidal, Olivia Mather, Louis Niebur, Glenn Pillsbury, Erica Scheinberg, Cecilia Sun, Jacqueline Warwick, and Stephanie Vander Wel. Our regular Zoom get-togethers were a lifesaver during the pandemic, providing much-needed connection and laughter. A special thanks to Charles "Chuck" H. Garrett, whose recent passing was a devastating loss for everyone who knew and loved him. Chuck read and commented on an earlier draft of several chapters, providing invaluable perspective and advice. Finally, another special thanks goes out to David Ake, who also read and commented on an earlier version of the manuscript. As always, his advice was supportive, sharp, and insightful.

The humanities and cultural studies department at the University of South Florida has been my academic home since 2006. Our interdisciplinary department, despite periodically baffling deans and administrators, continues to be a unique and wonderful place of intellectual ferment, collegiality, dedication, and passion. I need to thank all of my steady and encouraging colleagues, past and present: the late Priscilla Brewer, Sara Callahan, Brendan Cook, Annette Cozzi, Bill Cummings, Jim D'Emilio, Scott Ferguson, Benjamin Goldberg, Todd Jurgess, Deborah Kochman, Rachel May, Amy Rust, Brook Sadler, and Angsumala Tamang. A special thank-you to Daniel Belgrad, who read and commented on an earlier version of several chapters. USF has seen its challenges over the past several years—a pandemic, a budget crisis, cruel and divisive state laws—but the faculty have held firm. Caring and dedicated professionals, they have not been afraid to speak truth to power. Many have also listened patiently to my ideas about jazz. My thanks to Brian Connolly, Cass Fisher, McArthur Freeman, Margit Grieb, Cheryl Hall, Elizabeth Hordge-Freeman, David Johnson, Meredith Johnson, Nathan Johnson, Anne Latowsky, John Lennon, Alex Levine, Richard Manning, Susan Mooney, Chuck Owen, Laura Runge, Stephan Schindler, Bessie Skoures, Scott Solomon, Camilla Vásquez, Jack Wilkins, and Wallace Wilson. A special thanks to the multitalented Matt Knight, who finagled me access to some important digital archives. Our department office managers, first Edgardo Valentin, then Antonette Green, and now Meredith Donovan, have been extraordinarily helpful in too many ways to count.

The jazz studies world is large and growing, and there are many scholars who have listened to me talk about parts of this project. Many of them are members of the recently established Jazz and Improvisation Study Group of the American Musicological Society, an important moment for jazz studies vis-à-vis musicology more broadly. Thanks to Ben Bierman, Patrick Burke, Gretchen Carlson, Charles Carson, Scott DeVeaux, Stephanie Doktor, Krin Gabbard, Ken Ge, John Gennari, Ben Givan, Michael Heller, Charles Hersch, John Howland, Benjamin Lapidus, Mark Lomanno, Darren Mueller, Ken Prouty, Ron Radano, Bruce Boyd Raeburn, Gabriel Solis, Sarah Suhadolnik, Kimberly Hannon Teal, and Sherrie Tucker. Although focused on the US, I have been fortunate to share my work with a large coterie of international jazz scholars, many of whom I met at Rhythm Changes conferences over the years: Michael Borshuk, Andy Fry, Nicolas Pillai, Sarah Raine, Loes Rusch, Alan Stanbridge, Catherine Tackley, Walter van de Leur, Tony Whyton, and Katherine Williams. A special thank-you to Nick Gebhardt, who has been a sounding board for many of the ideas elaborated in this book.

I am very thankful to the University of Chicago Press, especially executive editor Elizabeth Branch Dyson, who first saw value in this project, gathered excellent reviews, and provided clear guidance to develop and improve the manuscript. Thank you also to assistant editor Mollie McFee, who was always available to answer my many questions. Leslie Keros's sharp, judicious editorial eye greatly improved the prose, and Christine Schwab gracefully guided the project through the production process. And thanks to all those in the design and production department who worked on making the book so beautiful.

Thank you to my parents, Robert and Ilene Berish: you were quite literally the beginning of all this. I am so grateful for your unwavering support and encouragement over the years. And also my sisters, Jennifer Wolfe and Bethanne Durell, and their families for all their love and inspiration. Finally, a huge thank-you to Maria Cizmic: I am so deeply thankful for your love, patience, and insight. The past few years have been challenging but also exciting, full of unexpected joys and sorrows, and I am so thankful to travel all of life's bumpy roads with you. Anthony and Julia—thank you for your effervescent intelligence, curiosity, and enthusiasm. You may not love jazz now, but maybe someday you at least won't hate it.

Notes

CHAPTER ONE

1. Ben Ratliff, "Jazz Hate," *Slate*, December 15, 2016, https://slate.com/culture/2016/12/la-la-lands-cliched-confused-depiction-of-jazz.html.
2. Ted Gioia, "What's with This Uncool Surge in Jazz Bashing?," *Daily Beast*, November 2, 2014, https://www.thedailybeast.com/whats-with-this-surge-in-jazz-bashing.
3. Justin Wm. Moyer, "All That Jazz Isn't All That Great," *Washington Post*, August, 8, 2014, https://www.washingtonpost.com/news/opinions/wp/2014/08/08/all-that-jazz-isnt-all-that-great/; Jason Gubbels, "Jazz Needs a Better Sense of Humor," *Deadspin*, September 11, 2014, https://deadspin.com/jazz-needs-a-better-sense-of-humor-1632954724; Django Gold, "Sonny Rollins: In His Own Words," Daily Shouts, *Shouts and Murmurs* (blog), *New Yorker*, July 31, 2014, https://www.newyorker.com/humor/daily-shouts/sonny-rollins-words.
4. For example, see Paul Lopes, *The Rise of a Jazz Art World* (Cambridge: Cambridge University Press, 2002).
5. Ratliff, "Jazz Hate."
6. Guthrie P. Ramsey Jr., *The Amazing Bud Powell: Black Genius, Jazz History, and the Challenge of Bebop* (Berkeley: University of California Press, 2013), 7.
7. Grover Sales, *Jazz: America's Classical Music* (Englewood Cliffs, NJ: Prentice-Hall, 1984); Bruno Nettl and Helen Myers, *Folk Music in the United States: An Introduction* (Detroit: Wayne State University Press, 1976), 88–102.
8. Albert Murray, *The Omni-Americans: Some Alternatives to the Folklore of White Supremacy* (1970; reprint, New York: Library of America, 2020).
9. "Black American Music and the Jazz Tradition," *Nicholas Payton* (blog), April 30, 2014, https://nicholaspayton.wordpress.com/2014/04/30/black-american-music-and-the-jazz-tradition/.
10. Max Roach, "Beyond Categories," in *Keeping Time: Readings in Jazz History*, ed. Robert Walser (New York: Oxford University Press, 1999), 307–8.

11. Ramsey, *Amazing Bud Powell*, 9. Ramsey is drawing on the rich music-studies literature on genre. See especially David Brackett, *Categorizing Sound: Genre and Twentieth-Century Popular Music* (Berkeley: University of California Press, 2016), a comprehensive look at genre theorizing in popular music, including jazz.

12. Following the changes in usage by the Associated Press and other journalistic and academic publications, I am capitalizing *Black*—and also *Blackness*—when used "in a racial, ethnic or cultural sense, conveying an essential and shared sense of history, identity, and community among people who identify as Black, including those in the African diaspora and within Africa." Also following recent changes, I retain lowercase *w* in *white* and *whiteness*. See "Explaining AP Style on Black and White," Associated Press News, July 20, 2020, https://apnews.com/article/archive-race-and-ethnicity-9105661462. See also Kelsey Klotz, *Dave Brubeck and the Performance of Whiteness* (New York: Oxford University Press, 2022), 1–2n2.

13. Not surprisingly, given the early attention and promotion of jazz by French-language music critics, there is a substantial body of literature in English on the reception of jazz in France. See Andy Fry, *Paris Blues: African American Music and French Popular Culture, 1920–1960* (Chicago: University of Chicago Press, 2014); Elizabeth Vihlen McGregor, *Jazz and Postwar French Identity: Improvising the Nation* (New York: Lexington Books, 2016); Colin W. Nettelbeck, *Dancing with DeBeauvoir: Jazz and the French* (Melbourne: Melbourne University Press, 2004); Tom Perchard, *After Django: Making Jazz in Postwar France* (Ann Arbor: University of Michigan Press, 2015); Jeffrey H. Jackson, *Making Jazz French: Music and Modern Life in Interwar Paris* (Durham, NC: Duke University Press, 2003); Matthew F. Jordan, *Le Jazz: Jazz and French Cultural Identity* (Urbana: University of Illinois Press, 2010). An excellent starting point for jazz reception across Europe is Francesco Martinelli, ed., *The History of European Jazz: The Music, Musicians and Audience in Context* (Bristol, CT: Equinox Publishing, 2017).

14. See, for example, Eugene Marlow, *Jazz in China: From Dance Hall Music to Individual Freedom of Expression* (Jackson: University Press of Mississippi, 2018); Christopher Ballantine, *Marabi Nights: Jazz, "Race" and Society in Early Apartheid South Africa*, 2nd ed. (Scottsville, South Africa: University of KwaZulu-Natal Press, 2012); Gwen Ansell, *Soweto Blues: Jazz, Popular Music, and Politics in South Africa* (New York: Continuum, 2004); Gerhard Kubik, *Jazz Transatlantic*, vol. 2, *Jazz Derivatives and Developments in Twentieth-Century Africa* (Jackson: University Press of Mississippi, 2017).

15. Birgitte Schepelern Johansen, "Locating Hatred: On the Materiality of Emotions," *Emotion, Space, and Society* 16 (2015): 50.

16. Annett Schirmer, *Emotion* (Thousand Oaks, CA: Sage, 2015), 91–182.

17. Johansen, "Locating Hatred," 51.

18. Ibid., 49–50.

19. Aristotle, *Rhetoric*, bk. 2, pt. 4, http://classics.mit.edu/Aristotle/rhetoric.2.ii.html.

20. Johansen, "Locating Hatred," 51.

21. Ibid.

Notes to Pages 6–8 159

22. Niza Yanay, *The Ideology of Hatred: The Psychic Power of Discourse* (New York: Fordham University Press, 2017), 4.
23. Sigmund Freud, "Instincts and Their Vicissitudes," *The Standard Edition of the Complete Psychological Works of Sigmund Freud*, vol. 14, *On the History of the Psychoanalytic Movement, Papers on Metapsychology and Other Works*, trans. and ed. James Strachey (London: Hogarth Press, 1957; reprint, New York: Vintage, 1999), 138.
24. Ibid., 134, 136–37.
25. Johansen, "Locating Hatred," 51.
26. Daniel Karlin, *Browning's Hatreds* (New York: Oxford University Press, 1993), 5.
27. Lara Langer Cohen and Brian Connolly, "Theses on Hating," *Avidly*, June 16, 2015, https://avidly.lareviewofbooks.org/2015/06/16/theses-on-hating/.
28. Melissa A. Click, ed., *Anti-fandom: Dislike and Hate in the Digital Age* (New York: New York University Press, 2019).
29. The most important figure in these discussions was philosopher Horace Kallen, who advocated the idea of an American pluralism in a series of essays, the most famous being "Democracy versus the Melting Pot," published in the *Nation* in 1915. William Toll, "Horace M. Kallen: Pluralism and American Jewish Identity," *American Jewish History* 85 (March 1997): 57–74; Daniel Greene, *The Jewish Origins of Cultural Pluralism: The Menorah Association and American Diversity* (Bloomington: Indiana University Press, 2011).
30. Philip Gleason, "Americans All: World War II and the Shaping of American Identity," *Review of Politics* 43 (October 1981): 483–518.
31. Charles King, *Gods of the Upper Air: How a Circle of Renegade Anthropologists Reinvented Race, Sex, and Gender in the Twentieth Century* (New York: Anchor, 2020).
32. In his 1927 book *The Appeal of Jazz*, British critic R. W. S. Mendl writes that "there are some people whose hostile reaction to syncopated dance music is attributed by them to their antipathy towards everything connected with the n[*****]." R. W. S. Mendl, *The Appeal of Jazz* (London: Philip Allan, 1927), 71.
33. Musical analytic approaches are diverse—some historically rooted, others aiming at more general conclusions—but all focus on connecting musical details to individual emotional experience. Leonard Meyers, *Emotion and Meaning in Music* (Chicago: University of Chicago Press, 1956), and Deryck Cook, *The Language of Music* (London: Oxford University Press, 1959), are two touchstones. Subsequent work expanded these investigations but applied other theoretical tools such as semiotics and cognitive theory: Leonard Ratner, *Classic Music: Expression, Form and Style* (New York: Schirmer, 1980); Kofi Agawu, *Playing with Signs* (Princeton, NJ: Princeton University Press, 1991); Robert Hatten, *Musical Meaning in Beethoven: Markedness, Correlation, and Interpretation* (Bloomington: Indiana University Press, 1994); Nicola Dibben, "Subjectivity and the Construction of Emotion in the Music of Björk," *Music Analysis* 25, no. 1/2 (March–July 2006): 171–97; Gregory Karl and Jenefer Robinson, "Shostakovich's Tenth Symphony and the Musical Expression of Cognitively Complex Emotions," in *Music and Meaning*, ed. Jenefer Robinson, 154–78 (Ithaca, NY: Cornell University Press, 1997).

A significant and larger body of work on music and emotion is rooted in psychology and its various subfields: see, for example, David Huron's influential *Sweet Anticipations: Music and the Psychology of Expectation* (Cambridge, MA: MIT Press, 2006); Patrik N. Juslin, *Musical Emotions* (New York: Oxford University Press, 2019); Patrik N. Juslin and John A. Sloboda, eds., *Handbook of Music and Emotion* (New York: Oxford University Press, 2010). In practice these two broad approaches frequently intersect and overlap. For a recent and comprehensive survey of musicological, ethnomusicological, music theoretical, and psychological approaches to music and emotion, see in particular the contributions of Stephen Davies, Nicholas Cook and Nicola Dibben, Judith Becker, and John A. Slobado and Patrik N. Juslin in the *Handbook of Music and Emotion*. For a comprehensive narrative account of all these trends, see Michael Spitzer, *A History of Emotion in Western Music: A Thousand Years from Chant to Pop* (New York: Oxford University Press, 2020).

34. Marie Thompson and Ian Biddle, introduction to *Sound, Music, Affect: Theorizing Sonic Experience*, ed. Thompson and Biddle (London: Bloomsbury, 2013), 10.
35. Anahid Kassabian, *Ubiquitous Listening: Affect, Attention, and Distributed Subjectivity* (Berkeley: University of California Press, 2013), 17–18.
36. Ruth Leys, *The Ascent of Affect: Genealogy and Critique* (Chicago: University of Chicago Press, 2017), 310.
37. Brian Massumi, *Parables for the Virtual: Movement, Affect, Sensation* (Durham, NC: Duke University Press, 2002).
38. Ben Anderson, *Encountering Affect: Capacities, Apparatuses, Conditions* (New York: Routledge, 2016), 85; Ben Highmore, "Taste as Feeling," *New Literary History* 47 (2016): 561, 547–66; Ben Highmore, *Cultural Feelings: Mood, Mediation and Cultural Politics* (New York: Routledge, 2017); Ben Highmore, "Bitter after Taste: Affect, Food, and Social Aesthetics," in *The Affect Theory Reader*, ed. Melissa Gregg and Gregory J. Seigworth (Durham, NC: Duke University Press, 2010), 118–37; Lawrence Grossberg, *We Gotta Get Out of This Place: Popular Conservatism and Postmodern Culture* (New York: Routledge, 1992), 79–87; Margaret Wetherell, *Affect and Emotion: A New Social Science Understanding* (Los Angeles: Sage, 2012).
39. Spitzer, *A History of Emotion in Western Music*, 337–39.
40. Wetherell, *Affect and Emotion*, 19.
41. Ibid., 12, 106. On habitus, Wetherell is quoting Pierre Bourdieu, *Distinction: A Social Critique of the Judgement of Taste*, trans. Richard Nice (Cambridge, MA: Harvard University Press, 1984), 474.
42. Jan Plamper, *The History of Emotions: An Introduction* (New York: Oxford University Press, 2015), 77. See Lila Abu-Lughod, *Veiled Sentiments: Honor and Poetry in a Bedouin Society* (Berkeley: University of California Press, 1986); Michelle Z. Rosaldo, *Knowledge and Passion: Ilongot Notions of Self and Social Life* (Cambridge: Cambridge University Press, 1980).

43. Herbert Spencer, "On the Origin and Function of Music," in *Essays on Education and Kindred Subjects* (New York: E. P. Dutton, 1911), https://www.gutenberg.org/cache/epub/16510/pg16510-images.html#page_310.
44. Ronald M. Radano and Philip V. Bohlman, *Music and the Racial Imagination* (Chicago: University of Chicago Press, 2000), 5.
45. Mark Tucker, *Duke Ellington: The Early Years* (Urbana: University of Illinois Press, 1991), 290n11; Christina D. Abreu, *Rhythms of Race: Cuban Musicians and the Making of Latino New York City and Miami, 1940–1960* (Chapel Hill: University of North Carolina Press, 2015), 20–55.
46. For example, see Pozo's treatment in Winthrop Sargeant, "Cuba's Tin Pan Alley," *Life*, October 6, 1947, 151. Sargeant describes the conguero as a "big, flashily dressed Negro."
47. Loren Kajikawa, "The Sound of Struggle: Black Revolutionary Nationalism and Asian American Jazz," in *Jazz/Not Jazz: The Music and Its Boundaries*, ed. David Ake, Charles Hiroshi Garrett, and Daniel Goldmark (Berkeley: University of California Press), 192.
48. Jon Panish, *The Color of Jazz: Race and Representation in Postwar American Culture* (Jackson: University Press of Mississippi, 1997), xvi.
49. Steve Garner, *Whiteness: An Introduction* (New York: Routledge, 2007), 6.
50. George Lipsitz, *The Possessive Investment in Whiteness: How White People Profit from Identity Politics* (1998; reprint, Philadelphia: Temple University Press, 2018), viii.
51. Klotz, *Dave Brubeck and the Performance of Whiteness*, 14, quoting Judith Butler, "Performative Acts and Gender Constitution: An Essay in Phenomenology and Feminist Theory," *Theatre Journal* 40 (December 1988): 523.
52. US Immigration Commission, *Dictionary of Races or Peoples*, S. Doc. No. 61-662 (Washington, DC: Government Printing Office, 1911; Detroit: Gale Research, 1969); Lary May, "Making the American Consensus: The Narrative of Conversion and Subversion in World War II Films," in *The War in American Culture: Society and Consciousness during World War II*, ed. Lewis Erenberg and Susan Hirsch (Chicago: University of Chicago Press, 1996), 71–102. In *The History of White People*, Nell Irvin Painter writes about the "enlargement of American whiteness," identifying four moments where the boundaries of whiteness were expanded to take in new, previously excluded peoples. Nell Irvin Painter, *The History of White People* (New York: W. W. Norton, 2010), 107.
53. Jennifer Lynn Stoever, *The Sonic Color Line: Race and the Cultural Politics of Listening* (New York: New York University Press, 2016); Klotz, *Dave Brubeck and the Performance of Whiteness*, 27.
54. Eric Lott, *Black Mirror: The Cultural Contradictions of American Racism* (Cambridge, MA: Harvard University Press, 2017), 7.
55. Matthew D. Morrison, "Race, Blacksound, and the (Re)Making of Musicological Discourse," *Journal of the American Musicological Society* 72, no. 3 (2019): 796.
56. Panish, *Color of Jazz*, x. On the "relative autonomy" of culture with respect to the economic base, see Raymond Williams, *Marxism and Literature* (New York: Oxford University Press, 1977), 83–89.

57. Ingrid Monson, *Freedom Sounds: Civil Rights Call Out to Jazz and Africa* (New York: Oxford University Press, 2007), 250.
58. Ibid., 249.
59. Radano and Bohlman, *Music and the Racial Imagination*, 5.
60. Judith Lochhead, Eduardo Mendieta, and Stephen Decatur Smith, eds., *Sound and Affect: Voice, Music, World* (Chicago: University of Chicago Press, 2021); Thompson and Biddle, *Sound, Music, Affect*.
61. Roger Mathew Grant, *Peculiar Attunements: How Affect Theory Turned Musical* (New York: Fordham University Press, 2020).
62. Lochhead, *Sound and Affect*, 22.
63. Anahid Kassabian, "Music for Sleeping," in Thompson and Biddle, *Sound, Music, Affect*, 179.
64. Kassabian, *Ubiquitous Listening*, xi.
65. Arnie Cox, *Music and Embodied Cognition: Listening, Moving, Feeling, and Thinking* (Bloomington: Indiana University Press, 2016), 176–99.
66. Mike Hobart, "Jazz: Love It or Hate It?," BBC, April 30, 2015, https://www.bbc.com/culture/article/20150430-jazz-do-you-love-it-or-hate-it.
67. Edward A. Berlin, *Ragtime: A Musical and Cultural History* (Berkeley: University of California Press, 1980), 43; on rap, see Jerry Adler, Jennifer Foote, and Ray Sawhill, "The Rap Attitude," *Newsweek*, March 19, 1990, 56–60.
68. Martin Williams, *Where's the Melody? A Listener's Introduction to Jazz* (New York: Pantheon Books, 1961); Jonny King, *What Jazz Is: An Insider's Guide to Understanding and Listening to Jazz* (New York: Walker, 1997).
69. Ronald Radano, *Lying Up a Nation: Race and Black Music* (Chicago: University of Chicago Press, 2003), 237.
70. Sara Ahmed, *The Cultural Politics of Emotion* (New York: Routledge, 2004), 11.
71. Ibid.
72. These are some of the key works: Richard Leppert, introduction and commentaries in Theodor W. Adorno, *Essays on Music*, ed. Leppert, trans. Susan H. Gillespie (Berkeley: University of California Press, 2002), 1–112, 213–50, 327–72, 513–63; Andrew Bowie, "Adorno and Jazz," in *A Companion to Adorno*, ed. Peter E. Gordon, Espen Hammer, and Max Pensky (Hoboken, NJ: Wiley Blackwell, 2020), 123–38; James Buhler, "Frankfurt School Blues: Rethinking Adorno's Critique of Jazz," in *Apparitions: New Perspectives on Adorno and Twentieth-Century Music*, ed. Berthold Hoeckner (New York: Routledge, 2006), 103–30; Fumi Okiji, *Jazz as Critique: Adorno and Black Expression Revisited* (Stanford, CA: Stanford University Press, 2018); Max Paddison, *Adorno's Aesthetics of Music* (Cambridge: Cambridge University Press, 1993); J. Bradford Robinson, "The Jazz Essays of Theodor Adorno: Some Thoughts on Jazz Reception in Weimar Germany," *Popular Music* 13, no. 1 (January 1994): 1–25; Robert W. Witkin, "Why Did Adorno 'Hate' Jazz?," *Sociological Theory* 18, no. 1 (March 2000): 145–70; Robert W. Witkin, *Adorno on Popular Culture* (New York: Routledge, 2003); and Robert W. Witkin, *Adorno on Music* (New York: Routledge, 1998).

73. These are Adorno's key writings on jazz: "On Jazz" (1936) and "Farewell to Jazz" (1933) in *Essays on Music*, 470–95, 496–500; "Perennial Fashion—Jazz" in *Prisms*, trans. Samuel Weber and Shierry Weber (1967; reprint, Cambridge, MA: MIT Press, 1981), 119–32; and parts of *Introduction to the Sociology of Music*, trans. E. B. Ashton (New York: Seabury Press, 1977).
74. Okiji, *Jazz as Critique*, 1–10.
75. Max Paddison, "The Critique Criticised: Adorno and Popular Music," *Popular Music* 2 (January 1982): 201–18. Also, Frederic Jameson, *Marxism and Form* (Princeton, NJ: Princeton University Press, 1971), 3–59.
76. Theodor Adorno, "Stravinsky and Reaction," in *Philosophy of New Music*, trans. Robert Hullot-Kentor (Minneapolis: University of Minnesota Press, 2006), 103–58.
77. Anna Parkinson, "Adorno on the Airwaves: Feeling Reason, Educating Emotions," *German Politics and Society* 32, no. 1 (110) (Spring 2014): 43–59; Espen Hammer, "Happiness and Pleasure in Adorno's Aesthetics," *Germanic Review: Literature, Culture, Theory* 90, no. 4 (2015): 247–59; Annika Thiem, "Adorno's Tears: Textures of Philosophical Emotionality," *MLN* 124, no. 3 (April 2009): 592–613.
78. Shannon L. Mariotti, *Adorno and Democracy: The American Years* (Lexington: University of Kentucky Press, 2016), 47, 56.
79. Theodor Adorno, *Negative Dialectics*, trans. E. B. Ashton (1966; New York: Continuum, 2007), 203.
80. Adorno, "Perennial Fashion," 129.
81. Mariotti, *Adorno and Democracy*, 62.
82. Theodor W. Adorno, "On Popular Music" (1941), in *Essays on Music*, ed. Richard Leppert, trans. Susan H. Gillespie (Berkeley: University of California Press, 2002), 467.
83. Ibid., 465.
84. Ibid.
85. Ibid., 463.
86. Paul Allen Anderson, "'My Foolish Heart': Bill Evans and the Public Life of Feeling," *Jazz Perspectives* 7, no. 3 (2013): 216.
87. Ibid., 206–7.
88. John Gennari, *Blowin' Hot and Cool: Jazz and Its Critics* (Chicago: University of Chicago Press, 2016), 199.
89. Nichole Rustin-Paschal, "'The Reason I Play the Way I Do Is': Jazzmen, Emotion, and Creating in Jazz," in *The Routledge Companion to Jazz Studies*, ed. Nicholas Gebhardt, Nichole Rustin-Paschal, and Tony Whyton (New York: Routledge, 2019), 401, 403.
90. Karlin, *Browning's Hatreds*, 7.
91. Kathy J. Ogren, *The Jazz Revolution: Twenties America and the Meaning of Jazz* (New York: Oxford University Press, 1989), 156–57.
92. Raymond Williams, *Marxism and Literature* (New York: Oxford University Press, 1977), 128–35.

93. Simon Frith, "What Is Bad Music?," in *Bad Music: The Music We Love to Hate*, ed. Christopher J. Washburne and Maiken Derno (New York: Routledge, 2004), 29.
94. Ogren, *Jazz Revolution*; David W. Stowe, *Swing Changes: Big-Band Jazz in New Deal America* (Cambridge, MA: Harvard University Press, 1994); Lewis A. Erenberg, *Swingin' the Dream: Big Band Jazz and the Rebirth of American Culture* (Chicago: University of Chicago Press, 1998); Lopes, *Rise of a Jazz Art World*; Scott Saul, *Freedom Is, Freedom Ain't: Jazz and the Making of the Sixties* (Cambridge, MA: Harvard University Press, 2009); Eric Porter, *What Is This Thing Called Jazz? African American Musicians as Artists, Critics, and Activists* (Berkeley: University of California Press, 2002); Gennari, *Blowin' Hot and Cool*; Tony Whyton, *Jazz Icons: Heroes, Myths and the Jazz Tradition* (Cambridge: Cambridge University Press, 2010).
95. Paul F. Berliner, *Thinking in Jazz: The Infinite Art of Improvisation* (Chicago: University of Chicago Press, 2009); Scott DeVeaux, *The Birth of Bebop: A Social and Musical History* (Berkeley: University of California Press, 1997); Ingrid Monson, *Saying Something: Jazz Improvisation and Interaction* (Chicago: University of Chicago Press, 2009); David Ake, *Jazz Cultures* (Berkeley: University of California Press, 2002).
96. Simon Frith, *Performing Rites: On the Value of Popular Music* (Cambridge, MA: Harvard University Press, 1996); Washburne and Derno, *Bad Music*; John J. Sheinbaum, *Good Music: What It Is and Who Gets to Decide* (Chicago: University of Chicago Press, 2018); Carl Wilson, *Let's Talk about Love: A Journey to the End of Taste* (New York: Continuum, 2007); John Howland, *Hearing Luxe Pop: Glorification, Glamour, and the Middlebrow in American Popular Music* (Berkeley: University of California Press, 2021), 1–8.
97. The reception of, and panic over, rock 'n' roll has been covered extensively. A good survey is in Glenn C. Altschuler, *All Shook Up: How Rock 'n' Roll Changed America* (New York: Oxford University Press, 2003). For an excellent summary of the attacks on rap and hip-hop, see Tricia Rose, *The Hip Hop Wars: What We Talk about When We Talk about Hip Hop—and Why It Matters* (New York: Basic Books, 2008). For an account of the specifically musical attacks on hip-hop, see Robert Walser, "Rhythm, Rhyme, and Rhetoric in the Music of Public Enemy," *Ethnomusicology* 39 (1995): 193–217.
98. Nadine Hubbs, *Rednecks, Queers, and Country Music* (Berkeley: University of California Press, 2014), 3.
99. Buddy Rich, interview by Mike Douglas, *The Mike Douglas Show*, 1971, video, 17:49, https://youtu.be/g67-LyG6JBY?si=3BD-CyRMCTsqubZ0. Rich's remarks on country music begin at 9:50.
100. On the multiple cultures of jazz, see Ake, *Jazz Cultures*, 1–9.
101. Michael H. Kater, *Different Drummers: Jazz in the Culture of Nazi Germany* (New York: Oxford University Press, 2003), 117.

CHAPTER TWO

1. Johnson's phrase comes from his definition of *passion* in the 1755 edition of his *Dictionary of the English Language*. The entire dictionary, in all its published variants, is available at https://johnsonsdictionaryonline.com/index.php.
2. Daniel Karlin, *Browning's Hatreds* (New York: Oxford University Press, 1993), 5.
3. Raymond Williams, *Keywords: A Vocabulary of Culture and Society* (New York: Oxford University Press, 1983), 313.
4. M. de Voltaire [François-Marie Arouet], Charles-Louis de Secondat, baron de La Brède et de Montesquieu, and Jean-Baptiste le Rond d'Alembert, "Taste," *The Encyclopedia: Selections: Diderot, d'Alembert and a Society of Men of Letters*, trans. Nelly S. Hoyt and Thomas Cassirer (Indianapolis: Bobbs-Merrill, 1965), http://hdl.handle.net/2027/spo.did2222.0000.168. First published as "Goût," *Encyclopédie ou Dictionnaire raisonné des sciences, des arts et des métiers*, 7:761–70 (Paris, 1757).
5. Williams, *Keywords*, 314.
6. Stephen Bayley, *Taste: The Secret Meaning of Things* (New York: Pantheon Books, 1991), xv.
7. Williams, *Keywords*, 315 (emphasis in original).
8. Luca Vercelloni, *The Invention of Taste: A Cultural Account of Desire, Delight and Disgust in Fashion, Food and Art*, trans. Kate Singleton (New York: Bloomsbury, 2016), 24–25.
9. Theodor W. Adorno, "On Popular Music" (1941), in *Essays on Music*, ed. Richard Leppert, trans. Susan H. Gillespie (Berkeley: University of California Press, 2002), 465.
10. For an important collection with examples by these writers and many others, see Bernard Rosenberg and David Manning White, eds., *Mass Culture: The Popular Arts in America* (New York: Free Press, 1957).
11. Herbert J. Gans, *Popular Culture and High Culture: An Analysis and Evaluation of Taste* (New York: Basic Books, 1974); Lawrence W. Levine, *Highbrow/Lowbrow: The Emergence of Cultural Hierarchy in America* (Cambridge, MA: Harvard University Press, 1988).
12. Pierre Bourdieu, *Distinction: A Social Critique of the Judgement of Taste*, trans. Richard Nice (Cambridge, MA: Harvard University Press, 1984), 466.
13. David Wright, *Understanding Cultural Taste: Sensation, Skill and Sensibility* (London: Palgrave Macmillan, 2015), 56. A good entry to Peterson's work is Richard A. Peterson and A. Simkus, "How Musical Tastes Mark Occupational Status Groups," in *Cultivating Differences*, ed. Michèle Lamont and Marcel Fournier (Chicago: University of Chicago Press, 1992), 152–86. Despite the criticism, Bourdieu's ideas remain influential and productive. See Keir Keightley's insightful genealogy of the jazz and pop "standard," a process driven not by the inherent quality of the music but by the elevation of generational mass-cultural preference. A similar dynamic happened with the baby boomer generation's elevation of its own music, rock of the 1960s and '70s. Keir Keightley, "You Keep Coming Back like a Song:

Adult Audiences, Taste Panics, and the Idea of the Standard," *Journal of Popular Music Studies* 13 (2001): 7–40.

14. Antoine Hennion, *The Passion for Music: A Sociology of Mediation*, trans. Margaret Rigaud and Peter Collier (New York: Routledge, 2020), 267–68.
15. Stephen Bayley, *Taste: The Secret Meaning of Things* (New York: Pantheon Books, 1991), xv.
16. Patrice Petro, "Mass Culture and the Feminine: The 'Place' of Television in Film Studies," *Cinema Journal* 25, no. 3 (Spring 1986): 5–21. Also, Andreas Huyssen, "Mass Culture as Woman," in *After the Great Divide: Modernism, Mass Culture, Postmodernism* (Bloomington: Indiana University Press, 1986), 44–62.
17. Simon Gikandi, *Slavery and the Culture of Taste* (Princeton, NJ: Princeton University Press, 2011), 16–21.
18. Ben Highmore, "Taste as Feeling," *New Literary History* 47 (2016): 547–48, 561.
19. Ibid., 557.
20. Melissa Gregg and Gregory J. Seigworth, *The Affect Theory Reader* (Durham, NC: Duke University Press, 2010), 1.
21. On taste and race, see Gikandi, *Slavery and the Culture of Taste*; on race and affect, see Ulla D. Berg and Ana Y. Ramos-Zaya, "Racializing Affect: A Theoretical Proposition," *Current Anthropology* 56, no. 5 (October 2018): 662.
22. Charles Hersch, *Subversive Sounds: Race and the Birth of Jazz in New Orleans* (Chicago: University of Chicago Press, 2007), 77.
23. Ibid., 59, 61, 72.
24. Following musicologist Kai West, I have chosen not to reproduce the racial slur Mendl uses and have indicated the change with asterisks and brackets. Although it is important to preserve the historical record, in this case I feel it is wrong to reprint such a damaging word. Kai West, "Buckra: Whiteness and *Porgy and Bess*," *Journal of the American Musicological Society* 75, no. 2 (2022): 319–77.
25. R. W. S. Mendl, *The Appeal of Jazz* (London: Philip Allan, 1927), 71–73.
26. Gikandi, *Slavery and the Culture of Taste*, 7, 25, 37–38.
27. John Gennari, *Blowin' Hot and Cool: Jazz and Its Critics* (Chicago: University of Chicago Press, 2016), 6.
28. Amiri Baraka (LeRoi Jones), "Jazz and the White Critic," in *The Jazz Cadence of American Culture*, ed. Robert G. O'Meally (New York: Columbia University Press, 1998), 137, 139 (emphasis in original).
29. Ibid., 142.
30. Gennari, *Blowin' Hot and Cool*, 66. And, as Krin Gabbard astutely notes, that aestheticization of black expressive culture by critics and record-collecting fans was an act of repression, one that sublimated an erotic fascination with black men. Krin Gabbard, *Black Magic: White Hollywood and African American Culture* (New Brunswick, NJ: Rutgers University Press, 2004), 212.
31. Wadada Leo Smith, "Creative Music and the AACM," in *Keeping Time: Readings in Jazz History*, ed. Robert Walser (New York: Oxford University Press, 1999), 318.

32. As George Lewis notes, Smith's aesthetic was far more expansive and mobile than those articulated by the leading figures of the Black Arts Music such as Amiri Baraka. George E. Lewis, *A Power Stronger Than Itself: The AACM and American Experimental Music* (Chicago: University of Chicago Press, 2008), 241–43.
33. Ibid., 210.
34. bell hooks, *Yearning: Race, Gender, and Cultural Politics* (Boston: South End Press, 1990), 110.
35. Katherine McKittrick, *Dear Science and Other Stories* (Durham, NC: Duke University Press, 2021), 50–51.
36. Gennari, *Blowin' Hot and Cool*, 8.
37. Reva Marin, *Outside and Inside: Race and Identity in White Jazz Autobiography* (Jackson: University of Mississippi Press, 2020). For a more detailed study of ethnic identity, race, and whiteness, see Charles Hersch, *Jews and Jazz: Improvising Ethnicity* (New York: Routledge, 2017); and John Gennari, *Flavor and Soul: Italian America at Its African American Edge* (Chicago: University of Chicago Press, 2017).
38. Christopher Coady, *John Lewis and the Challenge of "Real" Black Music* (Ann Arbor: University of Michigan Press, 2016), 1–23.
39. Albert Goldman, *Freakshow: The Rocksoulbluesjazzsickjewblackhumorsexpoppsych Gig and Other Scenes from the Counter-Culture* (New York: Atheneum, 1971), quoted in *Reading Jazz*, ed. David Meltzer (San Francisco: Mercury House, 1993), 267 (emphasis in *Reading Jazz*).
40. Creamysaxsolo, "To all the Jazz-Haters on Reddit, what is it that you dislike about Jazz?," accessed April 28, 2022, https://www.reddit.com/r/AskReddit/comments/14ekxh/to_all_the_jazzhaters_on_reddit_what_is_it_that/.
41. J. Bradford Robinson makes a compelling case for this argument, at least for the earlier essays. By the 1950s, however, it is harder to believe that "Adorno's ideas on jazz, however tempered by his experiences abroad, never entirely left the Weimar Republic and can only be understood in that context." J. Bradford Robinson, "The Jazz Essays of Theodor Adorno: Some Thoughts on Jazz Reception in Weimar Germany," *Popular Music* 13, no. 1 (January 1994): 3–4.
42. Tony Whyton, *Jazz Icons: Heroes, Myths and the Jazz Tradition* (Cambridge: Cambridge University Press, 2010), 80.
43. Simon Frith, "What Is Bad Music?," in *Bad Music: The Music We Love to Hate*, ed. Christopher J. Washburne and Maiken Derno (New York: Routledge, 2004), 19. Also, Robert Walser, "Review of *Bad Music: The Music We Love to Hate*, ed. Christopher J. Washburne and Maiken Derno," *Journal of the Society for American Music* 1, no. 4 (November 2007): 511–16.
44. Keightley, "You Keep Coming Back like a Song," 31.
45. Frith, "What Is Bad Music?," 15–36.
46. Ibid., 20–23.
47. Rudi Blesh, *Shining Trumpets: A History of Jazz* (New York: Alfred A. Knopf, 1946), 6.

48. B. S. Rogers, "Swing Is from the Heart," *Esquire*, April 1939, 43, 115, 118, 120.
49. Hugues Panassié, *The Real Jazz*, trans. Anne Sorell Williams (New York: Smith and Durrell, 1942), 46.
50. Frith, "What Is Bad Music?," 23–27; Anne Shaw Faulkner, "Does Jazz Put the Sin in Syncopation?," *Ladies Home Journal*, August 1921.
51. E. Elliott Rawlings, "Keeping Fit," *New York Amsterdam News*, April 1, 1925, 16.
52. Lewis A. Erenberg, *Swingin' the Dream: Big Band Jazz and the Rebirth of American Culture* (Chicago: University of Chicago Press, 1998), 37.
53. Record Labeling, Hearing before the U.S. Senate Committee on Commerce, Science, and Transportation, 99th Cong., 1st Sess. 13–17 (1985), quoted in *The Rock History Reader*, ed. Theo Cateforis, 3rd ed. (New York: Routledge, 2019), 243–50. For more on the PMRC, see Robert Walser, *Running with the Devil: Power, Gender, and Madness in Heavy Metal Music* (Hanover, NH: Wesleyan University Press, 1993), 137–51. For general reception of heavy metal, see Deena Weinstein, *Heavy Metal: Music and Its Culture* (New York: Da Capo Press, 2000), 237–75.
54. Tricia Rose, *The Hip Hop Wars: What We Talk about When We Talk about Hip Hop—and Why It Matters* (New York: Basic Books, 2008), 33–60.
55. Frith, "What Is Bad Music?," 27–28.
56. Neil Leonard, *Jazz and the White Americans* (Chicago: University of Chicago Press, 1962), 32.
57. J. W. Studebaker, "The Age of Jazz," *Journal of Education* 109, no. 3 (January 21, 1929): 68, reprinted in *Jazz in Print (1856–1929)*, ed. Karl Koenig (Hillsdale, NY: Pendragon Press, 2002), 550.
58. "Whiteman Senior, Long Foe of Jazz," *New York Times*, August 7, 1938, D5.
59. Max Scheler, *On Feeling, Knowing, and Valuing: Selected Writings*, ed. Harold J. Bershady (Chicago: University of Chicago Press, 1992), 117.
60. Ibid., 132.
61. Ibid., 137.
62. Justin Wm. Moyer, "All That Jazz Isn't All That Great," *Washington Post*, August 8, 2014, https://www.washingtonpost.com/news/opinions/wp/2014/08/08/all-that-jazz-isnt-all-that-great/.
63. Joseph V. Rubba, "Much Ado about Swinging," *Metronome* 52, no. 8 (August 1936): 9–10.
64. On the gender, race, and political implications of swing dancing, see Sherrie Tucker, *Dance Floor Democracy: The Social Geography of Memory at the Hollywood Canteen* (Durham, NC: Duke University Press, 2014); Christie Jay Wells, *Between the Beats: The Jazz Tradition and Black Vernacular Dance* (New York: Oxford University Press, 2021).
65. Gennari, *Blowin' Hot and Cool*, 87–88. Interpreting mass culture as feminine is a trope of much late nineteenth- and early twentieth-century writing on the intersection of popular art and modern capitalism. A classic survey of this association is Huyssen, "Mass Culture as Woman," 44–62.

66. Blesh, *Shining Trumpets*, 134. To be fair, Blesh makes this statement as a contrast to the great blues singers of the 1920s: "The blues of the classic period—despite the fine male singers—are pre-eminently the music of Negro women as jazz is the lusty music of Negro men. The one seems to embody healing, maternal sympathy, which gestates and conserves life; the other externalizes the vitality and power of male procreativeness."
67. Sherrie Tucker, *Swing Shift: "All-Girl" Bands of the 1940s* (Durham, NC: Duke University Press, 2000).
68. David Bindas, *Swing, That Modern Sound* (Jackson: University of Mississippi Press, 2001); Joel Dinerstein, *Swinging the Machine: Modernity, Technology, and African American Culture between the World Wars* (Amherst: University of Massachusetts Press, 2003); David W. Stowe, *Swing Changes: Big-Band Jazz in New Deal America* (Cambridge, MA: Harvard University Press, 1994); Erenberg, *Swingin' the Dream*; Andrew Berish, *Lonesome Roads and Streets of Dreams: Place, Mobility, and Race in Jazz of the 1930s and '40s* (Chicago: University of Chicago Press, 2012).
69. Erenberg, *Swingin' the Dream*, 36.
70. William Graebner, *The Age of Doubt: American Thought and Culture in the 1940s* (Boston: Twayne Publishing, 1991), 3.
71. Henry Luce, "The American Century," *Time*, February 17, 1941, 61–65.
72. Stowe, *Swing Changes*, 24.
73. Ibid., 30.
74. Harry Emerson Fosdick, *On Being a Real Person* (New York: Harper, 1943), 111.
75. Russ Morgan, "Why I Hate Swing," *Swing: The Guide to Modern Music* 1, no. 6 (October 1938): 14.
76. Paul Eduard Miller, "Judging and Appreciating Hot Music," *Music and Rhythm*, November 1940, 78–81.
77. Gama Gilbert, "Swing It! And Even in a Temple of Music: Hottest of Rhythms Vibrates in a Sanctum," *New York Times Magazine*, January 16, 1938, 7, 21.
78. Ibid., 7.
79. Ibid., 21.
80. Ingrid Monson, *Freedom Sounds: Civil Rights Call Out to Jazz and Africa* (New York: Oxford University Press, 2007), 94. For a more extensive analysis of Brubeck and whiteness in the 1950s, see Kelsey Klotz, *Dave Brubeck and the Performance of Whiteness* (New York: Oxford University Press, 2022), 73–118.
81. Marc Myers, *Why Jazz Happened* (Berkeley: University of California Press, 2013), 94.
82. For a broad history of the style, see Ted Gioia, *West Coast Jazz: Modern Jazz in California, 1945–1960* (Berkeley: University of California Press, 1992). On the era's color-blind aesthetic, see Monson, *Freedom Sounds*, 79.
83. Klotz, *Dave Brubeck and the Performance of Whiteness*, 97.
84. Georg Marek, "From the Dive to the Dean, Jazz Becomes Respectable," *Good Housekeeping*, June 1956, 120.

85. Tom Perchard, "Mid-century Modern Jazz: Music and Design in the Postwar Home," in "The Critical Imperative," special issue, *Popular Music* 36, no. 1 (2017): 55–74.
86. Lary May, *The Big Tomorrow: Hollywood and the Politics of the American Way* (Chicago: University of Chicago Press, 2000); Alan Nadel, *Containment Culture: American Narratives, Postmodernism, and the Atomic Age* (Durham, NC: Duke University Press, 1995); Robert Kolker, *Triumph over Containment: American Film in the 1950s* (New Brunswick, NJ: Rutgers University Press, 2021).
87. The analysis and examples here are indebted to conversations with Daniel Belgrad.
88. An excellent analysis of middlebrow culture in the 1950s is in Daniel Belgrad, "The Rockwell Syndrome," *Art in America* 88, no. 4 (April 2000): 61–63, 65–67.
89. John Howland, "Jazz with Strings: Between Jazz and the Great American Songbook," in *Jazz/Not Jazz: The Music and Its Boundaries*, ed. David Ake, Charles Hiroshi Garrett, and Daniel Goldmark (Berkeley: University of California Press), 197–99.
90. Elizabeth Fraterrigo, *"Playboy" and the Making of the Good Life in Modern America* (New York: Oxford University Press, 2009), 65–67.
91. David Rosenthal, *Hard Bop: Jazz and Black Music, 1955–1965* (New York: Oxford University Press, 1992), 62–84.
92. Kay Crisfield Grey, "The Lady Hated Jazz," *Saturday Evening Post*, December 24, 1955, 18, 50–51.
93. Scott DeVeaux, *The Birth of Bebop: A Social and Musical History* (Berkeley: University of California Press, 1997), 398. On drugs in the jazz world, especially among beboppers, see Rosenthal, *Hard Bop*, 16–17. Two classic sociological accounts are in Alan Merriam and Raymond Mack, "The Jazz Community," *Social Forces* 38 (1960): 211–22; and Howard S. Becker, *Outsiders: Studies in the Sociology of Deviance* (New York: Free Press, 1982).
94. Glenn C. Altschuler, *All Shook Up: How Rock 'n' Roll Changed America* (New York: Oxford University Press, 2003).
95. Keir Keightley, "You Keep Coming Back like a Song: Adult Audiences, Taste Panics, and the Idea of the Standard," *Journal of Popular Music Studies* 13 (2001): 7–40.
96. Kevin Whitehead, *Play the Way You Feel: The Essential Guide to Jazz Stories on Film* (New York: Oxford University Press, 2020), 151.
97. The association with drug use, particularly heroin, was not just fantasy. Scores of important bop and postbop 1950s jazz musicians, both black and white, battled addiction: Chet Baker, John Coltrane, Miles Davis, Billie Holiday, Stan Getz, Fats Navarro, and Charlie Parker, to name some of the most famous.
98. Mervyn Cooke notes that even with the rise of jazz-oriented scores in the 1950s and '60s, the genre was still strongly associated with sexual license and the seedier aspects of modern urban life. Jazz was caught between two essentialized

and racialized representations: a '20s- and '30s-era belief in jazz as the sound of modern America and the long-standing association of jazz with brothels and squalid nightclubs. Mervyn Cooke, *A History of Film Music* (New York: Cambridge University Press, 2012), 621–39. For extended analyses of the continuing tensions and contradictions in the relationship between jazz and film sound and scoring, see Nicolas Pillai, *Jazz as a Visual Language* (London: I. B. Tauris, 2017); Gretchen L. Carlson, *Improvising the Score: Rethinking Modern Film Music through Jazz* (Jackson: University of Mississippi Press, 2022).

99. Daniel Perlstein, "Imagined Authority: *Blackboard Jungle* and the Project of Educational Liberalism," *Paedogogica Historica* 36, no. 1 (2000): 407–24; for the specific role of sound in the film's liberal racialism, see Jennifer Stoever-Ackerman, "Reproducing U.S. Citizenship in *Blackboard Jungle*: Race, Cold War Liberalism, and the Tape Recorder," *American Quarterly* 63, no. 3 (2011): 781–806.

CHAPTER THREE

1. Brian McCulloch, "Jazz Schmazz," *The Kids in the Hall*, excerpt from episode 14, season 2, aired March 19, 1991, on CBC, https://youtu.be/WB6Ix1sw0iI?si=6jQpk23NBQG9zfdc.
2. David Denby, *Snark: A Polemic in Seven Fits* (New York: Simon & Schuster, 2009).
3. Here are a few: John Thompson, "Jazz Club: Donald Strong," *The Fast Show* (BBC), video, 1:19, https://youtu.be/8063h3KT6bY?si=A23h9NViDT0zTkzg; Julian Barratt and Noel Fielding, "Jazz Trance," *The Mighty Boosh* (BBC), video, 2:03, https://youtu.be/bKwQ_zeRwEs?si=uADiuPgHGpbYbhYy; Ricky Gervais and Eric Bana, "Oh God, Jazz," excerpt from the film *Special Correspondents* (2016), video, 0:32, https://youtu.be/fjRgpqhkRmw?si=jiDS6xRsC_zOJQnT; Kitty Flanagan, "Thoughts on Jazz Music," excerpt from the stage show *Seriously?* (DVD, 2017), video, 0:43, https://youtu.be/A8auId3Ocjw?si=EPBPix0bIXB2mxsb.
4. A. D. Amorosi, "Matt Groening on His Love of Jazz, How It Found Its Way into the 'Simpsons' and Curating a New Jazz Video Playlist for Qwest TV," *Variety*, October 26, 2014, https://variety.com/2021/music/news/matt-groening-jazz-playlist-qwest-tv-simpsons-interview-curated-jazz-video-playlist-drops-on-qwest-tv-1235098215/.
5. Michael Billig, *Laughter and Ridicule: Towards a Social Critique of Humour* (London: Sage, 2005), 16–19.
6. Simon Critchley, *On Humor* (New York: Routledge, 2002), 87.
7. Eric Lott, *Black Mirror: The Cultural Contradictions of American Racism* (Cambridge, MA: Belknap Press of Harvard University Press, 2017), xvii.
8. Joel Dinerstein, *The Origins of Cool in Postwar America* (Chicago: University of Chicago Press, 2017), 22–23.

9. Jon Panish, *The Color of Jazz: Race and Representation in Postwar American Culture* (Jackson: University Press of Mississippi, 1997), xi.
10. On the nature of African American humor, see Paul Beatty, *Hokum: An Anthology of African-American Humor* (New York: Bloomsbury, 2006); Dexter B. Gordon, "Humor in African American Discourse: Speaking of Oppression," *Journal of Black Studies* 29, no. 2 (November 1998): 254–76; Mel Watkins, *On the Real Side: Laughing, Lying, and Signifying—The Underground Tradition of African-American Humor That Transformed American Culture, from Slavery to Richard Pryor* (New York: Simon & Schuster, 1994).
11. Rod A. Martin, *The Psychology of Humor: An Integrative Approach* (San Diego: Elsevier, 2007), 8. For Hobbes on "sudden glory," see Thomas Hobbes, *Leviathan*, ed. J. C. A. Gaskin (New York: Oxford University Press, 1998), 38.
12. Martin, *The Psychology of Humor*, 8.
13. Annett Schirmer, *Emotion* (Thousand Oaks, CA: Sage, 2015), 72.
14. Sigmund Freud, *Jokes and Their Relation to the Unconscious*, trans. and ed. James Strachey (New York: W. W. Norton, 1989); Henri Bergson, *Laughter: An Essay on the Meaning of the Comic*, trans. Cloudesley Brererton and Fred Rothwell (1911), https://www.gutenberg.org/files/4352/4352-h/4352-h.htm. Freud divides up his discussion into jokes, the comic, and humor and treats each differently, particularly the joke, which has a specific structure and audience; its pleasure comes from a "compromise between the unconscious and the preconscious." Although I try to adhere to Freud's distinctions, his insights about humor and affect apply across types.
15. Freud, *Jokes*, 273–74.
16. Ibid., 284.
17. Bergson, *Laughter*.
18. Ibid. (emphasis in original).
19. Michael Billig, *Laughter and Ridicule: Towards a Social Critique of Humour* (New York: Sage, 2005), 202.
20. Bergson, *Laughter*.
21. Marie Thompson and Ian Biddle, introduction to *Sound, Music, Affect: Theorizing Sonic Experience*, ed. Thompson and Biddle (London: Bloomsbury, 2013), 10.
22. Jason Gubbels, "Jazz Needs a Better Sense of Humor," *Deadspin*, September 11, 2014, https://deadspin.com/jazz-needs-a-better-sense-of-humor-1632954724.
23. Charles Hiroshi Garrett, "The Humor of Jazz," in *Jazz/Not Jazz: The Music and Its Boundaries*, ed. David Ake, Charles Hiroshi Garrett, and Daniel Goldmark (Berkeley: University of California Press, 2012), 53.
24. Daniel Goldmark, *Tunes for 'Toons: Music and the Hollywood Cartoon* (Berkeley: University of California Press, 2005), 77–106.
25. "Louis Armstrong and Comedy, Part 2: 'Always a Showman!' 1922–1933," That's My Home: Louis Armstrong House Museum Virtual Exhibits, https://virtualexhibits.louisarmstronghouse.org/2020/10/20/louis-armstrong-and-comedy-part-2-always-a-showman-1922-1933.

26. Garrett, "The Humor of Jazz."
27. Ibid., 50.
28. On the changing places of jazz performance, see Kimberly Hannon Teal, *Jazz Places: How Performance Spaces Shape Jazz History* (Berkeley: University of California Press, 2021). On the neoliberal economics of jazz in the late twentieth and early twenty-first century, see Dale Chapman, *The Jazz Bubble: Neoclassical Jazz in Neoliberal Culture* (Berkeley: University of California Press, 2018).
29. "My Conversation with Horace Silver," All about Jazz, December 18, 2003, https://www.allaboutjazz.com/my-conversation-with-horace-silver-horace-silver-by-aaj-staff.
30. Jon Benjamin, Jazz Daredevil, *Well, I Should Have . . . * (*Learned to Play Piano)*, Sub Pop SP1151 (2015), 33⅓ rpm.
31. Jon Benjamin, Jazz Daredevil, *Well I Should Have . . . *Learned How to Play Piano*, video, 4:05, https://youtu.be/JuKJkghC2u0.
32. H. Jon Benjamin, *Failure Is an Option: An Attempted Memoir* (New York: Dutton, 2018).
33. H. Jon Benjamin, "'Failure Is an Option' Urges People to Let Go of the Constant Grind towards Success," interview by Mary Louise Kelly, *All Things Considered*, NPR, May 2, 2018, https://www.npr.org/2018/05/02/607817990/failure-is-an-option-urges-people-to-let-go-of-the-constant-grind-towards-success.
34. Ernest J. Hopkins, "In Praise of 'Jazz,' A Futurist Word Which Has Just Joined the Language," *San Francisco Bulletin*, April 5, 1913, in *Jazz: A Century of Change*, ed. Lewis Porter (New York: Schirmer Books, 1997), 6 (emphasis in original).
35. Ibid., 7–8. Variant spellings of *jazz* appear in the article.
36. See Alan P. Merriam and Fradley H. Garner, "Jazz—The Word," *Ethnomusicology* 12, no. 3 (1968): 373–96. This is still one of the best accounts of the many stories concerning the origins of the word *jazz*.
37. Walter Kingsley, "Whence Comes Jass? Facts from the Great Authority on the Subject," *New York Sun*, August 5, 1917, 3, reprinted in *Keeping Time: Readings in Jazz History*, ed. Robert Walser (New York: Oxford University Press, 1999), 6.
38. Leonard Feather, *The Book of Jazz* (New York: Horizon Press, 1957), 13.
39. Geoffrey C. Ward and Ken Burns, *Jazz: A History of America's Music* (New York: Alfred A. Knopf, 2000), xxi.
40. Donald Barthelme, "The King of Jazz," *New Yorker*, February 7, 1977, 31–32, in *Great Days* (New York: Farrar, Straus, Giroux, 1979), 55–60. All subsequent page references are to the *Great Days* edition.
41. Ibid., 59.
42. Ibid., 60.
43. Ibid., 57.
44. In "Jazz: A Few Definitions," published in 2017 in the *New Yorker*'s *Shouts and Murmurs* blog, author Riane Konc updates Barthelme's conceit. "What is jazz?" Konc begins. "No single definition can suffice. Jazz is all around us." After an

increasingly absurd list, Konc concludes: "Jazz is when you're tutoring a young musician and you give him a very large textbook called 'Jazz Information' and tell him, 'Everything you need to know about jazz is inside this book,' and he opens the book, and guess what's inside? A mirror." Riane Konc, "Jazz: A Few Definitions," Daily Shouts, *Shouts and Murmurs* (blog), *New Yorker*, March 2, 2017, https://www.newyorker.com/humor/daily-shouts/jazz-a-few-definitions.

45. Michael Billig, "Comic Racism and Violence," in *Beyond a Joke: The Limits of Humour*, ed. Sharon Lockyer and Michael Pickering (New York: Palgrave Macmillan, 2005), 33.

46. Ibid.

47. Garrett, "The Humor of Jazz."

48. Thomas Cunniffe, "Jazz and Standup Comedy," Jazz History Online, March 5, 2019, https://jazzhistoryonline.com/jazz-and-standup-comedy/.

49. George Crater [Ed Sherman], *Out of My Head*, Riverside RLP 841 (1960), 33⅓ rpm. For information on Sherman and his Crater persona, see John Corbett, *Vinyl Freak: Love Letters to a Dying Medium* (Durham, NC: Duke University Press, 2017), 28; Marc Myers, "Carly, Bruce and Barbara," *JazzWax* (blog), January 7, 2023, https://www.jazzwax.com/2023/01/carly-bruce-and-barbara.html; *Out of My Head* (blog), https://finster.wordpress.com/about/. On Crater's radio show, see Bob Rolontz, "George Crater—a Funny Cat," *Billboard*, December 18, 1961, 34.

50. Crater, "The Encyclopedic Critics," *Out of My Head*, available at https://www.youtube.com/watch?v=wE0au5MVHDE.

51. Hans Groiner [Larry Goldings], *The Music of Thelonious Monk, Part 1*, video, 4:00, https://www.youtube.com/watch?v=51bsCRv6kI0. See also Allen Morrison, "An Exclusive Interview with Hans Groiner: The Noted Austrian Musicologist and Monk Expert Grants *JazzTimes* an Audience," *JazzTimes*, June 10, 2021, https://jazztimes.com/features/interviews/an-exclusive-interview-with-hans-groiner/; Matt Phillips, "Hans Groiner: Does Humour Belong in Jazz?," Sounds of Surprise, November 6, 2011, https://soundsofsurprise.com/2015/11/06/hans-groiner-jazzs-last-taboo/. Larry Goldings also posts on X as Groiner, @HansGroiner.

52. Freud, *Jokes*, 175, 176–77, 163.

53. Simon Frith, "What Is Bad Music?," in *Bad Music: The Music We Love to Hate*, ed. Christopher J. Washburne and Maiken Derno (New York: Routledge, 2004), 29.

54. Paul F. Tompkins, "Jazz," *Impersonal*, Aspecialthing Records AST004 (2007), compact disc; all emphasis is in the original.

55. Billig, drawing on Bergson, analyzes the central role humiliation and embarrassment play in humor. These negative feelings have an important disciplinary function that enforces social norms. Children learn "how to laugh at those who behave inappropriately, for polite adults must be able to discipline the socially deviant with momentary heartless mockery." Billig, *Laughter and Ridicule*, 230. The cruelty of the mocker toward the mocked, however, is often covered over by the laughter experienced by onlookers.

56. Gillian Frank, "Discophobia: Antigay Prejudice and the 1979 Backlash against Disco," *Journal of the History of Sexuality* 16, no. 2 (May 2007): 288. Tim Lawrence extensively documents the roots of disco in Black and gay nightclubs. Tim Lawrence, *Love Saves the Day: A History of American Dance Music Culture, 1970–1979* (Durham, NC: Duke University Press, 2003).
57. Frank, "Discophobia," 293.
58. Ibid., 278.
59. Nishat Kurwa, "Behind the Rise of Xtranormal, A Hilarious DIY Deadpan," *Morning Edition*, NPR, January 5, 2011, https://www.npr.org/2011/01/05/132653525/behind-rise-of-xtranormal-a-hilarious-diy-deadpan.
60. Bergson, *Laughter*.
61. Joe Hundertmark, *Jazz Robots*, video, 1:48, October 27, 2010, https://www.youtube.com/watch?v=c1fWJKaUZ_4.
62. Margret Grebowicz, "The Internet and the Death of Jazz: Race, Improvisation, and the Crisis of Community," in *21st Century Perspectives on Music, Technology, and Culture: Listening Spaces*, ed. Richard Purcell and Richard Randall (London: Palgrave Macmillan, 2016), 74.
63. Nate Chinen, "Behold the Jazzbro," The Gig, *JazzTimes* 43, no. 6 (August 2013): 10.
64. In 2022, the most recent year for which data is available, 279 degrees in jazz or jazz studies were awarded to students who self-identified as white, 64 degrees to Hispanic or Latino students, and 46 to Black or African American students. "Jazz and Jazz Studies," Data USA, accessed August 13, 2024, https://datausa.io/profile/cip/jazz-jazz-studies#degree_obtainment (using data compiled by the Integrated Postsecondary Education System). In his essay, Chinen acknowledges that the jazzbro is mostly white, though not exclusively so. "Lest this begin to seem like a strictly white phenomenon, I'll point you toward Jonah Jones, the swing-era trumpeter whose errant spitball caused the rift between Cab Calloway and Dizzy Gillespie; trumpeter Lee Morgan, at least in the *Tom Cat* era; and bassist Stanley Clarke, whose defining solo album, *School Days*, literally shows him spray-painting musical graffiti on a subway wall." Chinen, "Behold the Jazzbro," 10.
65. Barbara Savage, *Broadcasting Freedom: Radio, War, and the Politics of Race, 1938–1948* (Chapel Hill: University of North Carolina Press, 1999), 7. On racial mimicry, see Jayne Brown, *Babylon Girls: Black Women Performers and the Shaping of the Modern* (Durham, NC: Duke University Press, 2008), 3.
66. Bergson is quoting René-François Sully Prudhomme's poem "Un bonhomme" (1866). Bergson, *Laughter*.
67. Bergson, *Laughter*.
68. George Colligan, "Jazz Is the Worst: LMAO," *Jazz Truth* (blog), December 25, 2014, http://jazztruth.blogspot.com/2014/12/jazz-is-worst-lmao.html.
69. See Alex Marianyi, "Who Is @JazzIsTheWorst?," Nextbop, July 26, 2013, https://nextbop.com/blog/whoisjazzistheworst.

70. "How to Become a Successful Jazz Musician in 2015," *Jazz Is the Worst... Reviews* (blog), December 21, 2014, https://jazzistheworst.blogspot.com/2014/12/.

71. Jazz Is the Worst (@JazzIsTheWorst), "Jazz Fact #65: There are more instructional books on 'How to Play Jazz' than there are people who can actually play Jazz," Twitter, October 13, 2015, https://x.com/JazzIsTheWorst/status/653950995878309889; "If Jazz had sex with *American Idol* their child would look like #JazzAtTheWhiteHouse," Twitter, April 30, 2016, https://x.com/JazzIsTheWorst/status/726572751314624512; "Jazz News: 'New jazz club set record by opening and subsequently going out of business within 30 minutes,'" Twitter, August 3, 2015, https://x.com/JazzIsTheWorst/status/628294139659034625; "Free Jazz: For when you're just too lazy to read a leadsheet, write a tune, or rehearse at all," Twitter, April 13, 2016, https://x.com/JazzIsTheWorst/status/720366831215620100.

72. Jazz Is the Worst (@JazzIsTheWorst), "I love Comedy-Jazz albums, like Jon Benjamin's 'I should have learned how to play piano' and Kamasi Washington's 'The Epic' #BothHilarious," Twitter, January 24, 2016.

73. Grebowicz, "Internet and the Death of Jazz," 73.

74. Ibid., 82–83.

75. Django Gold, "Sonny Rollins: In His Own Words," Daily Shouts, *Shouts and Murmurs* (blog), *New Yorker*, July 31, 2014, https://www.newyorker.com/humor/daily-shouts/sonny-rollins-words.

76. Howard Mandel, "Most Scurrilous, Unfunny *New Yorker* 'Humor' re Jazz," *Jazz beyond Jazz: Howard Mandel's Urban Improvisation* (blog), *ArtsJournal*, August 2, 2014, http://www.artsjournal.com/jazzbeyondjazz/2014/08/most-scurrilous-unfunny-new-yorker-humor-re-jazz.html; "On the *New Yorker* 'Satirizing' Sonny," *Nicholas Payton* (blog), August 4, 2014, https://nicholaspayton.wordpress.com/2014/08/04/on-the-new-yorker-satirizing-sonny/. For a more balanced take on the successes and failures of the satire as well as a summary of the responses to it, see Will Layman, "The Sonny Rollins/'New Yorker' Controversy and Jazz's Image Problem," *PopMatters*, August 18, 2014, https://www.popmatters.com/184681-the-sonny-rollins-new-yorker-controversy-and-jazzs-image-problem-2495629647.html.

77. Jazz Video Guy [Bret Primack], *"It Hurt Me"[:] Sonny Rollins' Response to the "New Yorker" Article*, August 5, 2014, https://www.youtube.com/watch?v=-j3LfPYqSZs. For Rollins, it wasn't the satire itself that was bothersome. He recognized it as the kind of blunt mockery that was common in *Mad* magazine. What did bother him was the way the piece was taken up on the internet, treated as "real," and then used to demean the music and its practitioners.

78. Dennis Howitt and Kwame Owusu-Bempah, "Race and Ethnicity in Popular Humour," in Lockyer and Pickering, *Beyond a Joke*, 47.

79. Jerry Palmer, "Parody and Decorum: Permission to Mock," in Lockyer and Pickering, *Beyond a Joke*, 82.

80. "On the *New Yorker* 'Satirizing' Sonny," *Nicholas Payton* (blog).
81. Matthew D. Morrison, "Race, Blacksound, and the (Re)Making of Musicological Discourse," *Journal of the American Musicological Society* 72, no. 3 (2019): 791. See also Greg Tate, ed., *Everything but the Burden: What White People Are Taking from Black Culture* (New York: Penguin, 2003).
82. Amy Rose Spiegel, "What's the Deal with Jazz?," *BuzzFeed*, February 14, 2013, https://www.buzzfeed.com/verymuchso/whats-the-deal-with-jazz.
83. Will Oremus, "Why a Young Writer Secretly Deleted Her Own *BuzzFeed* Post," *Slate*, August 15, 2014, https://slate.com/technology/2014/08/what-s-the-deal-with-jazz-why-a-buzzfeed-writer-secretly-deleted-her-post-in-shame.html.
84. Bergson, *Laughter*.
85. Birgitte Schepelern Johansen, "Locating Hatred: On the Materiality of Emotions," *Emotion, Space, and Society* 16 (2015): 51.
86. On the distinction between the more positive, socially useful *hating on* versus *hating*, see Lara Langer Cohen and Brian Connolly, "Theses on Hating," *Avidly*, June 16, 2015, https://avidly.lareviewofbooks.org/2015/06/16/theses-on-hating/.
87. Ken Willis, "Merry Hell: Humour Competence and Social Incompetence," in Lockyer and Pickering, *Beyond a Joke*, 129.

CHAPTER FOUR

1. Nichole Rustin-Paschal, "'The Reason I Play the Way I Do Is': Jazzmen, Emotion, and Creating in Jazz," in *The Routledge Companion to Jazz Studies*, ed. Nicholas Gebhardt, Nichole Rustin-Paschal, and Tony Whyton (New York: Routledge, 2019), 401–9.
2. Lawrence Grossberg, *Cultural Studies in the Future Tense* (Durham, NC: Duke University Press, 2010), 193–94.
3. Ken Prouty, *Knowing Jazz: Community, Pedagogy, and Canon in the Information Age* (Jackson: University Press of Mississippi, 2012), 3.
4. Michelle Mason, "Contempt as a Moral Attitude," *Ethics* 113 (January 2003): 239, 241.
5. Macalester Bell, *Hard Feelings: The Moral Psychology of Contempt* (New York: Oxford University Press, 2013), 40.
6. William Ian Miller, *The Anatomy of Disgust* (Cambridge, MA: Harvard University Press, 1997), 2.
7. Simon Frith, "What Is Bad Music?," in *Bad Music: The Music We Love to Hate*, ed. Christopher J. Washburne and Maiken Derno (New York: Routledge, 2004), 31.
8. Sara Ahmed, *The Cultural Politics of Emotion* (New York: Routledge, 2004), 55.
9. Not everyone agrees. In a 2009 blog post, jazz critic Patrick Jarenwattananon wonders if jazz critics today are too easy on the music. Are the records just very good, he wonders, or is the jazz world just too small to sustain a critical culture? Patrick Jarenwattananon, "Grade Inflation and the Jazz Critics," *A Blog Supreme*,

NPR, May 27, 2009, https://www.npr.org/sections/ablogsupreme/2009/05/grade_inflation_and_the_jazz_c_1.html.
10. Dan Morgenstern, "The Role of the Jazz Critic," *Program for the Twenty-Sixth Annual Notre Dame Collegiate Jazz Festival*, April 13–14, 1984, 1, 25, https://archives.nd.edu/ndcjf/dcjf1984.pdf.
11. John Gennari, *Blowin' Hot and Cool: Jazz and Its Critics* (Chicago: University of Chicago Press, 2016), 3.
12. Ibid., 14.
13. For a recent accounting of this situation, see Willard Jenkins's collection of writings and interviews with black jazz critics: Willard Jenkins, ed., *Ain't but a Few of Us: Black Music Writers Tell Their Story* (Durham, NC: Duke University Press, 2022).
14. For a history and selection of blindfold tests, see "Leonard Feather Blindfold Tests: Historic Interviews with Jazz Musicians, Recorded by Jazz Critic Leonard Feather," University of Idaho, Digital Initiatives, https://www.lib.uidaho.edu/digital/blindfold/about.html#the-blindfold-tests. For a recent study of the blindfold tests and 1950s "colorblind ideology," see Mikkel Vad, "Whiteness and the Problem of Colourblind Listening: Revisiting Leonard Feather's 1951 Blindfold Test with Roy Eldridge," *Twentieth-Century Music*, March 4, 2024, 1–28, https://doi.org/10.1017/S1478572224000033.
15. Gennari, *Blowin' Hot and Cool*, 56.
16. The recording Iyer hears is "Skipping," from the Fred Hersch Trio album *Live in Europe* (Palmetto PM2192 [2018], compact disc), with Fred Hersch on piano, John Hébert on bass, and Eric McPherson on drums. Dan Ouellette, "Vijay Iyer Blindfold Test at 2018 North Sea Jazz Festival," *DownBeat*, August 10, 2018, http://downbeat.com/news/detail/vijay-iyer-blindfold-test-at-2018-north-sea-jazz-festival (the blindfold test misidentifies the album title as *Live in Paris*).
17. David Hajdu, "Giant Steps: The Survival of a Great Jazz Pianist," *New York Times*, January 28, 2010, https://www.nytimes.com/2010/01/31/magazine/31Hersch-t.html.
18. See, for example, Fred Hersch's interview with Ethan Iverson on Iverson's blog, *Do the M@th*, https://ethaniverson.com/interviews/interview-with-fred-hersch.
19. Rachel Olding, "Why Is Jazz Unpopular? The Musicians 'Suck,' Says Branford Marsalis," *Sydney Morning Herald*, April 19, 2019, https://www.smh.com.au/entertainment/music/why-is-jazz-unpopular-the-musicians-suck-says-branford-marsalis-20190312-p513h2.html.
20. Gennari, *Blowin' Hot and Cool*, 16.
21. Kate Mann, *Down Girl: The Logic of Misogyny* (New York: Oxford University Press, 2017), 19–20. Sexism, for Manne, is the "branch of patriarchal ideology that justifies and rationalizes a patriarchal social order." Ibid., 20.
22. Kristin A. McGee, *Some Like It Hot: Jazz Women in Film and Television, 1928–1959* (Middletown, CT: Wesleyan University Press, 2009), 1–15.
23. Interviews with Viola Smith and Clora Bryant, *The Girls in the Band*, directed by Judy Chaikin (Studio City, CA: Artist Tribe and One Step Productions, 2011), DVD.

24. See Sherrie Tucker, *Swing Shift: "All-Girl" Bands of the 1940s* (Durham, NC: Duke University Press, 2000), 51.
25. Ibid.
26. Ibid., 59.
27. Ibid., 227–58.
28. Tammy L. Kernodle, *Soul on Soul: The Life and Music of Mary Lou Williams* (Urbana: University of Illinois Press, 2004), 219.
29. In *The Girls in the Band*, several of the younger musicians interviewed, such as trumpeter Ingrid Jensen, told positive stories about their career development. Jensen said, "In retrospect, to all of the things I've done to get to where I am in the music, very little of it has had anything to do with being a woman. The only thing that I can honestly say that has gotten me from point A to point B has been being in love with music, all kinds of music, and wanting to play music with people who want to play music with me." For an excellent summary of women jazz musicians on the positive changes in jazz culture, see Patrick Jarenwattananon, "Hey Ladies: Being a Woman in Jazz," *A Blog Supreme*, NPR, November 12, 2010, https://www.npr.org/sections/ablogsupreme/2010/11/12/131276820/hey-ladies-being-a-woman-in-jazz. That article is based on a larger project conducted by National Public Radio, "Hey Ladies: Being a Woman Musician Today," https://www.npr.org/series/128562443/hey-ladies-being-a-woman-musician-today.
30. Gillian Frank, "Discophobia: Antigay Prejudice and the 1979 Backlash against Disco," *Journal of the History of Sexuality* 16, no. 2 (May 2007): 276–306.
31. Grover Sales, *Jazz: America's Classical Music* (Englewood Cliffs, NJ: Prentice-Hall, 1984), 233–34.
32. Magdalena Fürnkranz, "Queer Aesthetics and the Performing Subject in Jazz in the 1920s," in *The Routledge Companion to Jazz and Gender*, ed. James Reddan, Monika Herzig, and Michael Kahr (New York: Routledge, 2023), 43–53. Also, from the same volume, Chloe Resler, "The Rise of Queermisia in Jazz: Medicalization, Legislation, and Its Effects," 119–30; Lisa Barg, *Queer Arrangements: Billy Strayhorn and Midcentury Jazz Collaboration* (Middletown, CT: Wesleyan University Press, 2023).
33. Sherrie Tucker, "When Did Jazz Go Straight? A Queer Question for Jazz Studies," *Critical Studies in Improvisation/Études critiques en improvisation* 4, no. 2 (2008): n.p., https://www.criticalimprov.com/index.php/csieci/article/view/850.
34. Fred Hersch, *Good Things Happen Slowly: A Life in and out of Jazz* (New York: Crown Archetype, 2017), 152.
35. The interview is no longer available on Iverson's blog, *Do the M@th*. The quotes in the text are from the original posting on Iverson's blog, but much of what I discuss and quote appears in other places. See Anthony Dean-Harris, "On Iverson on Glasper (Pause): Everyone Wants Everything, Even If It's Difference," Nextbop, n.d., https://nextbop.com/blog/oniversononglasperpauseeveryonewantseverythingevenifitsdifferent; Matthew

Kassel, "Q&A with Ethan Iverson: Addition through Subtraction," *DownBeat*, July 14, 2017, https://downbeat.com/news/detail/qa-with-ethan-iverson-addition-through-subtraction; Michelle Mercer, "Sexism from Two Leading Jazz Artists Draws Anger—and Presents an Opportunity," The Record, NPR, March 9, 2017, https://www.npr.org/sections/therecord/2017/03/09/519482385/sexism-from-two-leading-jazz-artists-draws-anger-and-presents-an-opportunity. Soon after the interview with Iverson, Glasper himself responded on his Facebook page: Robert Glasper, "I'm not much of a writer. I usually let my music speak for me," Facebook, March 18, 2017, https://www.facebook.com/robertglasper/posts/im-not-much-of-a-writer-i-usually-let-my-music-speak-for-me-its-what-i-do-best-a/10154647660178040/. Writer Sarah Deming, Iverson's wife, also posted a response to the controversy: Sarah Deming, "My Husband, the Misogynist: Ethan Iverson, Robert Glasper, Boxing, and Me," The Spiral Staircase (blog), March 12, 2017, https://sarahdeming.typepad.com/spiralstaircase/2017/03/my-husband-the-misogynist-ethan-iverson-robert-glasper-boxing-and-me.html.

36. Guthrie P. Ramsey Jr., "A New Kind of Blue: The Power of Suggestion and the Pleasure of Groove in Robert Glasper's 'Black Radio,'" *Daedalus* 142, no. 4 (Fall 2013): 120–25.
37. Iverson appears to have deleted the follow-up blog post. For a discussion of Iverson's postinterview response, see Mercer, "Sexism from Two Leading Jazz Artists Draws Anger."
38. Ibid.
39. Manne, *Down Girl*, 27.
40. Berklee Institute of Jazz and Gender Justice, https://college.berklee.edu/jazz-gender-justice. Also the video here: https://guides.library.berklee.edu/JGJ.
41. Terri Lyne Carrington, *New Standards: 101 Lead Sheets by Women Composers* (Boston: Berklee Press, 2022).
42. David Ake, Charles Hiroshi Garrett, and Daniel Goldmark, introduction to *Jazz/Not Jazz: The Music and Its Boundaries*, ed. Ake, Garrett, and Goldmark (Berkeley: University of California Press, 2012), 1.
43. Ahmed, *Cultural Politics of Emotion*, 51.
44. Bernard Gendron, *Between Montmartre and the Mudd Club* (Chicago: University of Chicago Press, 2002), 123.
45. Ibid., 125.
46. Rudi Blesh, *Shining Trumpets: A History of Jazz* (New York: Alfred A. Knopf, 1946), 290.
47. Ibid., 291.
48. Leonard Feather, "On Musical Fascism," *Metronome* 61, no. 9 (September 1945): 16.
49. John Tynan, "Take Five," *DownBeat*, November 23, 1961, 40. The uproar over Tynan's review and other criticisms by Leonard Feather (who also adopted the term *antijazz*) prompted the magazine to interview Coltrane and Dolphy the following year. Don DeMichael led the interview, where both musicians were able

to defend themselves at length. With thoughtfulness and poise, both musicians asked for more understanding from critics. Don DeMichael, "John Coltrane and Eric Dolphy Answer the Critics," *DownBeat*, April 12, 1962, 20–23.

50. David Ake, *Jazz Cultures* (Berkeley: University of California Press, 2002), 77, 82.
51. Years of verbal and, occasionally physical, abuse took a toll on Coleman's health. In 1963 and 1964, the saxophonist retreated from playing or recording. In a 1973 interview, Coleman believed that the ulcers he was suffering from in those years were, in part, the result of the stress caused by the "horrible things" he read by critics. John Litweiler, *Ornette Coleman: A Harmolodic Life* (New York: William Morrow, 1992), 108–9.
52. Kevin Fellezs, *Birds of Fire: Jazz, Rock, Funk, and the Creation of Fusion* (Durham, NC: Duke University Press, 2011), 5, 8.
53. For a detailed survey of this period, see Paul Tingen, *Miles Beyond: The Electric Explorations of Miles Davis, 1967–1991* (New York: Billboard Books, 2003); George Cole, *The Last Miles: The Music of Miles Davis, 1980–1991* (Ann Arbor: University of Michigan Press, 2007).
54. Paul Tingen, "The Most Hated Album in Jazz," *Guardian*, October 26, 2007, https://www.theguardian.com/music/2007/oct/26/jazz.shopping.
55. Will Smith, Review of *On the Corner*, by Miles Davis, *DownBeat*, March 29, 1973, 22–23.
56. A recent HBO documentary explores the broad hatred of Kenny G, with clips of people blowing up or shooting the saxophonist's CDs. *Listening to Kenny G*, Music Box series, directed by Penny Lane, aired December 2, 2021, on HBO, https://www.hbo.com/movies/music-box-listening-to-kenny-g.
57. Brian F. Wright, "Introduction: What Kenny G Can Teach Us about Jazz," part of "Colloquy: Revisiting Kenny G," *Journal of Jazz Studies* 14, no. 1 (2023): 1.
58. The post is no longer viewable on Metheny's website but has been copied to many other websites. You can view it here: Water Baby, "Great Article on Kenny G by Pat Metheny [sic]—Long but a Good Read," Sax on the Web, May 10, 2004, https://www.saxontheweb.net/threads/great-article-on-kenny-g-by-pat-metheny-long-but-a-good-read.12051/. All quotes in the text appear on this website.
59. Kenny G, *Classics in the Key of G*, Arista 07822-19085-2 (1999), compact disc, liner notes.
60. Quoted in Water Baby, "Great Article on Kenny G by Pat Metheny."
61. On the religiosity of jazz icons, see Whyton, *Jazz Icons*, 76–78.
62. Charles D. Carson, "'Bridging the Gap': Creed Taylor, Grover Washington Jr. and the Crossover Roots of Smooth Jazz," *Black Music Research Journal* 28, no. 1 (Spring 2008): 1.
63. Christopher J. Washburne, "Does Kenny G Play Bad Jazz? A Case Study," in *Bad Music: The Music We Love to Hate*, ed. Christopher J. Washburne and Maiken Derno (New York: Routledge, 2004), 125.

64. Critics continue to talk about Metheny's proximity to the much-derided genre. John Fordham, writing a review in the *Guardian*, describes Metheny "as a best-selling jazz fusion superstar with a songwriter's imagination" who "has negotiated the slippery ground between postbop, smooth jazz and edgy experiments." John Fordham, "Pat Metheny: *From This Place* Review—Wide-Horizons Music with Freewheeling Relish," *Guardian*, March 6, 2020, https://www.theguardian.com/music/2020/mar/06/pat-metheny-from-this-place-review.

65. As Tony Whyton notes, even though the jazz community is a social construction, "our sense of belonging and affiliation to communities creates intense feelings that are far from imaginary, as Metheny's comments on Kenny G reiterate." Whyton, *Jazz Icons*, 74.

66. Ibid., 58–81.

67. Listening to Kenny G, 25:40–26:12.

68. Whyton, *Jazz Icons*, 70.

69. Kelsey Klotz, "Kenny G and the Ignorance of Whiteness," part of "Colloquy: Revisiting Kenny G," *Journal of Jazz Studies* 14, no. 1 (2023): 21.

70. Stephen Witt, *How Music Got Free: A Story of Obsession and Invention* (New York: Penguin Books, 2016).

71. Will Layman, "R.I.P. Smooth Jazz, 1985–2008?," *PopMatters*, April 16, 2008, https://www.popmatters.com/rip-smooth-jazz-1985-2008-2496162968.html.

72. Whyton, *Jazz Icons*, 81.

73. Robert Walser, "Popular Music Analysis: Ten Apothegms and Four Instances," in *Analyzing Popular Music*, ed. Allan F. Moore (Cambridge: Cambridge University Press, 2003), 34–35.

74. Washburne, "Does Kenny G Play Bad Jazz?," 138. For the Harris quote, see Jerome Harris, "Jazz on the Global Stage," in *The African Diaspora: A Musical Perspective*, ed. Ingrid Monson (New York: Routledge, 2003), 118.

75. Charles Carson, "Listening Past Kenny G: Crossover Jazz and the Foregrounding of Black Sensualities," part of "Colloquy: Revisiting Kenny G," *Journal of Jazz Studies* 14, no. 1 (2023): 37–39.

76. Walser, "Popular Music Analysis," 36.

77. The battle, as depicted in Richard B. Woodward's 1994 *Village Voice* exposé, pitted critics against the Jazz at Lincoln Center leadership, although there is scattered documentation of musicians also speaking out about the situation. Richard B. Woodward, "The Jazz Wars: A Tale of Age, Rage, and Hash Brownies," *Village Voice*, August 9, 1994, 27–28. Also, Giovanni Russonello, "At 30, What Does Jazz at Lincoln Center Mean?," *New York Times*, September 13, 2017, https://www.nytimes.com/2017/09/13/arts/music/jazz-at-lincoln-center-30th-anniversary.html.

78. Sam Roberts, "Stanley Crouch, 74, a Critic Who Saw American Democracy in Jazz, Is Dead," *New York Times*, September 17, 2020.

79. Stanley Crouch, "Martin's Tempo," in *Considering Genius: Writings on Jazz* (New York: Basic Books, 2006), 154.

80. Stanley Crouch, "*On the Corner*: The Sellout of Miles Davis," in *Considering Genius*, 240–56. Other scholars, notably Eric Porter and Gary Tomlinson, have analyzed Crouch's attacks. Although I cover some of the same ground, my focus here is as much on the expression as it is on the substance of the critique. It is Crouch's contempt and disgust—his visceral, affective response—that is my starting point. Gary Tomlinson, "Cultural Dialogics and Jazz: A White Historian Signifies," *Black Music Research Journal* 11, no. 2 (1991): 229–64, reprinted in Supplement, *Black Music Research Journal* 22 (2002): 71–105; Eric Porter, "It's about That Time: The Response to Miles Davis's Electric Turn," in *Miles Davis and American Culture*, ed. Gerald Early (St. Louis: Missouri Historical Society Press, 2001), 130–46.
81. Bell, *Hard Feelings*, 54, citing Martha Nussbaum, *Hiding from Humanity: Disgust, Shame, and the Law* (Princeton: Princeton University Press, 2004).
82. Crouch, "*On the Corner*," 240.
83. Ibid., 246.
84. Ibid.
85. Stanley Crouch, "Miles Davis in the Fever of Spring, 1961," in Crouch, *Considering Genius*, 60.
86. Ahmed, *Cultural Politics of Emotion*, 54.
87. Jimmie L. Reeves, "Re-covering Racism: Crack Mothers, Reaganism, and the Network News," in *Living Color: Race and Television in the United States*, ed. Sasha Torres (Durham, NC: Duke University Press, 1998), 100–105.
88. Even with these massive systemic problems, the decade saw gains for certain segments of the African American community. A rising Black middle class tracked an increased representation of Black life in the mainstream media. In his book *Post-Soul Nation*, author Nelson George vividly reconstructs the era. Nelson George, *Post-Soul Nation: The Explosive, Contradictory, Triumphant, and Tragic 1980s as Experienced by African Americans (Previously Known as Blacks and Before That Negroes)* (New York: Viking, 2004), x–xi.
89. Ahmed, *Cultural Politics of Emotion*, 52.
90. "His outsized opinions were rendered in scalding, pugilistic prose—he even acquired a reputation for being willing to literally fight someone for disagreeing with him." Ethan Iverson, "Stanley Crouch, Towering Jazz Critic, Dead at 74," Music News, NPR, September 16, 2020, https://www.npr.org/2020/09/16/913619163/stanley-crouch-towering-jazz-critic-dead-at-74.
91. Leonard Feather, "Blindfold Test: Miles Davis," *DownBeat*, June 18, 1964, 31 (emphasis in original). *DownBeat* edited out Davis's profanities, replacing them with lines. But reconstructing Davis's word choice is not hard, and I have added the profanities back in. They are an index of affect.
92. Barbara H. Rosenwein, *Anger: The Conflicted History of an Emotion* (New Haven, CT: Yale University Press, 2020), 77–78.
93. See Nichole Rustin-Paschal, *The Kind of Man I Am: Jazzmasculinity and the World of Charles Mingus Jr.* (Middletown, CT: Wesleyan University Press, 2017), 56. Charles Mingus's public judgments on the jazz scene were strikingly similar

to Davis's. For example, see his 1955 and 1960 blindfold tests in *DownBeat*: Leonard Feather, "The Blindfold Test: 50 Stars for Bird!," *DownBeat*, June 15, 1955, 25, 33; Leonard Feather, "Blindfold Test: Charlie Mingus," *DownBeat*, April 28, 1960, https://www.charlesmingus.com/mingus/blindfold-test. In the 1955 test, Mingus, after hearing Oscar Peterson and Buddy DeFranco's 1954 recording of "Strike Up the Band" (Clef Records), says, "No stars! Because this is supposed to be a jazz review, and I don't think that's jazz—I think that's fascist music. Some cats that have listened and learned the lines and have no reason for playing them." Feather, "The Blindfold Test: 50 Stars for Bird!" 25.

94. Rustin-Paschal, *Kind of Man I Am*, 5.
95. See Geneva Smitherman's classic study, *Talkin' and Testifyin': The Language of Black America* (Detroit: Wayne State University Press, 1986); David E. Kirkland, "Black Masculine Language," in *Oxford Handbook of African American Language*, ed. Sonja Lanehart (New York: Oxford University Press, 2015), 834–49.
96. Katherine McKittrick, "Rebellion/Invention/Groove," *small axe* 20, no. 1 (49) (March 2016): 85.
97. Katherine McKittrick, *Dear Science and Other Stories* (Durham, NC: Duke University Press, 2021), 52.
98. Samuel Floyd, *The Power of Black Music: Interpreting Its History from Africa to the United States* (New York: Oxford University Press, 1995), 8.
99. Guthrie P. Ramsey Jr., *Race Music: Black Cultures from Bebop to Hip-Hop* (Berkeley: University of California Press, 2003), 36.
100. Prouty, *Knowing Jazz*, 6.

CHAPTER FIVE

1. Michael H. Kater, *Different Drummers: Jazz in the Culture of Nazi Germany* (New York: Oxford University Press, 2003); Frederick S. Starr, *Red and Hot: The Fate of Jazz in the Soviet Union, 1917–1991* (New York: Limelight Editions, 1994).
2. Robert J. Sternberg, *The Nature of Hate* (Cambridge: Cambridge University Press, 2008), 73.
3. "Goebbels [the Nazi propaganda minister]," Kater explains, "not only allowed such exploits but, within limits, actively encouraged them, for, as much as he realized the need for mollifying the civilian population, he valued the spiritual well-being of the armed forces even more." Kater, *Different Drummers*, 117; David Snowball, "Controlling Degenerate Music: Jazz in the Third Reich," in *Jazz and the Germans: Essays on the Influence of "Hot" American Idioms on 20th-Century German Music*, ed. Michael J. Budds (Hillsdale, NY: Pendragon Press, 2002), 149–66; Mike Zwerin, *La Tristesse de Saint Louis: Jazz under the Nazis* (New York: Beech Tree Books, 1985).
4. Sternberg, *Nature of Hate*, 60.

5. Martin Lücke, "Vilified, Venerated, Forbidden: Jazz in the Stalinist Era," trans. Anita Ip, *Music and Politics* 1, no. 2 (Summer 2007), https://doi.org/10.3998/mp.9460447.0001.201; Rüdiger Ritter, "Jazz in Moscow after Stalinism," in *Jazz and Totalitarianism*, ed. Bruce Johnson (New York: Routledge, 2017), 50–66.
6. Lücke, "Vilified, Venerated, Forbidden."
7. A translation of the essay under a different title appeared in *The Dial* magazine. Maxim Gorki, "The Music of the Degenerate," trans. Marie Budberg, *The Dial* 85, no. 6 (December 1928): 480–84.
8. Lücke, "Vilified, Venerated, Forbidden."
9. Ritter, "Jazz in Moscow after Stalinism," 50–66.
10. Birgitte Schepelern Johansen, "Locating Hatred: On the Materiality of Emotions," *Emotion, Space, and Society* 16 (2015): 51.
11. Sternberg, *Nature of Hate*, 73–75.
12. Jakob Norberg, "Anticapitalist Affect: Georg Lukács on Satire and Hate," *New German Critique* 45, no. 3 (135) (November 2018): 164.
13. Lara Langer Cohen and Brian Connolly, "Theses on Hating," *Avidly*, June 16, 2015, https://avidly.lareviewofbooks.org/2015/06/16/theses-on-hating/.
14. "Interview, Still in Rock: Mike Krol," *Still in Rock*, April 15, 2019, https://www.stillinrock.com/2019/04/interview-still-in-rock-mike-krol/.
15. Brad Cohan, "Mike Krol Hates Jazz and Wants No Part of Your SoCal Garage-Rock Scene," *Village Voice*, September 24, 2015, https://www.villagevoice.com/2015/09/24/mike-krol-hates-jazz-and-wants-no-part-of-your-socal-garage-rock-scene/.
16. "Interview, Still in Rock: Mike Krol."
17. Cohan, "Mike Krol Hates Jazz."
18. Cohen and Connolly, "Theses on Hating."
19. Cohan, "Mike Krol Hates Jazz."
20. The album is available on Bandcamp: https://ilovejazz1.bandcamp.com/releases.
21. Cohen and Connolly, "Theses on Hating."
22. Berit Brogaard, *Hatred: Understanding Our Most Dangerous Emotion* (New York: Oxford University Press, 2020), 88–89, 92–93.
23. For another take on hatred as reactive, see Thomas Brudholm, "Hatred as an Attitude," *Philosophical Papers* 39, no. 3 (November 2010): 289–313.
24. bell hooks, "Killing Rage: Militant Resistance," in *Killing Rage: Ending Racism* (New York: Henry Holt, 1996), 16.
25. Niza Yanay, *The Ideology of Hatred: The Psychic Power of Discourse* (New York: Fordham University Press, 2017), 4.
26. Norberg, "Anticapitalist Affect," 167.
27. Sianne Ngai, *Ugly Feelings* (Cambridge, MA: Harvard University Press, 2005), 336, 337–38.
28. Ibid., 335, 344–45.
29. Christopher Small, *Musicking: The Meanings of Performing and Listening* (Hanover, NH: Wesleyan University Press, 1998), 183–84.

30. Sara Ahmed, *The Cultural Politics of Emotion* (New York: Routledge, 2004), 45–46.
31. C. Fred Alford, "Hate," in *Routledge Handbook of Psychoanalytic Political Theory*, ed. Yannis Stavrakakis (New York: Routledge, 2020), 265.
32. William Hazlitt, "On the Pleasure of Hating," in *The Oxford Book of Essays*, ed. John Gross (New York: Oxford University Press, 1991), 112–21; Cohen and Connolly, "Theses on Hating."
33. Hazlitt, "On the Pleasure of Hating," 121.
34. Ibid., 122.
35. David Wright, *Understanding Cultural Taste: Sensation, Skill and Sensibility* (London: Palgrave Macmillan, 2015), 145 (emphasis in original).
36. Here are a few examples of these surveys: Scott DeVeaux, *Jazz in America: Who's Listening?* Research Division Report No. 31, National Endowment for the Arts (Carson, CA: Seven Locks Press, 1995), https://www.arts.gov/sites/default/files/NEA-Research-Report-31.pdf; Lee Mizell, Brett Crawford, and Caryn Anderson, *Music Preferences in the U.S.: 1982–2002*, prepared for the National Endowment for the Arts (June 2005), https://files.eric.ed.gov/fulltext/ED511715.pdf; Public Policy Polling, "Americans Hate Justin Bieber," press release, May 9, 2013, https://www.publicpolicypolling.com/wp-content/uploads/2017/09/PPP_Release_Music_050913.pdf; and Linley Sanders, "Americans' Opinions on 20 Different Music Genres, from Classic Rock to Hip-Hop and Rap," YouGov (US), May 11, 2023, https://today.yougov.com/entertainment/articles/45699-americans-opinions-different-music-genres-poll.
37. Michael Hardt and Antonio Negri, *Multitude: War and Democracy in the Age of Empire* (New York: Penguin, 2004), 142.
38. Ben Highmore, "Taste as Feeling," *New Literary History* 47, no. 4 (Autumn 2016): 548.
39. For example, on jazz radio stations trying to attract new listeners, see Leigh Giangreco, "Jazz Media Lab Stations Test Strategies for Cultivating Younger Audiences," Current, April 15, 2022, https://current.org/2022/04/jazz-media-lab-stations-test-new-strategies-for-cultivating-younger-audiences/. For a perspective from a prominent critic and jazz educator, see Willard Jenkins, "Jazz Audience Development: The Gender Factor," New Music USA, March 26, 2014,https://newmusicusa.org/nmbx/jazz-audience-development-the-gender-factor/.
40. DeVeaux, *Jazz in America: Who's Listening?*, 57.
41. Mizell, Crawford, and Anderson, *Music Preferences in the U.S.: 1982–2002*, i, 30.
42. David La Rosa, "Jazz Has Become the Least Popular Genre in the U.S.," *JazzLine News*, March 9, 2015, https://news.jazzline.com/news/jazz-least-popular-music-genre/ (citing *2014 Nielsen Music U.S. Report*, https://bird.jazzline.com/tjl/uploads/2015/03/nielsen-2014-year-end-music-report-us.pdf).
43. Eric Nisenson, *Blue: The Murder of Jazz* (New York: Da Capo, 1997), 235, 237–38.
44. Ibid., 240, 246.
45. Guthrie P. Ramsey Jr., "A New Kind of Blue: The Power of Suggestion and the Pleasure of Groove in Robert Glasper's 'Black Radio,'" *Daedalus* 142, no. 4 (Fall

2013): 120–25; Gabriel Solis, "Soul, Afrofuturism and the Timeliness of Contemporary Jazz Fusions," *Daedalus* 148, no. 2 (Spring 2019): 23–35.
46. Troy Collins, "Robert Glasper Experiment: *Black Radio*," All about Jazz, March 29, 2012, https://www.allaboutjazz.com/black-radio-blue-note-records-review-by-troy-collins.
47. On Murray's philosophy of music as a reaction to Baraka and the Black Arts Movement, see John Gennari, *Blowin' Hot and Cool: Jazz and Its Critics* (Chicago: University of Chicago Press, 2016), 339–71.
48. Richard Scheinin, "Grammy Winner Robert Glasper on 12 Topics: Chaka Khan, J Dilla, Jose James, and More," *San Jose Mercury News*, March 7, 2013, https://infoweb-newsbank-com.eu1.proxy.openathens.net/apps/news/document-view?p=WORLDNEWS&docref=news/144E5D4BF92CC7A0.
49. Robert Glasper, "Robert Glasper: A Unified Field Theory for Black Music," interview by Guy Raz, *Weekend All Things Considered*, NPR, February 25, 2012, https://link.gale.com/apps/doc/A281623490/LitRC?u=tamp44898&sid=ebsco&xid=4cd4d145.
50. Samantha Hunter, "Robert Glasper Talks about His Musical Roots, New August Greene Music and Why He Has No Regrets about His Lauryn Hill Comments," Okayplayer, December 4, 2018, https://www.okayplayer.com/music/robert-glasper-interview-lauryn-hill.html (emphasis in original).
51. Ibid.
52. Glasper, "Robert Glasper: A Unified Field Theory for Black Music."
53. Public Policy Polling, "Americans Hate Justin Bieber," press release, May 9, 2013, https://www.publicpolicypolling.com/wp-content/uploads/2017/09/PPP_Release_Music_050913.pdf. On the reputation of PPP's political polling, see Jonathan Easley, "Study Finds PPP Was the Most Accurate Pollster in 2012," *The Hill*, November 7, 2012, https://thehill.com/blogs/ballot-box/polls/133985-study-finds-ppp-was-the-most-accurate-pollster-in-2012.
54. Dale Chapman, *The Jazz Bubble: Neoclassical Jazz in Neoliberal Culture* (Berkeley: University of California Press, 2018).
55. Roddy Doyle, "Jimmy Jazz" (Toronto: Knopf Canada, 2013), e-book.
56. Roddy Doyle, *The Commitments* (New York: Vintage Contemporaries, 1989), 124–26, 133–34, 141–43.
57. Doyle, "Jimmy Jazz."
58. Ibid.
59. Ibid.
60. Ingrid Monson, *Freedom Sounds: Civil Rights Call Out to Jazz and Africa* (New York: Oxford University Press, 2007), 319.
61. Phil Freeman, *Ugly Beauty: Jazz in the 21st Century* (Washington, DC: Zero Books, 2021), 3–5.
62. Morgan Enos, "Three New Categories Added for the 2024 Grammys: Best African Music Performance, Best Alternative Jazz Album and Best Pop Dance Recording," Grammy, June 13, 2023, https://www.grammy.com/news/three-new-categories-added-for-the-2024-grammys.

63. Katherine McKittrick, *Dear Science and Other Stories* (Durham, NC: Duke University Press, 2021), 163 (emphasis in original).
64. "Black Lives Matter," SFJazz, n.d., accessed February 4, 2024, https://www.sfjazz.org/blm/.
65. Change, although slow, is happening. See Giovanni Russonello, "Jazz Has Always Been Protest Music. Can It Meet This Moment?," *New York Times*, September 3, 2020, https://www.nytimes.com/2020/09/03/arts/music/jazz-protest-academia.html.

Bibliography

Abreu, Christina D. *Rhythms of Race: Cuban Musicians and the Making of Latino New York City and Miami, 1940–1960*. Chapel Hill: University of North Carolina Press, 2015.
Abu-Lughod, Lila. *Veiled Sentiments: Honor and Poetry in a Bedouin Society*. Berkeley: University of California Press, 1986.
Adler, Jerry, Jennifer Foote, and Ray Sawhill. "The Rap Attitude." *Newsweek*, March 19, 1990, 56–60.
Adorno, Theodor W. *Essays on Music*. Edited by Richard Leppert. Translated by Susan H. Gillespie. Berkeley: University of California Press, 2002.
———. "Farewell to Jazz." In Adorno, *Essays on Music*, 470–95.
———. *Introduction to the Sociology of Music*. Translated by E. B. Ashton. New York: Seabury Press, 1977.
———. *Negative Dialectics*. Translated by E. B. Ashton. 1966. New York: Continuum, 2007.
———. "On Jazz." In Adorno, *Essays on Music*, 496–500.
———. "On Popular Music." In Adorno, *Essays on Music*, 437–69.
———. "Perennial Fashion—Jazz." In *Prisms*, translated by Samuel Weber and Shierry Weber, 119–32. 1967. Reprint, Cambridge, MA: MIT Press, 1981.
———. "Stravinsky and Reaction." In *Philosophy of New Music*, translated by Robert Hullot-Kentor, 103–58. Minneapolis: University of Minnesota Press, 2006.
Agawu, Kofi. *Playing with Signs*. Princeton, NJ: Princeton University Press, 1991.
Ahmed, Sara. *The Cultural Politics of Emotion*. New York: Routledge, 2004.
All about Jazz. "My Conversation with Horace Silver." All about Jazz, December 18, 2003. https://www.allaboutjazz.com/my-conversation-with-horace-silver-horace-silver-by-aaj-staff.
Ake, David. *Jazz Cultures*. Berkeley: University of California Press, 2002.
Ake, David, Charles Hiroshi Garrett, and Daniel Goldmark, eds. *Jazz/Not Jazz: The Music and Its Boundaries*. Berkeley: University of California Press, 2012.

Alford, C. Fred. "Hate." In *Routledge Handbook of Psychoanalytic Political Theory*, edited by Yannis Stavrakakis, 261–71. New York: Routledge, 2020.

Altschuler, Glenn C. *All Shook Up: How Rock 'n' Roll Changed America*. New York: Oxford University Press, 2003.

Amorosi, A. D. "Matt Groening on His Love of Jazz, How It Found Its Way into the 'Simpsons' and Curating a New Jazz Video Playlist for Qwest TV." *Variety*, October 26, 2014. https://variety.com/2021/music/news/matt-groening-jazz-playlist-qwest-tv-simpsons-interview-curated-jazz-video-playlist-drops-on-qwest-tv-1235098215.

Anderson, Ben. *Encountering Affect: Capacities, Apparatuses, Conditions*. New York: Routledge, 2016.

Anderson, Paul Allen. "'My Foolish Heart': Bill Evans and the Public Life of Feeling." *Jazz Perspectives* 7, no. 3 (2013): 205–49.

Ansell, Gwen. *Soweto Blues: Jazz, Popular Music, and Politics in South Africa*. New York: Continuum, 2004.

Aristotle. *Rhetoric*. Translated by W. Rhys Roberts. http://classics.mit.edu/Aristotle/rhetoric.2.ii.html.

Associated Press. "Explaining AP Style on Black and White." Associated Press News, July 20, 2020. https://apnews.com/article/archive-race-and-ethnicity-9105661462.

Ballantine, Christopher. *Marabi Nights: Jazz, "Race" and Society in Early Apartheid South Africa*. 2nd ed. Scottsville, South Africa: University of KwaZulu-Natal Press, 2012.

Baraka, Amiri (LeRoi Jones). "Jazz and the White Critic." In *The Jazz Cadence of American Culture*, edited by Robert G. O'Meally, 137–42. New York: Columbia University Press, 1998.

Barg, Lisa. *Queer Arrangements: Billy Strayhorn and Midcentury Jazz Collaboration*. Middletown, CT: Wesleyan University Press, 2023.

Barthelme, Donald. "The King of Jazz." *New Yorker*, February 7, 1977, 31–32. In *Great Days*, 55–60. New York: Farrar, Straus, Giroux, 1979.

Bayley, Stephen. *Taste: The Secret Meaning of Things*. New York: Pantheon Books, 1991.

Beatty, Paul. *Hokum: An Anthology of African-American Humor*. New York: Bloomsbury, 2006.

Becker, Howard S. *Outsiders: Studies in the Sociology of Deviance*. New York: Free Press, 1982.

Belgrad, Daniel. "The Rockwell Syndrome." *Art in America* 88, no. 4 (April 2000): 61–63, 65–67.

Bell, Macalester. *Hard Feelings: The Moral Psychology of Contempt*. New York: Oxford University Press, 2013.

Benjamin, H. Jon. *Failure Is an Option: An Attempted Memoir*. New York: Dutton, 2018.

———. "'Failure Is an Option' Urges People to Let Go of the Constant Grind towards Success." Interview by Mary Louise Kelly. *All Things Considered*, NPR, May 2, 2018. https://www.npr.org/2018/05/02/607817990/failure-is-an-option-urges-people-to-let-go-of-the-constant-grind-towards-success.

Berg, Ulla D., and Ana Y. Ramos-Zaya. "Racializing Affect: A Theoretical Proposition." *Current Anthropology* 56, no. 5 (October 2018): 654–65.

Bergson, Henri. *Laughter: An Essay on the Meaning of the Comic*. Translated by Cloudesley Brereton and Fred Rothwell. 1911. https://www.gutenberg.org/files/4352/4352-h/4352-h.htm.

Berish, Andrew. *Lonesome Roads and Streets of Dreams: Place, Mobility, and Race in Jazz of the 1930s and '40s*. Chicago: University of Chicago Press, 2012.

Berlin, Edward A. *Ragtime: A Musical and Cultural History*. Berkeley: University of California Press, 1980.

Berliner, Paul F. *Thinking in Jazz: The Infinite Art of Improvisation*. Chicago: University of Chicago Press, 2009.

Billig, Michael. "Comic Racism and Violence." In Lockyer and Pickering, *Beyond a Joke*, 25–44.

———. *Laughter and Ridicule: Towards a Social Critique of Humour*. New York: Sage, 2005.

Bindas, David. *Swing, That Modern Sound*. Jackson: University of Mississippi Press, 2001.

Blesh, Rudi. *Shining Trumpets: A History of Jazz*. New York: Alfred A. Knopf, 1946.

Bourdieu, Pierre. *Distinction: A Social Critique of the Judgement of Taste*. Translated by Richard Nice. Cambridge, MA: Harvard University Press, 1984.

Bowie, Andrew. "Adorno and Jazz." In *A Companion to Adorno*, edited by Peter E. Gordon, Espen Hammer, and Max Pensky, 123–38. Hoboken, NJ: Wiley Blackwell, 2020.

Brackett, David. *Categorizing Sound: Genre and Twentieth-Century Popular Music*. Berkeley: University of California Press, 2016.

Brogaard, Berit. *Hatred: Understanding Our Most Dangerous Emotion*. New York: Oxford University Press, 2020.

Brown, Jayne. *Babylon Girls: Black Women Performers and the Shaping of the Modern*. Durham, NC: Duke University Press, 2008.

Brudholm, Thomas. "Hatred as an Attitude." *Philosophical Papers* 39, no. 3 (November 2010): 289–313.

Buhler, James. "Frankfurt School Blues: Rethinking Adorno's Critique of Jazz." In *Apparitions: New Perspectives on Adorno and Twentieth-Century Music*, edited by Berthold Hoeckner, 103–30. New York: Routledge, 2006.

Carlson, Gretchen L. *Improvising the Score: Rethinking Modern Film Music through Jazz*. Jackson: University of Mississippi Press, 2022.

Carrington, Terri Lyne. *New Standards: 101 Lead Sheets by Women Composers*. Boston: Berklee Press, 2022.

Carson, Charles D. "'Bridging the Gap': Creed Taylor, Grover Washington Jr. and the Crossover Roots of Smooth Jazz." *Black Music Research Journal* 28, no. 1 (Spring 2008): 1–15.

———. "Listening Past Kenny G: Crossover Jazz and the Foregrounding of Black Sensualities," part of "Colloquy: Revisiting Kenny G." *Journal of Jazz Studies* 14, no. 1 (2023): 35–46.

Cateforis, Theo, ed. *The Rock History Reader*. 3rd ed. New York: Routledge, 2019.

Chaikin, Judy, dir. *The Girls in the Band*. Studio City, CA: Artist Tribe and One Step Productions, 2011. DVD, 88 min.

Chapman, Dale. *The Jazz Bubble: Neoclassical Jazz in Neoliberal Culture*. Berkeley: University of California Press, 2018.

Chinen, Nate. "Behold the Jazzbro." The Gig. *JazzTimes* 43, no. 6 (August 2013): 10.

Click, Melissa A., ed. *Anti-fandom: Dislike and Hate in the Digital Age*. New York: New York University Press, 2019.

Coady, Christopher. *John Lewis and the Challenge of "Real" Black Music*. Ann Arbor: University of Michigan Press, 2016.

Cohan, Brad. "Mike Krol Hates Jazz and Wants No Part of Your SoCal Garage-Rock Scene." *Village Voice*, September 24, 2015. https://www.villagevoice.com/2015/09/24/mike-krol-hates-jazz-and-wants-no-part-of-your-socal-garage-rock-scene.

Cohen, Lara Langer, and Brian Connolly. "Theses on Hating." *Avidly*, June 16, 2015. https://avidly.lareviewofbooks.org/2015/06/16/theses-on-hating/.

Cole, George. *The Last Miles: The Music of Miles Davis, 1980–1991*. Ann Arbor: University of Michigan Press, 2007.

Colligan, George. "Jazz Is the Worst: LMAO." *Jazz Truth* (blog), December 25, 2014. http://jazztruth.blogspot.com/2014/12/jazz-is-worst-lmao.html.

Collins, Troy. "Robert Glasper Experiment: *Black Radio*." All about Jazz, March 29, 2012. https://www.allaboutjazz.com/black-radio-blue-note-records-review-by-troy-collins.

Cook, Deryck. *The Language of Music*. London: Oxford University Press, 1959.

Cooke, Mervyn. *A History of Film Music*. New York: Cambridge University Press, 2012.

Corbett, John. *Vinyl Freak: Love Letters to a Dying Medium*. Durham, NC: Duke University Press, 2017.

Cox, Arnie. *Music and Embodied Cognition: Listening, Moving, Feeling, and Thinking*. Bloomington: Indiana University Press, 2016.

Creamysaxsolo. "To all the Jazz-Haters on Reddit, what is it that you dislike about Jazz?" Reddit, n.d., accessed April 28, 2022, https://www.reddit.com/r/AskReddit/comments/14ekxh/to_all_the_jazzhaters_on_reddit_what_is_it_that/.

Critchley, Simon. *On Humor*. New York: Routledge, 2002.

Crouch, Stanley. *Considering Genius: Writings on Jazz*. New York: Basic Books, 2006.

———. "Martin's Tempo." In Crouch, *Considering Genius*, 154–56.
———. "Miles Davis in the Fever of Spring, 1961." In Crouch, *Considering Genius*, 40–65.
———. "*On the Corner*: The Sellout of Miles Davis." In Crouch, *Considering Genius*, 240–56.
Cunniffe, Thomas. "Jazz and Standup Comedy." Jazz History Online, March 5, 2019. https://jazzhistoryonline.com/jazz-and-standup-comedy.
DeMichael, Don. "John Coltrane and Eric Dolphy Answer the Critics." *DownBeat*, April 12, 1962, 20–23.
Denby, David. *Snark: A Polemic in Seven Fits*. New York: Simon & Schuster, 2009.
DeVeaux, Scott. *The Birth of Bebop: A Social and Musical History*. Berkeley: University of California Press, 1997.
———. *Jazz in America: Who's Listening?* Research Division Report No. 31, National Endowment for the Arts. Carson, CA: Seven Locks Press, 1995. https://www.arts.gov/sites/default/files/NEA-Research-Report-31.pdf.
Dibben, Nicola. "Subjectivity and the Construction of Emotion in the Music of Björk." *Music Analysis* 25, no. 1/2 (March–July 2006): 171–97.
Dinerstein, Joel. *The Origins of Cool in Postwar America*. Chicago: University of Chicago Press, 2017.
———. *Swinging the Machine: Modernity, Technology, and African American Culture between the World Wars*. Amherst: University of Massachusetts Press, 2003.
Douglas, Ann. *The Feminization of American Culture*. 1977. Reprint, New York: Noonday Press, 1998.
Doyle, Roddy. *The Commitments*. New York: Vintage Contemporaries, 1989.
———. "Jimmy Jazz." Toronto: Knopf Canada, 2013. E-book.
Easley, Jonathan. "Study Finds PPP Was the Most Accurate Pollster in 2012." *The Hill*, November 7, 2012. https://thehill.com/blogs/ballot-box/polls/133985-study-finds-ppp-was-the-most-accurate-pollster-in-2012.
Enos, Morgan. "Three New Categories Added for the 2024 Grammys: Best African Music Performance, Best Alternative Jazz Album and Best Pop Dance Recording." Grammy, June 13, 2023. https://www.grammy.com/news/three-new-categories-added-for-the-2024-grammys.
Erenberg, Lewis A. *Swingin' the Dream: Big Band Jazz and the Rebirth of American Culture*. Chicago: University of Chicago Press, 1998.
Faulkner, Anne Shaw. "Does Jazz Put the Sin in Syncopation?" *Ladies Home Journal*, August 1921.
Feather, Leonard. "Blindfold Test: Charlie Mingus." *DownBeat*, April 28, 1960, https://www.charlesmingus.com/mingus/blindfold-test.
———. "The Blindfold Test: 50 Stars for Bird! Mingus Exclaims." *DownBeat*, June 15, 1955, 25, 33.
———. "Blindfold Test: Miles Davis." *DownBeat*, June 18, 1964, 31.
———. *The Book of Jazz*. New York: Horizon Press, 1957.

———. "Leonard Feather Blindfold Tests: Historic Interviews with Jazz Musicians, Recorded by Jazz Critic Leonard Feather." University of Idaho, Digital Initiatives. https://www.lib.uidaho.edu/digital/blindfold/about.html#the-blindfold-tests.

———. "On Musical Fascism." *Metronome* 61, no. 9 (September 1945): 16, 31.

Fellezs, Kevin. *Birds of Fire: Jazz, Rock, Funk, and the Creation of Fusion*. Durham, NC: Duke University Press, 2011.

Floyd, Samuel. *The Power of Black Music: Interpreting Its History from Africa to the United States*. New York: Oxford University Press, 1995.

Fordham, John. "Pat Metheny: *From This Place* Review—Wide-Horizons Music with Freewheeling Relish." *Guardian*, March 6, 2020. https://www.theguardian.com/music/2020/mar/06/pat-metheny-from-this-place-review.

Fosdick, Harry Emerson. *On Being a Real Person*. New York: Harper, 1943.

Frank, Gillian. "Discophobia: Antigay Prejudice and the 1979 Backlash against Disco." *Journal of the History of Sexuality* 16, no. 2 (May 2007): 276–306.

Fraterrigo, Elizabeth. *"Playboy" and the Making of the Good Life in Modern America*. New York: Oxford University Press, 2009.

Freeman, Phil. *Ugly Beauty: Jazz in the 21st Century*. Washington, DC: Zero Books, 2021.

Freud, Sigmund. "Instincts and Their Vicissitudes." *The Standard Edition of the Complete Psychological Works of Sigmund Freud*. Vol. 14, *On the History of the Psycho-analytic Movement, Papers on Metapsychology and Other Works*, translated and edited by James Strachey. London: Hogarth Press, 1957; reprint, New York: Vintage, 1999.

———. *Jokes and Their Relation to the Unconscious*. Translated and edited by James Strachey. New York: W. W. Norton, 1989.

Frith, Simon. *Performing Rites: On the Value of Popular Music*. Cambridge, MA: Harvard University Press, 1996.

———. "What Is Bad Music?" In Washburne and Derno, *Bad Music*, 15–36.

Fry, Andy. *Paris Blues: African American Music and French Popular Culture, 1920–1960*. Chicago: University of Chicago Press, 2014.

Fürnkranz, Magdalena. "Queer Aesthetics and the Performing Subject in Jazz in the 1920s." In Reddan, Herzig, and Kahr, *Routledge Companion to Jazz and Gender*, 43–53.

Gabbard, Krin. *Black Magic: White Hollywood and African American Culture*. New Brunswick, NJ: Rutgers University Press, 2004.

Gans, Herbert J. *Popular Culture and High Culture: An Analysis and Evaluation of Taste*. New York: Basic Books, 1974.

Garner, Steve. *Whiteness: An Introduction*. New York: Routledge, 2007.

Garrett, Charles Hiroshi. "The Humor of Jazz." In Ake, Garrett, and Goldmark, *Jazz/Not Jazz*, 49–69.

Gendron, Bernard. *Between Montmartre and the Mudd Club*. Chicago: University of Chicago Press, 2002.

Gennari, John. *Blowin' Hot and Cool: Jazz and Its Critics*. Chicago: University of Chicago Press, 2016.

———. *Flavor and Soul: Italian America at Its African American Edge*. Chicago: University of Chicago Press, 2017.

George, Nelson. *Post-Soul Nation: The Explosive, Contradictory, Triumphant, and Tragic 1980s as Experienced by African Americans (Previously Known as Blacks and Before That Negroes)*. New York: Viking, 2004.

Giangreco, Leigh. "Jazz Media Lab Stations Test Strategies for Cultivating Younger Audiences." Current, April 15, 2022. https://current.org/2022/04/jazz-media-lab-stations-test-new-strategies-for-cultivating-younger-audiences/.

Gikandi, Simon. *Slavery and the Culture of Taste*. Princeton, NJ: Princeton University Press, 2011.

Gilbert, Gama. "Swing It! And Even in a Temple of Music: Hottest of Rhythms Vibrates in a Sanctum." *New York Times Magazine*, January 16, 1938, 7, 21.

Gioia, Ted. *West Coast Jazz: Modern Jazz in California, 1945–1960*. Berkeley: University of California Press, 1992.

———. "What's with This Uncool Surge in Jazz Bashing?" *Daily Beast*, November 2, 2014. https://www.thedailybeast.com/whats-with-this-surge-in-jazz-bashing.

Glasper, Robert. "Robert Glasper: A Unified Field Theory for Black Music." Interview by Guy Raz. *Weekend All Things Considered*, NPR, February 25, 2012. https://link.gale.com/apps/doc/A281623490/LitRC?u=tamp44898&sid=ebsco&xid=4cd4d145.

Gleason, Philip. "Americans All: World War II and the Shaping of American Identity." *Review of Politics* 43, no. 4 (October 1981): 483–518.

Gold, Django. "Sonny Rollins: In His Own Words." Daily Shouts, *Shouts and Murmurs* (blog). *New Yorker*, July 31, 2014. https://www.newyorker.com/humor/daily-shouts/sonny-rollins-words.

Goldmark, Daniel. *Tunes for 'Toons: Music and the Hollywood Cartoon*. Berkeley: University of California Press, 2005.

Gordon, Dexter B. "Humor in African American Discourse: Speaking of Oppression." *Journal of Black Studies* 29, no. 2 (November 1998): 254–76.

Graebner, William. *The Age of Doubt: American Thought and Culture in the 1940s*. Boston: Twayne Publishing, 1991.

Grant, Roger Mathew. *Peculiar Attunements: How Affect Theory Turned Musical*. New York: Fordham University Press, 2020.

Grebowicz, Margret. "The Internet and the Death of Jazz: Race, Improvisation, and the Crisis of Community." In *21st Century Perspectives on Music, Technology, and Culture: Listening Spaces*, edited by Richard Purcell and Richard Randall, 72–83. London: Palgrave Macmillan, 2016.

Greene, Daniel. *The Jewish Origins of Cultural Pluralism: The Menorah Association and American Diversity*. Bloomington: Indiana University Press, 2011.

Gregg, Melissa, and Gregory J. Seigworth. *The Affect Theory Reader*. Durham, NC: Duke University Press, 2010.

Grey, Kay Crisfield. "The Lady Hated Jazz." *Saturday Evening Post*, December 24, 1955, 18, 50–51.

Grossberg, Lawrence. *Cultural Studies in the Future Tense*. Durham, NC: Duke University Press, 2010.

———. *We Gotta Get Out of This Place: Popular Conservatism and Postmodern Culture*. New York: Routledge, 1992.

Gubbels, Jason. "Jazz Needs a Better Sense of Humor." *Deadspin*, September 11, 2014. https://deadspin.com/jazz-needs-a-better-sense-of-humor-1632954724.

Hajdu, David. "Giant Steps: The Survival of a Great Jazz Pianist." *New York Times*, January 28, 2010. https://www.nytimes.com/2010/01/31/magazine/31Hersch-t.html.

Hammer, Espen. "Happiness and Pleasure in Adorno's Aesthetics." *Germanic Review: Literature, Culture, Theory* 90, no. 4 (2015): 247–59.

Hardt, Michael, and Antonio Negri. *Multitude: War and Democracy in the Age of Empire*. New York: Penguin, 2004.

Harris, Jerome. "Jazz on the Global Stage." In *The African Diaspora: A Musical Perspective*, edited by Ingrid Monson, 101–34. New York: Routledge, 2003.

Hatten, Robert. *Musical Meaning in Beethoven: Markedness, Correlation, and Interpretation*. Bloomington: Indiana University Press, 1994.

Hazlitt, William. "On the Pleasure of Hating." In *The Oxford Book of Essays*, edited by John Gross, 112–21. New York: Oxford University Press, 1991.

Hennion, Antoine. *The Passion for Music: A Sociology of Mediation*. Translated by Margaret Rigaud and Peter Collier. New York: Routledge, 2020.

Hersch, Charles. *Jews and Jazz: Improvising Ethnicity*. New York: Routledge, 2017.

———. *Subversive Sounds: Race and the Birth of Jazz in New Orleans*. Chicago: University of Chicago Press, 2007.

Hersch, Fred. *Good Things Happen Slowly: A Life in and out of Jazz*. New York: Crown Archetype, 2017.

———. "Interview with Fred Hersch." By Ethan Iverson. *Do the M@th* (blog), n.d. [July 2012]. https://ethaniverson.com/interviews/interview-with-fred-hersch.

Highmore, Ben. "Bitter after Taste: Affect, Food, and Social Aesthetics." In *The Affect Theory Reader*, edited by Melissa Gregg and Gregory J. Seigworth, 118–37. Durham, NC: Duke University Press, 2010.

———. *Cultural Feelings: Mood, Mediation and Cultural Politics*. New York: Routledge, 2017.

———. "Taste as Feeling." *New Literary History* 47 (2016): 547–66.

Hobart, Mike. "Jazz: Love It or Hate It?" BBC, April 30, 2015. https://www.bbc.com/culture/article/20150430-jazz-do-you-love-it-or-hate-it.

Hobbes, Thomas. *Leviathan*. Edited by J. C. A. Gaskin. New York: Oxford University Press, 1998.

hooks, bell. "Killing Rage: Militant Resistance." In *Killing Rage: Ending Racism*, 8–20. New York: Henry Holt, 1996.

———. *Yearning: Race, Gender, and Cultural Politics*. Boston: South End Press, 1990.

Hopkins, Ernest J. "In Praise of 'Jazz,' A Futurist Word Which Has Just Joined the Language." *San Francisco Bulletin*, April 5, 1913. In *Jazz: A Century of Change*, edited by Lewis Porter, 6–8. New York: Schirmer Books, 1997.

Howitt, Dennis, and Kwame Owusu-Bempah. "Race and Ethnicity in Popular Humour." In Lockyer and Pickering, *Beyond a Joke*, 45–62.

Howland, John. *Hearing Luxe Pop: Glorification, Glamour, and the Middlebrow in American Popular Music*. Berkeley: University of California Press, 2021.

———. "Jazz with Strings: Between Jazz and the Great American Songbook." In Ake, Garrett, and Goldmark, *Jazz/Not Jazz*, 197–99.

Hubbs, Nadine. *Rednecks, Queers, and Country Music*. Berkeley: University of California Press, 2014.

Hunter, Samantha. "Robert Glasper Talks about His Musical Roots, New August Greene Music and Why He Has No Regrets about His Lauryn Hill Comments." Okayplayer, December 4, 2018. https://www.okayplayer.com/music/robert-glasper-interview-lauryn-hill.html.

Huron, David. *Sweet Anticipations: Music and the Psychology of Expectation*. Cambridge, MA: MIT Press, 2006.

Huyssen, Andreas. "Mass Culture as Woman." In *After the Great Divide: Modernism, Mass Culture, Postmodernism*, 44–62. Bloomington: Indiana University Press, 1986.

Iverson, Ethan. "Stanley Crouch, Towering Jazz Critic, Dead at 74." Music News, NPR, September 16, 2020. https://www.npr.org/2020/09/16/913619163/stanley-crouch-towering-jazz-critic-dead-at-74.

Jackson, Jeffrey H. *Making Jazz French: Music and Modern Life in Interwar Paris*. Durham, NC: Duke University Press, 2003.

Jameson, Frederic. *Marxism and Form*. Princeton, NJ: Princeton University Press, 1971.

Jarenwattananon, Patrick. "Grade Inflation and the Jazz Critics." *A Blog Supreme*, NPR, May 27, 2009. https://www.npr.org/sections/ablogsupreme/2009/05/grade_inflation_and_the_jazz_c_1.html.

———. "Hey Ladies: Being a Woman in Jazz." *A Blog Supreme*, NPR, November 12, 2010. https://www.npr.org/sections/ablogsupreme/2010/11/12/131276820/hey-ladies-being-a-woman-in-jazz.

Jenkins, Willard, ed. *Ain't but a Few of Us: Black Music Writers Tell Their Story*. Durham, NC: Duke University Press, 2022.

———. "Jazz Audience Development: The Gender Factor." New Music USA, March 26, 2014. https://newmusicusa.org/nmbx/jazz-audience-development-the-gender-factor/.

Johansen, Birgitte Schepelern. "Locating Hatred: On the Materiality of Emotions." *Emotion, Space, and Society* 16 (2015): 48–55.

Jordan, Matthew F. *Le Jazz: Jazz and French Cultural Identity*. Urbana: University of Illinois Press, 2010.

Juslin, Patrik N. *Musical Emotions*. New York: Oxford University Press, 2019.

Juslin, Patrik N., and John A. Sloboda, eds. *Handbook of Music and Emotion*. New York: Oxford University Press, 2010.

Kajikawa, Loren. "The Sound of Struggle: Black Revolutionary Nationalism and Asian American Jazz." In Ake, Garrett, and Goldmark, *Jazz/Not Jazz*, 190–216.

Kallen, Horace. "Democracy versus the Melting Pot." *The Nation*, February 25, 1915, 190–94.

Karl, Gregory, and Jenefer Robinson. "Shostakovich's Tenth Symphony and the Musical Expression of Cognitively Complex Emotions." In *Music and Meaning*, edited by Jenefer Robinson, 154–78. Ithaca, NY: Cornell University Press, 1997.

Karlin, Daniel. *Browning's Hatreds*. New York: Oxford University Press, 1993.

Kassabian, Anahid. "Music for Sleeping." In Thompson and Biddle, *Sound, Music, Affect*, 165–81.

———. *Ubiquitous Listening: Affect, Attention, and Distributed Subjectivity*. Berkeley: University of California Press, 2013.

Kater, Michael H. *Different Drummers: Jazz in the Culture of Nazi Germany*. New York: Oxford University Press, 2003.

Keightley, Keir. "You Keep Coming Back like a Song: Adult Audiences, Taste Panics, and the Idea of the Standard." *Journal of Popular Music Studies* 13 (2001): 7–40.

Kernodle, Tammy L. *Soul on Soul: The Life and Music of Mary Lou Williams*. Urbana: University of Illinois Press, 2004.

King, Charles. *Gods of the Upper Air: How a Circle of Renegade Anthropologists Reinvented Race, Sex, and Gender in the Twentieth Century*. New York: Anchor, 2020.

King, Jonny. *What Jazz Is: An Insider's Guide to Understanding and Listening to Jazz*. New York: Walker, 1997.

Kingsley, Walter. "Whence Comes Jass? Facts from the Great Authority on the Subject." *New York Sun*, August 5, 1917, 3. In Walser, *Keeping Time*, 6–7.

Kirkland, David E. "Black Masculine Language." In *Oxford Handbook of African American Language*, edited by Sonja Lanehart, 834–49. New York: Oxford University Press, 2015.

Klotz, Kelsey. *Dave Brubeck and the Performance of Whiteness*. New York: Oxford University Press, 2022.

———. "Kenny G and the Ignorance of Whiteness," part of "Colloquy: Revisiting Kenny G." *Journal of Jazz Studies* 14, no. 1 (2023): 20–34.

Kolker, Robert. *Triumph over Containment: American Film in the 1950s*. New Brunswick, NJ: Rutgers University Press, 2021.

Konc, Riane. "Jazz: A Few Definitions." Daily Shouts, *Shouts and Murmurs* (blog). *New Yorker*, March 2, 2017. https://www.newyorker.com/humor/daily-shouts/jazz-a-few-definitions.

Krol, Mike. "Interview, Still in Rock: Mike Krol." *Still in Rock*, April 15, 2019. https://www.stillinrock.com/2019/04/interview-still-in-rock-mike-krol.

Kubik, Gerhard. *Jazz Transatlantic*. Vol. 2, *Jazz Derivatives and Developments in Twentieth-Century Africa*. Jackson: University Press of Mississippi, 2017.

Kurwa, Nishat. "Behind the Rise of Xtranormal, A Hilarious DIY Deadpan." *Morning Edition*, NPR, January 5, 2011. https://www.npr.org/2011/01/05/132653525/behind-rise-of-xtranormal-a-hilarious-diy-deadpan.

La Rosa, David. "Jazz Has Become the Least Popular Genre in the U.S." *JazzLine News*, March 9, 2015. https://news.jazzline.com/news/jazz-least-popular-music-genre.

Lawrence, Tim. *Love Saves the Day: A History of American Dance Music Culture, 1970–1979*. Durham, NC: Duke University Press, 2003.

Layman, Will. "R.I.P. Smooth Jazz, 1985–2008?" *PopMatters*, April 16, 2008. https://www.popmatters.com/rip-smooth-jazz-1985-2008-2496162968.html.

———. "The Sonny Rollins/'New Yorker' Controversy and Jazz's Image Problem." *PopMatters*, August 18, 2014. https://www.popmatters.com/184681-the-sonny-rollins-new-yorker-controversy-and-jazzs-image-problem-2495629647.html.

Leonard, Neil. *Jazz and the White Americans*. Chicago: University of Chicago Press, 1962.

Levine, Lawrence W. *Highbrow/Lowbrow: The Emergence of Cultural Hierarchy in America*. Cambridge, MA: Harvard University Press, 1988.

Lewis, George E. *A Power Stronger Than Itself: The AACM and American Experimental Music*. Chicago: University of Chicago Press, 2008.

Leys, Ruth. *The Ascent of Affect: Genealogy and Critique*. Chicago: University of Chicago Press, 2017.

Lipsitz, George. *The Possessive Investment in Whiteness: How White People Profit from Identity Politics*. 1998. Reprint, Philadelphia: Temple University Press, 2018.

Litweiler, John. *Ornette Coleman: A Harmolodic Life*. New York: William Morrow, 1992.

Lochhead, Judith, Eduardo Mendieta, and Stephen Decatur Smith, eds. *Sound and Affect: Voice, Music, World*. Chicago: University of Chicago Press, 2021.

Lockyer, Sharon, and Michael Pickering, eds. *Beyond a Joke: The Limits of Humour*. New York: Palgrave Macmillan, 2005.

Lopes, Paul. *The Rise of a Jazz Art World*. Cambridge: Cambridge University Press, 2002.

Lott, Eric. *Black Mirror: The Cultural Contradictions of American Racism*. Cambridge, MA: Belknap Press of Harvard University Press, 2017.

Luce, Henry. "The American Century." *Time*, February 17, 1941, 61–65.

Lücke, Martin. "Vilified, Venerated, Forbidden: Jazz in the Stalinist Era." Translated by Anita Ip. *Music and Politics* 1, no. 2 (Summer 2007), https://doi.org/10.3998/mp.9460447.0001.201.

Mandel, Howard. "Most Scurrilous, Unfunny *New Yorker* 'Humor' re Jazz." *Jazz beyond Jazz: Howard Mandel's Urban Improvisation* (blog). *ArtsJournal*, August 2, 2014. https://www.artsjournal.com/jazzbeyondjazz/2014/08/most-scurrilous-unfunny-new-yorker-humor-re-jazz.html.

Manne, Kate. *Down Girl: The Logic of Misogyny*. New York: Oxford University Press, 2017.

Marek, Georg. "From the Dive to the Dean, Jazz Becomes Respectable." *Good Housekeeping*, June 1956, 120.

Marianyi, Alex. "Who Is @JazzIsTheWorst?" Nextbop, July 26, 2013, https://nextbop.com/blog/whoisjazzistheworst.

Marin, Reva. *Outside and Inside: Race and Identity in White Jazz Autobiography*. Jackson: University of Mississippi Press, 2020.

Mariotti, Shannon L. *Adorno and Democracy: The American Years*. Lexington: University of Kentucky Press, 2016.

Marlow, Eugene. *Jazz in China: From Dance Hall Music to Individual Freedom of Expression*. Jackson: University Press of Mississippi, 2018.

Martin, Rod A. *The Psychology of Humor: An Integrative Approach*. San Diego: Elsevier, 2007.

Martinelli, Francesco, ed. *The History of European Jazz: The Music, Musicians and Audience in Context*. Bristol, CT: Equinox Publishing, 2017.

Mason, Michelle. "Contempt as a Moral Attitude." *Ethics* 113 (January 2003): 234–72.

Massumi, Brian. *Parables for the Virtual: Movement, Affect, Sensation*. Durham, NC: Duke University Press, 2002.

May, Lary. *The Big Tomorrow: Hollywood and the Politics of the American Way*. Chicago: University of Chicago Press, 2000.

———. "Making the American Consensus: The Narrative of Conversion and Subversion in World War II Films." In *The War in American Culture: Society and Consciousness during World War II*, edited by Lewis Erenberg and Susan Hirsch, 71–102. Chicago: University of Chicago Press, 1996.

McGee, Kristin A. *Some Like It Hot: Jazz Women in Film and Television, 1928–1959*. Middletown, CT: Wesleyan University Press, 2009.

McGregor, Elizabeth Vihlen. *Jazz and Postwar French Identity: Improvising the Nation*. New York: Lexington Books, 2016.

McKittrick, Katherine. *Dear Science and Other Stories*. Durham, NC: Duke University Press, 2021.

———. "Rebellion/Invention/Groove." *small axe* 20, no. 1 (49) (March 2016): 79–91.

Meltzer, David, ed. *Reading Jazz*. San Francisco: Mercury House, 1993.

Mendl, R. W. S. *The Appeal of Jazz*. London: Philip Allan, 1927.

Mercer, Michelle. "Sexism from Two Leading Jazz Artists Draws anger—and Presents an Opportunity." The Record, NPR, March 9, 2017, https://www.npr.org/sections/therecord/2017/03/09/519482385/sexism-from-two-leading-jazz-artists-draws-anger-and-presents-an-opportunity.

Merriam, Alan, and Raymond Mack. "The Jazz Community." *Social Forces* 38, no. 3 (1960): 211–22.

Merriam, Alan P., and Fradley H. Garner. "Jazz—The Word." *Ethnomusicology* 12, no. 3 (1968): 373–96.

Meyers, Leonard. *Emotion and Meaning in Music*. Chicago: University of Chicago Press, 1956.

Miller, Paul Eduard. "Judging and Appreciating Hot Music." *Music and Rhythm*, November 1940, 78–81.

Miller, William Ian. *The Anatomy of Disgust*. Cambridge, MA: Harvard University Press, 1997.

Mizell, Lee, Brett Crawford, and Caryn Anderson. *Music Preferences in the U.S.: 1982–2002*. Prepared for the National Endowment for the Arts, June 2005. https://files.eric.ed.gov/fulltext/ED511715.pdf.

Monson, Ingrid. *Freedom Sounds: Civil Rights Call Out to Jazz and Africa*. New York: Oxford University Press, 2007.

———. *Saying Something: Jazz Improvisation and Interaction*. Chicago: University of Chicago Press, 2009.

Morgan, Russ. "Why I Hate Swing." *Swing: The Guide to Modern Music* 1, no. 6 (October 1938): 14, 18–19, 20–24.

Morgenstern, Dan. "The Role of the Jazz Critic." *Program for the Twenty-Sixth Annual Notre Dame Collegiate Jazz Festival*, April 13–14, 1984. https://archives.nd.edu/ndcjf/dcjf1984.pdf.

Morrison, Allen. "An Exclusive Interview with Hans Groiner: The Noted Austrian Musicologist and Monk Expert Grants *JazzTimes* an Audience." *JazzTimes*, June 10, 2021, https://jazztimes.com/features/interviews/an-exclusive-interview-with-hans-groiner.

Morrison, Matthew D. "Race, Blacksound, and the (Re)Making of Musicological Discourse." *Journal of the American Musicological Society* 72, no. 3 (2019): 781–823.

Moyer, Justin Wm. "All That Jazz Isn't All That Great." *Washington Post*, August 8, 2014, https://www.washingtonpost.com/news/opinions/wp/2014/08/08/all-that-jazz-isnt-all-that-great.

Mueller, John H. *The American Symphony Orchestra: A Social History of Musical Taste*. Bloomington: Indiana University Press, 1951.

Murray, Albert. *The Omni-Americans: Some Alternatives to the Folklore of White Supremacy*. 1970. Reprint, New York: Library of America, 2020.

Myers, Marc. "Carly, Bruce and Barbara." *JazzWax* (blog), January 7, 2023. https://www.jazzwax.com/2023/01/carly-bruce-and-barbara.html.

———. *Why Jazz Happened*. Berkeley: University of California Press, 2013.

Nadel, Alan. *Containment Culture: American Narratives, Postmodernism, and the Atomic Age*. Durham, NC: Duke University Press, 1995.

Nettelbeck, Colin W. *Dancing with DeBeauvoir: Jazz and the French*. Melbourne: Melbourne University Press, 2004.

Nettl, Bruno, and Helen Myers. *Folk Music in the United States: An Introduction*. Detroit: Wayne State University Press, 1976.

New York Times. "Whiteman Senior, Long Foe of Jazz." August 7, 1938, D5.

Ngai, Sianne. *Ugly Feelings.* Cambridge, MA: Harvard University Press, 2005.

Nisenson, Eric. *Blue: The Murder of Jazz.* New York: Da Capo, 1997.

Norberg, Jakob. "Anticapitalist Affect: Georg Lukács on Satire and Hate." *New German Critique* 45, no. 3 (135) (November 2018): 155–74.

NPR. "Hey Ladies: Being a Woman Musician Today." NPR, https://www.npr.org/series/128562443/hey-ladies-being-a-woman-musician-today.

Ogren, Kathy J. *The Jazz Revolution: Twenties America and the Meaning of Jazz.* New York: Oxford University Press, 1989.

Okiji, Fumi. *Jazz as Critique: Adorno and Black Expression Revisited.* Stanford, CA: Stanford University Press, 2018.

Olding, Rachel. "Why Is Jazz Unpopular? The Musicians 'Suck,' Says Branford Marsalis." *Sydney Morning Herald*, April 19, 2019. https://www.smh.com.au/entertainment/music/why-is-jazz-unpopular-the-musicians-suck-says-branford-marsalis-20190312-p513h2.html.

Oremus, Will. "Why a Young Writer Secretly Deleted Her Own *BuzzFeed* Post." *Slate*, August 15, 2014. https://slate.com/technology/2014/08/what-s-the-deal-with-jazz-why-a-buzzfeed-writer-secretly-deleted-her-post-in-shame.html.

Ouellette, Dan. "Vijay Iyer Blindfold Test at 2018 North Sea Jazz Festival." *DownBeat*, August 10, 2018. http://downbeat.com/news/detail/vijay-iyer-blindfold-test-at-2018-north-sea-jazz-festival.

Out of My Head (blog). https://finster.wordpress.com/about/.

Paddison, Max. *Adorno's Aesthetics of Music.* Cambridge: Cambridge University Press, 1993.

——. "The Critique Criticised: Adorno and Popular Music." *Popular Music* 2 (January 1982): 201–18.

Painter, Nell Irvin. *The History of White People.* New York: W. W. Norton, 2010.

Palmer, Jerry. "Parody and Decorum: Permission to Mock." In Lockyer and Pickering, *Beyond a Joke*, 79–97.

Panassié, Hugues. *The Real Jazz.* Translated by Anne Sorell Williams. New York: Smith and Durrell, 1942.

Panish, Jon. *The Color of Jazz: Race and Representation in Postwar American Culture.* Jackson: University Press of Mississippi, 1997.

Parkinson, Anna. "Adorno on the Airwaves: Feeling Reason, Educating Emotions." *German Politics and Society* 32, no. 1 (110) (Spring 2014): 43–59.

Payton, Nicholas. "Black American Music and the Jazz Tradition." April 30, 2014. https://nicholaspayton.wordpress.com/2014/04/30/black-american-music-and-the-jazz-tradition.

Perchard, Tom. *After Django: Making Jazz in Postwar France.* Ann Arbor: University of Michigan Press, 2015.

——. "Mid-century Modern Jazz: Music and Design in the Postwar Home." In "The Critical Imperative," special issue, *Popular Music* 36, no. 1 (2017): 55–74.

Perlstein, Daniel. "Imagined Authority: *Blackboard Jungle* and the Project of Educational Liberalism." *Paedogogica Historica* 36, no. 1 (2000): 407–24.

Peterson, Richard A., and A. Simkus. "How Musical Tastes Mark Occupational Status Groups." In *Cultivating Differences*, edited by Michèle Lamont and Marcel Fournier, 152–86. Chicago: University of Chicago Press, 1992.

Petro, Patrice. "Mass Culture and the Feminine: The 'Place' of Television in Film Studies." *Cinema Journal* 25, no. 3 (Spring 1986): 5–21.

Phillips, Matt. "Hans Groiner: Does Humour Belong in Jazz?" Sounds of Surprise, November 6, 2011. https://soundsofsurprise.com/2015/11/06/hans-groiner-jazzs-last-taboo.

Pillai, Nicolas. *Jazz as a Visual Language*. London: I. B. Tauris, 2017.

Plamper, Jan. *The History of Emotions: An Introduction*. New York: Oxford University Press, 2015.

Porter, Eric. "It's about That Time: The Response to Miles Davis's Electric Turn." In *Miles Davis and American Culture*, edited by Gerald Early, 130–46. St. Louis: Missouri Historical Society Press, 2001.

———. *What Is This Thing Called Jazz? African American Musicians as Artists, Critics, and Activists*. Berkeley: University of California Press, 2002.

Prouty, Ken. *Knowing Jazz: Community, Pedagogy, and Canon in the Information Age*. Jackson: University Press of Mississippi, 2012.

Public Policy Polling. "Americans Hate Justin Bieber." Press Release, May 9, 2013, https://www.publicpolicypolling.com/wp-content/uploads/2017/09/PPP_Release_Music_050913.pdf.

Radano, Ronald. *Lying Up a Nation: Race and Black Music*. Chicago: University of Chicago Press, 2003.

Radano, Ronald M., and Philip V. Bohlman. *Music and the Racial Imagination*. Chicago: University of Chicago Press, 2000.

Ramsey Jr., Guthrie P. *The Amazing Bud Powell: Black Genius, Jazz History, and the Challenge of Bebop*. Berkeley: University of California Press, 2013.

———. "A New Kind of Blue: The Power of Suggestion and the Pleasure of Groove in Robert Glasper's 'Black Radio,'" *Daedalus* 142, no. 4 (Fall 2013): 120–25.

———. *Race Music: Black Cultures from Bebop to Hip-Hop*. Berkeley: University of California Press, 2003.

Ratliff, Ben. "Jazz Hate." *Slate*, December 15, 2016. https://slate.com/culture/2016/12/la-la-lands-cliched-confused-depiction-of-jazz.html.

Ratner, Leonard. *Classic Music: Expression, Form and Style*. New York: Schirmer, 1980.

Rawlings, E. Elliott. "Keeping Fit." *New York Amsterdam News*, April 1, 1925.

Reddan, James, Monika Herzig, and Michael Kahr, eds. *The Routledge Companion to Jazz and Gender*. New York: Routledge, 2023.

Reeves, Jimmie L. "Re-covering Racism: Crack Mothers, Reaganism, and the Network News." In *Living Color: Race and Television in the United States*, edited by Sasha Torres, 97–117. Durham, NC: Duke University Press, 1998.

Resler, Chloe. "The Rise of Queermisia in Jazz: Medicalization, Legislation, and Its Effects." In Reddan, Herzig, and Kahr, *Routledge Companion to Jazz and Gender*, 119–30.

Ritter, Rüdiger. "Jazz in Moscow after Stalinism." In *Jazz and Totalitarianism*, edited by Bruce Johnson, 50–66. New York: Routledge, 2017.

Roach, Max. "Beyond Categories." In Walser, *Keeping Time*, 305–10.

Roberts, Sam. "Stanley Crouch, 74, a Critic Who Saw American Democracy in Jazz, Is Dead." *New York Times*, September 17, 2020.

Robinson, J. Bradford. "The Jazz Essays of Theodor Adorno: Some Thoughts on Jazz Reception in Weimar Germany." *Popular Music* 13, no. 1 (January 1994): 1–25.

Rogers, B. S. "Swing Is from the Heart." *Esquire*, April 1939, 43, 115, 118, 120.

Rolontz, Bob. "George Crater—a Funny Cat." *Billboard*, December 18, 1961, 2.

Rosaldo, Michelle Z. *Knowledge and Passion: Ilongot Notions of Self and Social Life*. Cambridge: Cambridge University Press, 1980.

Rose, Tricia. *The Hip Hop Wars: What We Talk about When We Talk about Hip Hop—and Why It Matters*. New York: Basic Books, 2008.

Rosenberg, Bernard, and David Manning White, eds. *Mass Culture: The Popular Arts in America*. New York: Free Press, 1957.

Rosenthal, David. *Hard Bop: Jazz and Black Music, 1955–1965*. New York: Oxford University Press, 1992.

Rosenwein, Barbara H. *Anger: The Conflicted History of an Emotion*. New Haven, CT: Yale University Press, 2020.

Rubba, Joseph V. "Much Ado about Swinging." *Metronome* 52, no. 8 (August 1936), 9–10.

Russonello, Giovanni. "At 30, What Does Jazz at Lincoln Center Mean?" *New York Times*, September 13, 2017. https://www.nytimes.com/2017/09/13/arts/music/jazz-at-lincoln-center-30th-anniversary.html.

———. "Jazz Has Always Been Protest Music. Can It Meet This Moment?" *New York Times*, September 3, 2020. https://www.nytimes.com/2020/09/03/arts/music/jazz-protest-academia.html.

Rustin-Paschal, Nichole. *The Kind of Man I Am: Jazzmasculinity and the World of Charles Mingus Jr*. Middletown, CT: Wesleyan University Press, 2017.

———. "'The Reason I Play the Way I Do Is': Jazzmen, Emotion, and Creating in Jazz." In *The Routledge Companion to Jazz Studies*, edited by Nicholas Gebhardt, Nichole Rustin-Paschal, and Tony Whyton, 401–9. New York: Routledge, 2019.

Sales, Grover. *Jazz: America's Classical Music*. Englewood Cliffs, NJ: Prentice-Hall, 1984.

Sanders, Linley. "Americans' Opinions on 20 Different Music Genres, from Classic Rock to Hip-Hop and Rap." YouGov (US), May 11, 2023. https://today.yougov.com/entertainment/articles/45699-americans-opinions-different-music-genres-poll.

Sargeant, Winthrop. "Cuba's Tin Pan Alley." *Life*, October 6, 1947.

Saul, Scott. *Freedom Is, Freedom Ain't: Jazz and the Making of the Sixties*. Cambridge, MA: Harvard University Press, 2009.

Savage, Barbara. *Broadcasting Freedom: Radio, War, and the Politics of Race, 1938–1948*. Chapel Hill: University of North Carolina Press, 1999.

Scheinin, Richard. "Grammy Winner Robert Glasper on 12 Topics: Chaka Khan, J Dilla, Jose James, and more," *San Jose Mercury News*, March 7, 2013. https://infoweb-newsbank-com.eu1.proxy.openathens.net/apps/news/document-view?p=WORLDNEWS&docref=news/144E5D4BF92CC7A0.

Scheler, Max. *On Feeling, Knowing, and Valuing: Selected Writings*. Edited by Harold J. Bershady. Chicago: University of Chicago Press, 1992.

Schirmer, Annett. *Emotion*. Thousand Oaks, CA: Sage, 2015.

Sheinbaum, John J. *Good Music: What It Is and Who Gets to Decide*. Chicago: University of Chicago Press, 2018.

Small, Christopher. *Musicking: The Meanings of Performing and Listening*. Hanover, NH: Wesleyan University Press, 1998.

Smith, Wadada Leo. "Creative Music and the AACM." In Walser, *Keeping Time*, 315–23.

Smith, Will. Review of *On the Corner*, by Miles Davis. *DownBeat*, March 29, 1973, 22–23.

Smitherman, Geneva. *Talkin' and Testifyin': The Language of Black America*. Detroit: Wayne State University Press, 1986.

Snowball, David. "Controlling Degenerate Music: Jazz in the Third Reich." In *Jazz and the Germans: Essays on the Influence of "Hot" American Idioms on 20th-Century German Music*, edited by Michael J. Budds, 149–66. Hillsdale, NY: Pendragon Press, 2002.

Solis, Gabriel. "Soul, Afrofuturism and the Timeliness of Contemporary Jazz Fusions." *Daedalus* 148, no. 2 (Spring 2019): 23–35.

Spencer, Herbert. "On the Origin and Function of Music." In *Essays on Education and Kindred Subjects*. New York: E. P. Dutton, 1911. https://www.gutenberg.org/cache/epub/16510/pg16510-images.html#page_310.

Spiegel, Amy Rose. "What's the Deal with Jazz?" *BuzzFeed*, February 14, 2013. https://www.buzzfeed.com/verymuchso/whats-the-deal-with-jazz.

Spitzer, Michael. *A History of Emotion in Western Music: A Thousand Years from Chant to Pop*. New York: Oxford University Press, 2020.

Starr, Frederick S. *Red and Hot: The Fate of Jazz in the Soviet Union, 1917–1991*. New York: Limelight Editions, 1994.

Sternberg, Robert J. *The Nature of Hate*. Cambridge: Cambridge University Press, 2008.

Stoever, Jennifer Lynn. *The Sonic Color Line: Race and the Cultural Politics of Listening*. New York: New York University Press, 2016.

Stoever-Ackerman, Jennifer. "Reproducing U.S. Citizenship in Blackboard Jungle: Race, Cold War Liberalism, and the Tape Recorder." *American Quarterly* 63, no. 3 (2011): 781–806.

Stowe, David W. *Swing Changes: Big-Band Jazz in New Deal America*. Cambridge, MA: Harvard University Press, 1994.

Studebaker, J. W. "The Age of Jazz." *Journal of Education* 109, no. 3 (January 21, 1929): 68. Reprint, *Jazz in Print (1856–1929)*, edited by Karl Koenig, 550. Hillsdale, NY: Pendragon Press, 2002.

Tate, Greg, ed. *Everything but the Burden: What White People Are Taking from Black Culture*. New York: Penguin, 2003.

Teal, Kimberly Hannon. *Jazz Places: How Performance Spaces Shape Jazz History*. Berkeley: University of California Press, 2021.

Thiem, Annika. "Adorno's Tears: Textures of Philosophical Emotionality." *MLN* 124, no. 3 (April 2009): 592–613.

Thompson, Marie, and Ian Biddle, eds. *Sound, Music, Affect: Theorizing Sonic Experience*. London: Bloomsbury, 2013.

Tingen, Paul. *Miles Beyond: The Electric Explorations of Miles Davis, 1967–1991*. New York: Billboard Books, 2003.

———. "The Most Hated Album in Jazz." *Guardian*, October 26, 2007. https://www.theguardian.com/music/2007/oct/26/jazz.shopping.

Toll, William. "Horace M. Kallen: Pluralism and American Jewish Identity." *American Jewish History* 85 (March 1997): 57–74.

Tomlinson, Gary. "Cultural Dialogics and Jazz: A White Historian Signifies." *Black Music Research Journal* 11, no. 2 (1991): 229–64. Reprint, Supplement, *Black Music Research Journal* 22 (2002): 71–105.

Tucker, Mark. *Duke Ellington: The Early Years*. Urbana: University of Illinois Press, 1991.

Tucker, Sherrie. *Dance Floor Democracy: The Social Geography of Memory at the Hollywood Canteen*. Durham, NC: Duke University Press, 2014.

———. *Swing Shift: "All-Girl" Bands of the 1940s*. Durham, NC: Duke University Press, 2000.

———. "When Did Jazz Go Straight? A Queer Question for Jazz Studies." *Critical Studies in Improvisation/Études critiques en improvisation* 4, no. 2 (2008). https://www.criticalimprov.com/index.php/csieci/article/view/850.

Tynan, John. "Take Five." *DownBeat*, November 23, 1961, 40.

US Immigration Commission. *Dictionary of Races or Peoples*, S. Doc. No. 61-662. Washington, DC: Government Printing Office, 1911; Detroit: Gale Research, 1969.

Vad, Mikkel. "Whiteness and the Problem of Colourblind Listening: Revisiting Leonard Feather's 1951 Blindfold Test with Roy Eldridge." *Twentieth-Century Music*, March 4, 2024, 1–28. https://doi.org/10.1017/S1478572224000033.

Vercelloni, Luca. *The Invention of Taste: A Cultural Account of Desire, Delight and Disgust in Fashion, Food and Art*. Translated by Kate Singleton. New York: Bloomsbury, 2016.

Voltaire [François-Marie Arouet], M. de, Charles-Louis de Secondat, baron de La Brède et de Montesquieu, and Jean-Baptiste le Rond d'Alembert. "Taste." In *The Encyclopedia: Selections: Diderot, d'Alembert and a Society of Men of Letters*, trans. Nelly S. Hoyt and Thomas Cassirer. Indianapolis: Bobbs-Merrill, 1965. http://hdl.handle.net/2027/spo.did2222.0000.168. First published as "Goût," *Encyclopédie ou Dictionnaire raisonné des sciences, des arts et des métiers*, 7:761–70 (Paris, 1757).

Walser, Robert, ed. *Keeping Time: Readings in Jazz History*. New York: Oxford University Press, 1999.

———. "Popular Music Analysis: Ten Apothegms and Four Instances." In *Analyzing Popular Music*, edited by Allan F. Moore, 16–38. Cambridge: Cambridge University Press, 2003.

———. Review of *Bad Music: The Music We Love to Hate*, edited by Christopher J. Washburne and Maiken Derno. *Journal of the Society for American Music* 1, no. 4 (November 2007): 511–16.

———. "Rhythm, Rhyme, and Rhetoric in the Music of Public Enemy." *Ethnomusicology* 39 (1995): 193–217.

———. *Running with the Devil: Power, Gender, and Madness in Heavy Metal Music*. Hanover, NH: Wesleyan University Press, 1993.

Ward, Geoffrey C., and Ken Burns. *Jazz: A History of America's Music*. New York: Alfred A. Knopf, 2000.

Washburne, Christopher J., and Maiken Derno, eds. *Bad Music: The Music We Love to Hate*. New York: Routledge, 2004.

Watkins, Mel. *On the Real Side: Laughing, Lying, and Signifying—The Underground Tradition of African-American Humor That Transformed American Culture, from Slavery to Richard Pryor*. New York: Simon & Schuster, 1994.

Weinstein, Deena. *Heavy Metal: Music and Its Culture*. New York: Da Capo Press, 2000.

Wells, Christie Jay. *Between the Beats: The Jazz Tradition and Black Vernacular Dance*. New York: Oxford University Press, 2021.

West, Kai. "Buckra: Whiteness and *Porgy and Bess*." *Journal of the American Musicological Society* 75, no. 2 (2022): 319–77.

Wetherell, Margaret. *Affect and Emotion: A New Social Science Understanding*. Los Angeles: Sage, 2012.

Whitehead, Kevin. *Play the Way You Feel: The Essential Guide to Jazz Stories on Film*. New York: Oxford University Press, 2020.

Whyton, Tony. *Jazz Icons: Heroes, Myths and the Jazz Tradition*. Cambridge: Cambridge University Press, 2010.

Williams, Martin. *Where's the Melody? A Listener's Introduction to Jazz*. New York: Pantheon Books, 1961.

Williams, Raymond. *Keywords: A Vocabulary of Culture and Society*. New York: Oxford University Press, 1983.

———. *Marxism and Literature*. New York: Oxford University Press, 1977.

Willis, Ken. "Merry Hell: Humour Competence and Social Incompetence." In Lockyer and Pickering, *Beyond a Joke*, 126–45.

Wilson, Carl. *Let's Talk about Love: A Journey to the End of Taste*. New York: Continuum, 2007.

Witkin, Robert W. *Adorno on Music*. New York: Routledge, 1998.

———. *Adorno on Popular Culture*. New York: Routledge, 2003.

———. "Why Did Adorno 'Hate' Jazz?" *Sociological Theory* 18, no. 1 (March 2000): 145–70.

Witt, Stephen. *How Music Got Free: A Story of Obsession and Invention.* New York: Penguin Books, 2016.

Woodward, Richard B. "The Jazz Wars: A Tale of Age, Rage, and Hash Brownies." *Village Voice*, August 9, 1994, 27–28.

Wright, Brian F. "Introduction: What Kenny G Can Teach Us about Jazz," part of "Colloquy: Revisiting Kenny G." *Journal of Jazz Studies* 14, no. 1 (2023): 1–19.

Wright, David. *Understanding Cultural Taste: Sensation, Skill and Sensibility.* London: Palgrave Macmillan, 2015.

Yanay, Niza. *The Ideology of Hatred: The Psychic Power of Discourse.* New York: Fordham University Press, 2017.

Zwerin, Mike. *La Tristesse de Saint Louis: Jazz under the Nazis.* New York: Beech Tree Books, 1985.

Index

Page numbers in italics refer to figures and tables.

AACM (Association for the Advancement of Creative Musicians), 39, 150
Abu-Lughod, Lila, 10
Adorno, Theodor: and affect, 18–20; jazz writings of, 17–20; and jitterbugs, 19; *Negative Dialectics*, 18; "On Popular Music," 19; rhetorical strategies of, 17–18
aesthetics, connection to taste, 34, 37–38
affect: autonomy of, 9; definitions of, 8–10; and habitus, 9–10; and music, 14–16; as practice, 9; as "trajectory toward emotion," 9
Affektenlehre (doctrine of affects), 14
Aftab, Arooj, 151
Ahmed, Sara: on hate and bodies, 124; on hate and boundaries, 113; on hate as narcissism, 125; on hate as "negative attachment," 101
Ake, David, 24, 112, 115
Aldana, Melissa, 92, 112
Alford, Fred C., 136–37
Allen, Woody, 80, 83
Allison, Mose, 74, 83
Anderson, Ben, 9

Anderson, Caryn, 140–41, *142*
Anderson, Paul Allen, 20–21
Aristotle, 6
Armstrong, Louis, 43, 74, 118, 120, 121
Arnold, Magda, 5
Association for the Advancement of Creative Musicians (AACM), 39, 150

Bach, J. S., 4
Baraka, Amiri (LeRoi Jones), 40, 82, 144, 167n32, 187n47; "Jazz and the White Critic," 38–39
Barnet, Charlie, 63
Barthelme, Donald, "The King of Jazz," 78–79, 94, 96, 173n44
Beatles, 4
Beiderbecke, Bix, 62–63
Benjamin, H. Jon, 75–77, 176n72
Benjamin, Lakecia, 112, 150
Benson, George, 116, 138
Berg, Alban, 17
Bergson, Henri, 89, 91, 174n55, 175n66; and affect in humor, 72–73; on humor's disciplinary function, 97
Berklee College of Music, 112, 152
Berliner, Paul, 23
Bey, Andy, 110

Biddle, Ian, 14
Bieber, Justin, 147
Billig, Michael, 69, 72, 80, 174n55
Bitches Brew (album), 116
Blackboard Jungle (film), 59, 61–64
blackface minstrelsy, 13, 91, 95, 97
Black Lives Matter, 151
Blackness, 3, 27, 28, 31, 35, 65, 69, 87, 94, 113, 125, 147, 158n12; as "a combination of cultural inheritances and diasporic experiences," 11; and disco, 87; and Kenny G, 119, 121; and Robert Glasper's aesthetics, 144, 146; and "racial imagination," 12–14; and rock 'n' roll, 63–64; and Sonny Rollins parody, 94–96; and swing, 54–56
Blanchard, Terence, 122
Blesh, Rudi, 44, 49; *Shining Trumpets*, 113–14, 169n66
"Blindfold Test, The," 103–5, 178n14, 184n93; Miles Davis 1964, 125–26
Bohlman, Philip, 10, 13
Bourdieu, Pierre: *Distinction*, 27, 33–34, 165n13; and habitus, 9
Brogaard, Berit, 134
Brown, Marion, 20
Brown, Wendy, 134
Bruce, Lenny, 80, 81, 82
Bryant, Clora, 107
Burns, Ken, *Jazz* (film), 48, 78, 120, 122
Burns, Ralph, 110
Burton, Gary, 110
Butler, Judith, 12

Calloway, Cab, 74, 175n64
Cannon, Walter, 5
Carrington, Terri Lyne, 108–9; Berklee Institute of Jazz and Gender Justice, 112
Carson, Charles, 118, 121
Chaikin, Judy, *The Girls in the Band* (film), 107, 108–9
Chapman, Dale, 147
Chazelle, Damien, *La La Land* (film), 1–2, 7, 30–31, 42, 65, 139, 149

Chinen, Nate, 90–91, 96, 175n64
Christian, Charlie, 119
Cohan, Brad, 132
Cohen, Lara Langer, 7, 131–32, 133, 134, 137, 138
Cole, Louis, 151
Coleman, Ornette, 46, 81, 115, 181n51
Coltrane, John, 20, 114–15, 170n97, 180n49
Commitments, The (Doyle), 148
Connick, Harry, Jr., 141
Connolly, Brian, 131–32, 133, 134, 137
containment, 58–59
contempt, defined, 100
Cosby, Bill, 80
country music, 3, 26, 164n99
"Cow-Cow Boogie" (recording), 62, 63
Cox, Arnie, 15
Crater, George (Ed Sherman), 24, 81–82, 83, 174n49
Crawford, Brett, 140–41, 142
Croker, Theo, 150
Crouch, Stanley, 21, 102, 120, 126–27, 136, 183n80, 183n90; criticism of 1980s and '90s "blaxploitation" culture, 125; "On the Corner: The Sellout of Miles Davis," 122–25

Davis, Kris, 112
Davis, Miles, 28, 68, 78, 81, 96, 110, 115, 122–25, 127, 128, 136, 170n97, 183n80, 183n91; 1964 blindfold test, 125–26; *On the Corner*, 116
Deleuze, Gilles, and Felix Guattari, 9
Derno, Maiken, 26
DeVeaux, Scott, 24, 146, 147, 150; *Jazz in America*, 140–41, 142
Dictionary of Races or Peoples (US Immigration Commission), 12
disco, 3, 87–88, 109, 175n56
disgust: and Stanley Crouch on Miles Davis, 123–24; defined, 100–101; "negation of intimacy" and, 129; political possibilities of, 135
Donegan, Dorothy, 74
Do the M@th (blog). *See* Iverson, Ethan

DownBeat (magazine), 38, 81, 94, 114, 116; and blindfold test, 103–5, 125–26, 180n49, 183n91, 183n93
Doyle, Roddy: *The Commitments*, 148; "Jimmy Jazz," 147–49
Du Bois, W. E. B., 12

Elling, Kurt, 151
Ellington, Edward "Duke," 53, 56, 57, 120, 125–26
emotion: appraisal theory of, 5, 70; as bodily sensation, 5; as culturally determined, 10; in Bill Evans's music, 20, 109–10; limbic theory of, 5; in music scholarship, 8, 159n33
Erenberg, Lewis, 49
Evans, Bill, 20, 109–10

Feather, Leonard, 78, 102, 180n49, 183n93; creator of "The Blindfold Test," 103; and Miles Davis's blindfold test, 125–26; and defense of modern jazz, 113–14
Fellezs, Kevin, 115–16
Floyd, Samuel, 127
Frankfurt school, 17
Freberg, Stan, 80–81
Freeman, Phil, four "key zones" of jazz practice, 150
Freud, Sigmund, 19, 88, 101, 172n14; on affect and humor, 71–73, 97; on hate as ego protection, 6–7; on love as "ambivalent" emotion, 6; on structure of the joke's audience, 84–85; and "tendentious" humor, 28, 80
Frith, Simon, 22–23, 25, 43, 44, 45, 86

G, Kenny, 24, 28, 30, 116–21, 136, 138, 181n56, 182n65
Gaillard, Slim, 74
Garcia, Nubya, 150
Garrett, Charles Hiroshi, 73–75, 112–13
Gennari, John, 23, 38, 102, 106; and "critics pose," 39

genre: defined, 2–3, 158n11; and Kenny G, 116–17; and Robert Glasper, 144–46; and historical fluidity of jazz genre, 42–43; and Pat Metheny, 118–21, 182n64; *Music Preferences in the U.S.*, 140–42; policing boundaries of, 100–101, 113; 2013 Public Policy Polling (PPP) survey of musical tastes, 146–47
Getz, Stan, 109, 125, 170n97
Gikandi, Simon, 37–38, 39, 40
Gilbert, Gama, 54–55
Gilbert, Peggy, 107
Gilberto, João, 125
Gillespie, Dizzy, 73, 74, 81, 82, 175n64
Gioia, Ted, 1
Girls in the Band, The (film), 107, 108–9
Glasper, Robert, 24, 150; on commercial viability versus social relevance, 144–46, 147; interview with Ethan Iverson, 110–12, 179n35
Glover, Nicole, 112
Gold, Django, 48, 93–96
Goldings, Larry, 82–83
Goldman, Albert, 41
Goldmark, Daniel, 112–13
Goodman, Benny, 8, 41, 44, 51, 54–55, 56, 68
Gordon, Dexter, 119
Gorelick, Kenneth. *See* G, Kenny
Gorky, Maxim, "On the Music of the Gross," 130
Grammy Awards, Best Alternative Jazz Album, 155
Grant, Roger Mathew, 14
"Great Pretender, The" (recording) 80–81
Grey, Kay Crisfield, 59–60, 61, 64
groove, 16, 23, 83, 111
Grossberg, Lawrence, 9, 99
Gubbels, Jason, 1, 73, 74

Haley, Bill, and His Comets, 61, 63, 64
Halvorson, Mary, 112
Hancock, Herbie, 108–9, 116, 138
Hardt, Michael, 139–40

Hargrove, Roy, 122
Harris, Jerome, "canonical" versus "process" approach to jazz, 121
hate: and bodies, 124; and boundaries, 6–7, 113; defined, 5–7; and discourse on popular music, 24–25; ethics of, 29, 131–38; versus hating on, 7, 131–34, 138; William Hazlitt on, 131, 137–38; "holy hate," 135; as hypostatizing and reifying, 6, 7, 106; objective versus ideological, 134; and "reactive attitude," 134; relationship to love, 5, 6, 101, 125, 136, 137; reputation of, 7, 131; as set of "intolerable traits," 6, 97; Robert Sternberg's categories of, 129, 131; strong and weak versions of, 7, 31, 64–65, 92, 97, 100, 101, 105
"Hate the Sport" (recording), 132
Hazlitt, William, 131; "On the Pleasure of Hating," 137–38
heavy metal, 3, 45, 142
Henry, Cory, 151
Hersch, Fred, 104; *Good Things Happen Slowly*, 109–10
Highmore, Ben, 9; and "orchestration of sensibilities," 27, 34–35, 40, 140, 149
hip-hop and rap, 3, 13, 44, 46, 48, 110, 111, 141, 142, 144, 145, 150, 164n97
Hobart, Mike, 15
Hodeir, André, 102
hooks, bell: and aesthetics, 40; "Killing Rage," 134–35
Horkheimer, Max, 17
Howland, John, 25
Hubbs, Nadine, 26
humor: affect of, 70–73, 97; in attacks on disco, 87–88; Bergson on, 72–73; Freud on, 71–72, 84–85, 172n14; and jazz hate, 27–28; and jazz musicians, 73–75; parody, 94; in power relations, 98; and race, 69, 83, 87, 93–97; ridicule and mockery in, 69, 72–73, 75, 174n55; and satire, 67, 88–97; "tendentious," 28, 84–85
Hundertmark, Joe, 88–89
Hunter, Charlie, 151

I Hate Jazz (album), 132–34, *133*
"Invention for Guitar and Trumpet" (recording), 63
Ismaily, Shahzad, 151
Iverson, Ethan, 110–11, 178n18, 179n35, 180n37
Iyer, Vijay, 92, 103–4, 151

James, William, 5
Jarrett, Keith, 148–49
jazz: and Asian Americans, 11; and avant-garde, 20–21, 46, 114–15, 150; battle between "revivalists" and "modernists," 113–15; and Black creativity, 10; and Black mirror, 12–13, 23, 28, 69; as "complex signifier" of race, 13–14; critics, 8, 13, 15–16, 20, 21, 23, 24, 28, 35, 36, 38–41, 44–45, 47, 50, 51–52, 54, 56, 65, 67, 75, 82, 101–3, 109–10, 111, 113–16, 118, 121, 122, 126, 138, 139, 140, 142–43, 144, 151, 152, 158n13; and cultural asymmetry, 13; as cultural "site" saturated with affect, 16; and drug use, 61, 63, 170n93; as elitist, 27, 47, 66, 67, 85–87, 90–91; as formless, 15, 42, 45, 84; as having no melody, 15–16, 28, 42; internal criticism of, 103–5; and masculinity, 21, 27, 59, 109, 110–12, 115; and Nazi Germany, 3, 28–29, 63, 114, 129–30, 131, 184n3; and queer musicians, 109–10; semantic indeterminacy of, 2, 43; and sexual licentiousness, 21–22, 25, 35–36, 51, 108, 128, 130, 170n98; and Soviet Union, 3, 130–31; and Spanish tinge, 11; West Coast, 57–58, 59
Jazz (film), 48, 78, 120, 122
Jazz at Lincoln Center, 75, 122, 182n77

jazzbro, 90–91, 96, 175n64
Jazz for People Who Hate Jazz (album), 56, 57
Jazz Is the Worst (blog), 1, 91–93, 96
@JazzIsTheWorst (social media), 1, 91–93, 96
"Jazz Me Blues" (recording), 62–63
"Jazz Robots" (video), 88–89
"Jimmy Jazz" (Doyle), 147–49
Johansen, Birgitte, 5
Johnson, Samuel, 7, 31
Jones, Elvin, 114
Jones, LeRoi. *See* Baraka, Amiri (LeRoi Jones)
Joy, Samara, 112
Juilliard School, 152

Kajikawa, Loren, 11
Kant, Immanuel, 4, 34, 40
Karlin, Daniel, 7, 21
Kassabian, Anahid, 9, 14
Kater, Michael, 29, 129, 184n3
Kenny G, 24, 28, 30, 116–21, 136, 138, 181n56, 182n65
Kernodle, Tammy, 108
Kids in the Hall, 66–67
King, Jonny, 16
Klotz, Kelsey, 12, 58, 119, 158n12
Klugh, Earl, 116
Krol, Mike, 132–34

"Lady Hated Jazz, The," 59–61, 60, 64
La La Land (film), 1–2, 7, 30–31, 42, 65, 139, 149
Lange, Carl, 5
La Rosa, David, 141–42
Levitt, Rod, 125
Lewis, George, 40, 167n32
Lewis, John, 41
Leys, Ruth, 9
Lipsitz, George, 12
Listening to Kenny G (film), 119
"Livery Stable Blues" (recording), 8, 73
Lochhead, Judith, 14

Lombardo, Guy, 44, 83
Lopes, Paul, 23
Lott, Eric, and Black mirror, 12–13, 23, 28, 69
Luce, Henry, 50
Lücke, Martin, 130
Lukács, Georg, and "holy hate," 134–35

MacLean, Paul, 5
Mandel, Howard, 93–94
Mangione, Chuck, 116
Mann, Kate, 106, 107, 111
Mariotti, Shannon L., 18–19
Marsalis, Branford, 105
Marsalis, Wynton, 105, 106, 120, 143; and Jazz at Lincoln Center, 122
Massumi, Brian, 9
McBride, Christian, 122
McCann, Les, and the Jazz Crusaders, 112
McCraven, Makaya, 150
McGee, Kristin, 107
McKittrick, Katherine, 40, 127, 151
McLaughlin, John, 116
Mendieta, Eduardo, 14
Mendl, R. W. S., 36–37, 38, 58, 159n32, 166n24
Mendoza, Ava, 112
Mercer, Michelle, 111
Metheny, Pat, 24, 117–21, 136, 138, 182nn64–65
Mike Douglas Show (television show), 26
Miller, Allison, 90
Miller, Paul Eduard, 54
Mingus, Charles, 20–21, 73, 81, 82, 126–27, 183n93
misogyny, 2, 7, 21–22, 28, 49, 87, 90, 100, 106–12; defined, 106
Mizell, Lee, 140, 141, 142
Money Jungle (album), 126
Monk, Thelonious, 81, 82–83, 119
Monson, Ingrid, 13, 24, 150
Moodysson, Lucas, 132

Morgan, Russ, 52–54, 53, 56
Morgenstern, Dan, 102
Morrison, Matthew D., 13, 95
Morrissey, 147
Morton, Jelly Roll, 11, 82
Moyer, Justin Wm., 1, 47–48
Moynihan, Daniel Patrick, Moynihan Report (*The Negro Family*), 124–25
Music Preferences in the U.S. (Mizell, Crawford, and Anderson), 140–42

Nazis, 3, 28–29, 63, 114, 129–30, 131, 184n3
Ndegeocello, Meshell, 151
Negri, Antonio, 139–40
networks, as common form of digital age, 139–40
New Yorker (magazine), 1, 69, 73, 78, 93–96, 173n44
Ngai, Sianne, 135
Nisenson, Eric, *Blue*, 143
Norberg, Jakob, 131, 135

Office, The (television show), 84–86, 87
Ogren, Kathy, 23
Oh, Linda May Han, 112
Original Dixieland Jazz Band, 8, 73–74, 77
Ouellette, Dan, 103–4
"Out of My Head" (magazine column). *See* Crater, George (Ed Sherman)
Overall, Kassa, 150

Panish, Jon, 11–12, 13, 69
Papez, James, 5
Parks and Recreation (television show), 68–69, 75
parody, 1, 48, 73, 80, 93, 94–96
Payton, Nicholas, 69, 92, 93, 94–96
Peterson, Richard A., 33, 165n13
Porter, Eric, 23, 183n80
Pozo, Chano, 11, 161n46
Pravda (newspaper), 130
Prince, 123

Prouty, Ken, 99–100, 127–28
Public Policy Polling (PPP), 146–47

race: and concept of taste, 27, 35–41; defined, 10–14
racism, 2, 7, 8, 13, 21, 22, 28, 35, 38, 40, 86, 96, 101–2, 108, 125, 126, 131, 151; and disco, 87–88
Radano, Ronald, 10, 13, 16
ragtime, 13, 15, 16, 35, 43, 45
Ramsey, Guthrie P., 2–3, 127, 158n11
R&B, 1, 3, 44, 58, 110, 111, 116, 118, 141, 142, 144–45, 150, 151
rap. *See* hip-hop and rap
Ratliff, Ben, 1, 2
Recording Academy, 151
Reeves, Jimmie, and "cultural Moynihanism" 124–25
ressentiment, 46–48
Rich, Buddy, 26–27
Roach, Max, 2, 126
rock, 64, 67, 88, 115, 122, 123, 132, 133, 138, 142, 150, 151, 164n97, 165n13
"Rock around the Clock" (recording), 61, 63, 64
rock 'n' roll. *See* rock
Rollins, Sonny, 1, 48, 69, 73, 93–97, 125, 176n77
Rosaldo, Michelle Zimbalist, 10
Rustin-Paschal, Nichole, 20–21, 99, 126

Sahl, Mort, 80
Sales, Grover, 109
Salvant, Cécile McLorin, 112
satire, 24, 65, 69, 83, 87, 89, 90, 93, 94, 95, 176nn76–77; defined, 88
Saturday Evening Post, 59–61, 60
Saul, Scott, 23
Scheler, Max, 46–48
Schoenberg, Arnold, 17
sexism, 49, 100, 107, 108, 110, 178n21; defined, 106
SFJazz, 75, 151
Sheinbaum, John J., 25

Shepp, Archie, 20
Sherman, Ed. *See* Crater, George (Ed Sherman)
Silver, Horace, 75
Simpsons, The (television show), 68
Skrillex, 147
Small, Christopher, 136
Smith, Stephen Decatur, 14
Smith, Viola, 107
Smith, Wadada Leo, 39–40
Soviet Union, 3, 130–31
spalding, esperanza, 92, 112
Spyro Gyra, 116
Stalin, Joseph, 129–30
Sternberg, Robert J., 129, 131
Stowe, David, 23, 49
Stravinksy, Igor, 18
Strawson, Peter, 134
Strayhorn, Billy, 109, 110
Survey of Public Participation in the Arts (SPPA), 140–41, 146, 147, 150
swing (musical style), 23, 24, 31, 42, 48, 62, 63, 69, 112, 141, 175n64; criticism of, 7–8, 43–44, 45, 46, 48–56; and gender, 107–8; and jitterbugs, 19, 51, 61; "revivalists" versus "modernists," 113–14
swing (rhythm), 2, 16, 20, 49, 51, 52, 53, 63, 89, 90, 138

Tarantino, Alexa, 112
taste, 1, 4, 7, 23, 24, 25, 27, 28, 31, 43, 61, 64, 100, 101, 102, 113–14, 123, 126, 128, 144, 145, 146; algorithms and digital media, 139–40; Bourdieu on, 27, 33–34; and consumerism, 32; and "cultural omnivores," 26, 33, 165n13; defined, 31–32; as feeling, 27, 34; Marxist critiques of, 32; as "orchestration of sensibility," 34–35; and polling, 140–42; and race, 31, 37–41, 166n21
Taylor, Cecil, 20, 125, 126

Terry, Clark, 125
Thompson, Maria, 14
Tingen, Paul, 116
Tizol, Juan, 11
Tompkins, Paul F., 86–87, 88, 96
Tucker, Sherry, 107–8, 109
Tynan, John, 114–15, 180n49
Tyner, McCoy, 114

Voltaire, 32

Walser, Robert, 120–21
Ward, Geoffrey C., 78
Washburne, Christopher, 25
Washington, Grover, Jr., 116
We Are the Best! (film), 132
Weather Report, 138
Webern, Anton, 17
West Coast jazz, 57, 58, 59
Wetherell, Margaret, 9–10
Whiteman, Paul, 41, 54, 83
whiteness, 3, 4, 13, 14, 28, 31, 35, 57, 158n12, 167n37, 169n80; defined, 11–12; expansion of, 12, 161n52; and Kenny G, 119; "possessive investment in," 12
"Why I Hate Swing" (Morgan), 52–54, 53
Whyton, Tony, 23, 43, 120
Williams, Martin, 15–16, 102–3
Williams, Mary Lou, 108
Williams, Raymond, 13, 31, 161n56; and "structures of feeling," 22
Williams, Tony, 116
Wilson, Carl, 25
Wolcott, Charles, 62, 63
Workman, Reggie, 114
Wright, David, 139
Wynter, Sylvia, 127, 151

Yanay, Niza, 6, 134
Younger, Brandee, 150

www.ingramcontent.com/pod-product-compliance
Ingram Content Group UK Ltd.
Pitfield, Milton Keynes, MK11 3LW, UK
UKHW011816110625
459582UK00005B/523